The product of a lifetime of teaching and research, this book addresses a broad range of issues concerning mind and consciousness, for example, the differing ways in which psychiatry and neurology view consciousness; whether animals think abstractly; whether consciousness has a function; trial and error versus insight; the question of innate ideas; whether information and consciousness are equivalent; the suicidal consciousness; whether the right and left brain hemispheres differ in consciousness; the aging consciousness; whether consciousness is dynamic or motivated.

Viewing these and related issues against the background of their beginnings with thinkers like Aristotle, Descartes, Spinoza, and Locke, the author stresses an underlying belief in the unity or integration of mind or consciousness. He notes that this belief is at variance with teaching now prevalent that attributes different modes of consciousness to each brain hemisphere, and assembles an array of evidence for the concept of unity.

Klein also devotes considerable discussion to the idea of motivation, which has resulted in a troublesome number of theories. Unlike Freud, he draws a distinction between motivation and causation; and, with a tri-dimensional schema of motivation, he brings clarifying order to the welter of theories.

Throughout, Klein emphasizes the complexity of what he calls the "mystery of mind," which he likens to a jigsaw puzzle being worked on by experts in a multitude of disciplines — cognitive and humanistic psychology, psycholinguistics, information theory, epistemology, neurology, endocrinology, psychopharmacology — and takes into account the contributions of each. In closing, the book offers a progress report on current research and suggests areas for additional exploration.

David Ballin Klein was professor emeritus of psychology at the University of Southern California. During his distinguished career he wrote many books and articles, including *Mental Hygiene: A Survey of Personality Disorders and Mental Health* (rev. ed., 1956), *A History of Scientific Psychology: Its Origins and Philosophic Backgrounds* (1970), and *The Unconscious: Invention or Discovery? A Historico-critical Inquiry* (1977).

*I regard consciousness as fundamental.
I regard matter as derivative from
consciousness.*
— Max Planck

*To suppose that consciousness or
the mind has localization is a failure to
understand neurophysiology.*
— Wilder Penfield

The Concept of
Consciousness

A Survey

David Ballin Klein

University of Nebraska Press

Lincoln & London

The paper in this book meets the guidelines for permanence
and durability of the Committee on Production Guidelines
for Book Longevity of the Council on Library Resources.

Library of Congress Cataloging in Publication Data

Klein, David Ballin, 1897–1983
  The concept of consciousness.

  Includes index.
  1. Consciousness. I. Title.
BF311.K625 1984   154   83-5851
ISBN 0-8032-2707-8

To the memory of Gardner Murphy

Contents

Preface

This work is an outgrowth of one of my earlier books, which traced the history of psychology from its prescientific philosophic origins to its identification with the methodology of science. In writing it I gained intermittent glimpses of consciousness from the varying perspectives of those influential in its long philosophic and short scientific history. During the planning stages of my inquiry into the concept of consciousness I recalled many of those glimpses—for example, the common sensibles of Aristotle, Spinoza's *conatus,* Locke's reflection, Kant's categories, Hamilton's redintegration, and Marbe's conscious attitudes—what might be called nonphysiological glimpses.

By contrast, there were also reminders of the persistent mind/brain problem: the *res extensa* of Descartes, Hartley's neural vibrations, Gall's phrenology, Lotze's *Medical Psychology,* Müller's specific nerve energy, and the physiological psychology of Wundt, for instance. These and kindred recollections made me consider what segments of the complex psychoneural problem to deal with in this book. I had to be selective. I finally decided to limit the account to current interest in cerebral lateralization, split-brain studies, and, to some extent, the psychophysiology of motivation.

What consciousness has come to mean is a product of two broad lines of influence, involving contributions from such fields as information theory, epistemology, cognitive psychology, psycholinguistics, and humanistic psychology, the other involving workers in fields like neurochemistry, electroencephalography, psychopharmacology, endocrinology, gerontology, otology, and ophthalmology. To do justice to all of them is beyond the competence of any one author, so here too I had to be selective. The mere enumeration of these fields, however, reveals the complexity of the concept of consciousness.

One of my aims has been to enhance the readers' appreciation of that complexity; hence many of these specialized lines of influence are mentioned as occasion warrants. I shall show how this complex concept of consciousness has grown out of psychology's philosophic antecedents and its later scientific aspirations. Since I had in mind readers who may be unfamiliar with this historical background, the work developed into both a historical and a contemporary treatise.

The study reflects the multifaceted nature of consciousness and thus, at least by implication, the mystery of mind, which is closely related to certain neural mysteries. To cite a familiar example: neural pathways tend to cross the median plane so that each brain hemisphere controls contralateral bodily functions; yet the reason for this remains unexplained. A less familiar example involves a troublesome exception to the established finding that the cerebellum regulates muscular coordination so that cerebellar injury may disturb gait and motor control. Yet sometimes there is no such disturbance despite congenital absence of a cerebellum. Presumably other brain structures compensate, but what they are remains unknown. In fact, the essential nature of psychoneural processes remains unknown; despite striking advances in neurology, the precise nature of the transition from nerve impulse to conscious experience is not understood. Thus we do not know, for example, how a neural impulse from the retina gives rise to a sensation of light or color upon reaching the striate or visual cortex. Until such neural puzzles are solved, aspects of consciousness will continue to elude understanding. I hope this work will show how the lure of this unsolved mystery of the mind prompts persistent studies of mental life and behavior from generation to generation, not only by psychologists but also by workers from a wide array of specialized disciplines.

To the Reader:

On the day that the page proof for this book arrived, my father died. He was not, therefore, able to make the final inspection of the text, nor to construct the index himself as he had planned. Although we have completed these tasks for him, the reader should know that all essential parts of this book are the work of the author.

September 28, 1983   Philip A. Klein

1 / Consciousness as a Problem: Introductory Survey

Most people readily understand the ordinary use of the word *consciousness*. They are not puzzled by references to "loss of consciousness" or "return of consciousness," and they have general notions of consciousness as related to awareness, brain concussion, anesthetics, and the sleep of exhaustion. They probably take it for granted that consciousness ceases with death. As an everyday term in familiar contexts, consciousness is not a problem. Their curiosity is not aroused by the shifts of meaning in different contexts. They do not ask why chemicals like chloroform or carbon monoxide cause loss of consciousness. Nor do they question the nature of brain changes associated with self-consciousness, anxiety, elation, confusion, and other conscious states. Despite their familiarity with the word, or rather because of it, they fail to ask questions of this sort.

The same is true for other terms in daily use. Thus we can talk about digestion without understanding its physiology and chemistry. In the same way we use a word like *law* with blithe indifference to the history of jurisprudence. We all act as if we understand a word like *money*, though for monetary theorists the concept is a problem. Spinoza had in mind this difference between familiar words and their problem aspects when he wrote that we believe we understand something when we cease to wonder about it.

In reality there is a great deal to wonder about in the problem aspects of consciousness, which are phases of a single problem and possibly also of different problems. As long ago as 1904 Ralph Barton Perry had this to say about the term (1904, p. 282):

> There is no philosophical term at once so popular and so devoid of standard meaning. How can a term mean anything when it is employed to connote anything and everything, including its own

negation? One hears of the object of consciousness and the subject of consciousness, and the union of the two in self-consciousness; of the private consciousness, the social consciousness, and the transcendental consciousness; the inner and the outer, the higher and the lower, the temporal and the eternal consciousness; the activity and the state of consciousness. Then there is consciousness-stuff, and unconscious consciousness, called respectively mind-stuff for short, and unconscious physical states or subconsciousness to avoid a verbal contradiction. This list is not complete, but sufficiently amazing. Consciousness comprises everything that is, and indefinitely much more. It is small wonder that the definition of it is little attempted.

As Perry's title indicates, there is no one concept of consciousness. Even from the restricted viewpoint of the philosophical psychology of the time, he perceived an amazing variety of conceptions. Today he could extend his list from the viewpoints of workers in many other specialties.

Consciousness, the Concern of Many

A general symposium on consciousness would draw many specialists besides psychologists.[1] Because of the effects on consciousness of alcohol, cocaine, and other drugs, pharmacologists would be invited. Neurosurgeons would share their observations of how brain surgery affects consciousness in terms of lateralization or possible differences between brain hemispheres. Electroencephalographers—students of brain waves—would tell how the EEG records conscious states. Neurologists and internists would discuss the effects of cerebral arteriosclerosis, vascular accidents, encephalitis, and kindred afflictions on the integrity of conscious functions. And psychiatrists would explain abnormalities of consciousness associated with schizophrenia, affective disorders, neuroses, and other psychiatric conditions.

1. Such an idea is not entirely fanciful. Some years ago, five conferences were held on the topic "Problems of Consciousness," under the sponsorship of the Josiah Macy, Jr., Foundation. They took place in successive years starting in 1950, and the transactions were published in annual monographs. Twenty-five to thirty speakers participated, including specialists in physiology, electroencephalography, anesthesia, anthropology, sleep, psychiatry, emotion, schizophrenia, sociology, and embryology, and their talks covered a diversity of topics. For example, through the years the participants discussed papers on the following themes: "The Role of the Cerebral Cortex in the Development and Maintenance of Consciousness"; "The Phenomena of Hypnosis"; "Three Dimensions of Emotion"; "Consciousness and the Metabolism of the Brain"; "Variations in States of Awareness in Schizophrenic Patients"; "Consciousness: A Psychopathological and Psychodynamic View"; and "Experimental Work on Sleep and Other Variations of Consciousness." The five monographs were published by the Josiah Macy, Jr., Foundation, 16 West Forty-sixth Street, New York, New York 10036.

Psychologists are concerned with the findings of these other groups, depending on their own varied fields of interest. There are some forty divisions of the American Psychological Association. Thus members of the Division of Clinical Psychology would take special interest in the findings of neurologists and psychiatrists, while those belonging to the Division of Psychopharmacology would be alert for findings by professional pharmacologists. There is also a division whose members are mindful of developments in technical philosophy and related areas, the Division of Philosophical and Theoretical Psychology. In a "review . . . of some of psychology's intractable philosophic problems," Royce had this to say about the division (1982, p. 261): "It is important to take a historical perspective when confronted with perennial philosophic issues such as the mind-body problem, free will versus determinism, and the nature of humankind." Closely related to this division is one concerned with the history of psychology. None of these divisions are divorced in interest from the others. Directly or indirectly, they all come to grips with phenomena of consciousness. This explains why there is no Division of Consciousness.

Consciousness and Mind

The members of all divisions have a comparable interest in the subject of mind; just as there is no Division of Consciousness, so there is no Division of Mind. The closely related concepts of mind and consciousness are brought together when psychology is designated as the study of mind and/or consciousness. It is redundant to speak of the psychology of mind or the psychology of consciousness—like referring to the chemistry of chemicals or the economics of economy. This is why I have been writing about the *concept,* not the *psychology* of consciousness.

Although consciousness and mind are closely related, their connotations are different. Thus to lose consciousness is not the same as losing one's mind. We all lose consciousness when fast asleep; this is normal. But to lose one's mind is manifestly abnormal. Inasmuch as psychology investigates both mind and consciousness, we might expect the psychologist to account for the difference. Many educated people think of psychology as the science of consciousness or the science of mind, and they are not entirely mistaken, though modern psychology textbooks are not content with such an unqualified definition.

Both terms seem to give psychologists trouble. Many of their definitions of psychology make no mention either of mind or of consciousness. Instead, some define psychology as the study of experience, while others regard it as the study of behavior. This goes back to psychology's initial efforts to win recognition as an experimental science. As a founding father of this "new" experimental psychology, Wilhelm Wundt (1832–1920) was one of the first to define psychology in terms of the concept of experience rather than the concept of consciousness or of mind.

In 1886, not long after Wundt established his laboratory at Leipzig in 1879, John Dewey (1859–1952) published the first American textbook dealing with the "new" psychology. He wrote, "Psychology is the Science of the facts or Phenomena of Self" (1893, p. 1). In explaining this definition he introduced the concept of consciousness, but he found it refractory, as is shown in these excerpts (p. 2):

> The self not only exists, but may know that it exists; psychical phenomena are not only facts, but they are facts of consciousness. . . . What distinguishes the facts of psychology from the facts of every other science is, accordingly, that they are conscious facts. . . . Consciousness can neither be defined nor described. We can define or describe anything only by the employment of consciousness. It is presupposed, accordingly, in all definitions and all attempts to define it must move in a circle. . . . Consciousness is necessary for the definition of what is in itself unconscious. Psychology, accordingly, can study only the various *forms* of consciousness, showing the *conditions* under which they arise.

In his reference to "what is in itself unconscious" Dewey mentioned both a stick and a stone, neither of which is "aware . . . of its existence." He thus implied that to be unconscious is to be unaware, and that to be conscious is to be aware. Nevertheless, he evidently did not regard this as a satisfactory definition of consciousness. Apparently he did not find dictionary definitions of the time sufficient, since he assuredly had them at his disposal. Lexicographers can never follow his example of maintaining that a given word "can neither be defined nor described." It is their professional obligation to state what every term means or has meant.

Accordingly, it may prove enlightening to consult current general and psychological dictionaries to see whether modern lexicographers have been able to define *consciousness* and its derivatives so as to make the concept congruent with psychology's scientific aspirations.

Dictionary Definitions

Modern dictionaries, unlike those of the 1880s, mention the psychoanalytic contrast between the conscious and the unconscious. They also confirm the close relation between mind and consciousness. However, among other definitions, the word *unconscious* is said to have "to do with those of one's mental processes that one is unable to bring into his consciousness." This suggests that the mind's processes take place independently of consciousness in a paradoxical realm of unconscious consciousness. How is this to be understood? Does it refer to mental processes that once were conscious or to those not yet conscious? If the latter, what renders them mental? If consciousness is the hallmark of mind, how can a *mental* process be unconscious?

From one point of view "unconsciousness" presupposes prior understanding of consciousness, just as *unprejudiced* calls for a prior definition of *prejudiced*. Accordingly, one might expect an unabridged dictionary's definition of consciousness to set the stage for the antithetical notion of unconsciousness. Unfortunately, of about six definitions of consciousness, none is antithetical to the meaning of unconsciousness. Thus being awake is often given as one meaning of consciousness. Does this mean being asleep is the same as being unconscious? After all, a sleeping person is conscious to the extent of noting dream content. Moreover, the victim of a nightmare is vividly aware of terror. The transition from nightmare to wakefulness is not a shift from unconsciousness to consciousness but from one state of awareness to another. Consequently, to regard sleep as antithetical to consciousness is wrong unless we include only dreamless sleep. Even so, the dreamless sleep of a healthy person is different from the unconsciousness of a comatose patient; there is a distinction between normal and abnormal unconsciousness.

There is also a distinction between being comatose and being dead. To be in a coma is to be unconscious, but to be dead is to be nonconscious. Inanimate objects like bricks and bottles are nonconscious. The lifeless corpse, unlike the unconscious patient, can never become conscious; like other inanimate objects, it is nonconscious.

Actually the word *nonconscious* is not well known. It is not included in all unabridged dictionaries, and even some psychiatric dictionaries fail to mention it. But it can be found in dictionaries of psychology. For example, Warren's *Dictionary of Psychology* (1934, p. 181), after noting that the literal meaning of nonconscious is "without consciousness," qualifies this by adding: "Best confined to lifeless beings or substances, using *unconscious* to denote conditions in living beings." Similarly, English and English (1958, p. 348) make the same point by calling "lifeless substance" nonconscious, in contrast to "unconscious, which refers to a special condition or activity of a living organism." By implication this distinction allocates the concept of consciousness to the life sciences as opposed to the physical sciences. Unconsciousness is biological while nonconsciousness is a physical condition. Metaphysically considered, the distinction involves such dichotomies as monism/dualism, mechanism/vitalism, and materialism/spiritualism, an indication of the broad scope of the problem of consciousness.

Of course some dictionary allusions to consciousness suggest the antithetical connotations of *unconsciousness.* Thus, awareness suggests unawareness, knowing suggests unknowing, intentional suggests unintentional, and mindfulness suggests mindlessness. It is difficult to bring all these connotations within the confines of a single comprehensive definition. After listing some of the meanings of *consciousness,* English and English (p. 113) wrote that it "has many other shades of meaning, few of them explicitly defended or consistently used." In fact, they concluded that "the term has lost usefulness and should be replaced in technical discussion" by some less "confusing" term. Needless to say, no satisfactory replacement has come to light, and the term continues to appear in technical books and journals as well as in popular fiction and ordinary discourse. Nor are references to consciousness in all contexts "confusing." For instance, most people would not be confused by a simple statement like "I am conscious." They would understand it to mean knowing what is taking place, being aware of one's surroundings, and being sensitive to internal cravings, aches, thoughts, and feelings. Such understanding is in accord with the word's derivation from the Latin *scire,* "to know," the root of the word *science.* Thus consciousness connotes capacity for reflection in the sense of knowing that one knows or being able to think about what one knows.

Awareness, commonly regarded as a synonym for consciousness, has a different connotation. According to the dictionary, the word is of Anglo-Saxon rather than Latin origin and is derived from the root *waere,* meaning "cautious" or "watchfully alert." As a result, being aware has a slightly different meaning from being conscious. Both terms have to do with perceiving a source of stimulation, either external or internal. In general, awareness is concerned with external and consciousness with internal events. Thus we are aware of a police siren and conscious of being startled by it. To be aware implies being attentive—being watchful or wary or vigilant toward impersonal outside events—while to be conscious implies being sensitive to changes in more personal internal events. The tired driver is aware of traffic signals and conscious of his weariness. He might exclaim, "My, but I'm tired," not only giving expression to tiredness, but also acknowledging its existence as a personal possession, as if the fatigue belongs to him while the traffic lights belong to the outside world.

Awareness is less personal and reflective than consciousness, so unreflective animals may be aware but not conscious in the sense of recognizing or thinking about their own awareness. Aristotle appears to have referred to this idea when he endowed animals with sensitive but not rational souls.

Victims of embarrassment or stage fright are said to be self-conscious. In fact, the terms *self-aware* and *self-awareness* are not found in dictionaries, whereas *self-conscious* and *self-consciousness* not only are included there but are also familiar everyday expressions. In recent years, however, as brought out by Wicklund (1979), both *self-aware* and *self-awareness* have been used in studies concerned with the self as the object of analysis. This recent usage has not yet come to the attention of lexicographers. When they do deal with the terms, they will not present them as precise synonyms for consciousness of self, since there is a distinction between viewing the self subjectively, as in stage fright, and objectively, as in critical self-analysis. In some respects the subjective connotation is more akin to the historical meaning of consciousness.

Some Facts of History in Broad Perspective

Both the word *consciousness* and systematic interest in the psychological concept had their origins in the seventeenth century. This was the century of two influential thinkers, René Descartes (1596–1650) and John Locke (1632–1704). Both were concerned with the concept of consciousness, which had virtually been ignored before their time. Klemm called attention to this: "The discovery of consciousness as a fundamental psychical fact was not made before Descartes" (1914, p. 169). This "discovery," he was careful to note, is connected with "the development of the modern concept of consciousness." He was not saying that phenomena commonly regarded as facts of consciousness had previously been overlooked. It is easy to find mention of such facts in the Bible, from the dreams of Joseph to Job's catalog of human afflictions. In the Psalms consciousness of self is reflected in such verses as "Mine eye is dimmed because of grief."[2]

Consciousness of self was especially prominent in the writings of Plotinus (205–70), the Neoplatonist whose *Enneads* raised many questions of psychological significance. In connection with emotional changes he asked, "Pleasure and distress, fear and courage, desire and aversion, where have these affections their seat?" (1957, p. 21). Plotinus was curious about loss of consciousness, wondering about "the suspension which drugs or disease may bring about" (p. 44). In his quest for self-understanding he called attention to a wide range of psychological phenomena, especially those pertaining to consciousness of self. As George Brett noted: "In Plotinus, for the first time in its history, psychology becomes the science of the phenomena of consciousness, conceived as self-consciousness" (1912,

---

2. This reference to visual changes associated with "grief" is from Ps. 6:7. For another interesting psychological observation see Ps. 19:14, which distinguishes between covert thoughts and overt expression by calling the latter "the words of my mouth" as contrasted with "the meditation of my heart." A biblical use of a contemporary spatial metaphor as in "depth psychology," with its differentiation between "deep" thoughts and "shallow" ones, is in Ps. 92:5—thy "thoughts are very deep."

1:302). Brett thus was recognizing knowledge of self as a product of introspective observation, a relatively sophisticated process that entails reflecting upon one's experience. This is tantamount to holding that without
some capacity for reflection there can be no self-consciousness.

To reflect is to be conscious of being conscious or to know that one
knows. This was brought out in John Locke's famous *Essay Concerning
Human Understanding* of 1690 (1901, p. 207):

> [Reflection] is the perception of the operation of our own mind
> within us, as it is employed about the ideas it has got; which opera-
> tions . . . are perception, thinking, doubting, believing, reasoning,
> knowing, willing, and all the different actings of our own minds;
> which we being conscious of, and observing in ourselves, do from
> these receive into our understandings as distinct ideas, as we do from
> bodies affecting our senses.

Reflection for Locke was evidently far from a simple operation. It
embraced all cognitive functions involved in the life of the intellect; hence
"all the different actings of our . . . minds." In another passage Locke
explained that when he reflects man is "conscious to himself that he thinks."
This view of reflection may be identical with what Aristotle, in *De anima,*
attributed to "that in the soul which is called mind" and then added, "by
mind I mean that whereby the soul thinks and judges" (McKeon, 1947,
p. 218).

There may be some question about the precise meaning of these Aristotelian references to "mind," a frequent translation of the Greek word *nous.*
Nous may also be translated as "reason," so that the preceding excerpt
would read, "by reason I mean that whereby the soul thinks and judges."
Reason, of course, has to do with thinking, as suggested by the Greek
noesis, so *nous* may be said to connote thought, reason, mind, intellect,
or cognitive functions in general. Close to two thousand years later this
Aristotelian *nous* became Descartes's *res cogitans,* or "thing which thinks,"
brought out in his *Metaphysical Meditations* of 1641 in a striking passage
concerned with his quest for identity (Descartes, n.d., pp. 132–33):

> But what, then, am I? *A thing which thinks.* What is a thing which
> thinks? It is a thing which doubts, understands, conceives, affirms,
> denies, wills, wills not, which also imagines, and feels. Certainly it
> is no small matter, if all these things belong to my nature. But why
> should they not belong to it? Am I not that which now doubts of
> almost everything which nevertheless understands and conceives
> certain things, which asserts and affirms these alone to be true, and
> denies the rest . . . ? Is there, besides, any of these attributes which
> can be distinguished from my thought, or which can be said to be
> separated from myself? For it is so self-evident that it is I who doubt,

understand, and desire that there is no need to add here anything to explain it.

Descartes saw this conclusion as "self-evident" in part because he had already considered the issue in his *Discourse on Method*,[3] published in 1637. In that work he had explained how confidence in the reality of *res cogitans* had emerged from his quest for a solid basis for knowledge, in which he took no belief or teaching for granted but subjected each one to systematic doubt. But he found it impossible to doubt that he was doubting, and so thinking, since to doubt is to think; hence his famous conclusion, "I think, therefore I am"—*cogito ergo sum*.

Now *cogito,* customarily translated in this context as "I think," has additional meanings. For example, according to one Latin-English dictionary, the verb *cogito* means "*to turn over in the mind, to think, reflect;* sometimes *to intend, plan,*" just as the noun *cogitatio* refers to "*thinking, conception, reflection, reasoning:* sometimes a particular *thought, idea* or *intention*" (*Cassell's* 1964, p. 40). In terms of these extended meanings *cogitatio,* "reflection,"[4] and *nous,* "reason," are seen to be synonymous, with Descartes, Locke, and Aristotle in substantial agreement regarding their psychological implications.

Implications of the Cartesian Cogito

One of these implications refers to self-consciousness in the "*cogito*" of Descartes and the "reflection" of Locke. Locke had made this explicit by noting that during reflection man is "conscious to himself that he thinks." Descartes was equally explicit in using the phrase "*ergo sum*" as if to argue that "because I think, I know that I exist or have a mind or soul." This enlarged interpretation of *sum* is justified because of the sharp distinction Descartes had made between mind as thinking substance and body as extended substance—the *res cogitans* as contrasted with *res extensa.*[5] The "I" as mind or soul or thinking substance and the brain as extended substance thus were allocated to different realms of being. Mere possession of a brain did not establish the existence of a mind.

3. This is a contraction of the actual title, *Discourse upon the Method of Rightly Conducting the Reason and the Research of Truth in the Sciences.*

4. In the *Metaphysical Meditations* (p. 104) Descartes supports this interpretation by writing that "the human mind in *reflecting* on itself, knows itself to be nothing else but a thing which thinks" (italics added).

5. In making this distinction between mind as inextended or nonspatial and body as extended or spatial, Descartes may have been influenced by Aristotle. This distinction is mentioned in *De anima* when Aristotle asks whether thinking is "spatially" separate and concludes that mind "cannot reasonably be regarded as blended with the body" (McKeon 1947, pp. 217–18).

Mind as *res cogitans* was an exclusive human endowment and could function independently of the brain. Brett quotes Descartes: "I have often shown that the mind can work independently of the brain; for clearly there can be no use of the brain for pure intelligence, but only for imagination and sensation" (Brett 1921, p. 205). In somewhat arbitrary fashion Descartes thus denied animals any cognitive functions beyond sensation and imagination, following the Aristotelian view that man has a rational soul and animals only sensitive souls. But, unlike Aristotle, he did this in terms of his understanding of the function of brain and nerves. As James noted (1890, p. 130).

To Descartes belongs the credit of having first been bold enough to conceive of a completely self-sufficing nervous mechanism which should be able to perform complicated and apparently intelligent acts. By a singularly arbitrary restriction, however, Descartes stopped short at man, and while contending that in beasts the nervous machinery was all, he held that the higher acts of man were the result of the agency of his rational soul.

The Cartesian *cogito* and all it implied for self-consciousness was thus unique to man, as attribute of his rational soul.

The "I" of the Cartesian *cogito* is not an immediately and directly apprehended sensory datum like a blinding light or a sudden pain. Instead, its status is entirely inferential. This was brought out forcefully some years ago in C. A. Strong's book *Why the Mind Has a Body,* which E. G. Boring praised as "the best book on the mind-body problem" (1950, p. 688). According to Strong's trenchant argument (1903, p. 198):

> Soul is not an empirical fact, but an inference. This appears from Descartes' argument for it, the famous "*cogito ergo sum.*" Here the conclusion, the "sum" does not simply mean that "my thought exists"; it means that there is a "*res cogitans,*" distinct from the "*cogitatio,*" and not immediately given as the "*cogitatio*" is given. If the Soul were an immediate datum, it would not have to be inferred but merely noted, and the argument would shrink to the observational proposition "*sum.*" The real premise, as Descartes intends it, is not "*cogito,*" but "*cogitatio fit,*" "thinking goes on," and the conclusion being drawn "*ergo sum,*" "I am": the "I" thus being given in the conclusion but not in the premise.

Here Strong uses "soul" as a synonym for "I" or self or ego, as if he had written "ego is not an empirical fact, but an inference" and "the self is not an immediate datum." A more modern idiom would call the "I" of the Cartesian maxim a hypothetical construct. Like all intervening variables, hypothetical constructs are not amenable to direct observation. They are *inferred* processes not open to direct sensory perception. That the self or "I" cannot be grasped apart from perceptions is clearly brought out by David Hume (1711–76) (Chappell 1963, p. 84):

> For my part, when I enter most intimately into what I call *myself,*
> I always stumble on some particular perception or other, of heat or
> cold, light or shade, love or hatred, pain or pleasure. I never can
> catch *myself* at any time without a perception, and never can observe
> any thing but the perception. When my perceptions are removed for
> any time, as by sound sleep; so long am I insensible of *myself,* and
> may truly be said not to exist.

In thus equating existence with perceptibility Hume echoed the convic-
tion George Berkeley (1685–1753), expressed in his maxim *"esse est percipi"*
— "to be is to be perceived." But Hume differed from Berkeley in an important respect when he argued that he might "truly be said not to exist" during
"sound sleep." He did not infer an independent percipient. Unlike Descartes, he was not saying "perception is taking place, therefore I am a separate mind or soul or spirit."[6] Berkeley seemed to endorse the Cartesian
inference, for he acknowledged the existence of a spiritual principle even
though spirit "cannot of itself be perceived." In one passage (1910, p. 126)
he referred to spirit as synonymous with "understanding, mind, soul" and
as "an incorporeal active substance" that "perceives ideas."

As a *nonperceptible* inferred entity this Berkeleyan spiritual mind, conceived of as "one simple, undivided, active being," amounts to an *unconscious*[7] mind. The skeptical Hume could not endorse belief in such "an
incorporeal active substance," and in accordance with the maxim *esse est
percipi* he could never "catch" himself observing an ego or self or thinker
distinct from the cognitive item being noted or observed. About a century
after Hume's death, William James (1842–1910) also found no support for
an independent "Non-phenominal Thinker" or a "Transcendental Ego."
Instead, he found each "passing thought" to be its own thinker (1890,
pp. 339–40):

> Each pulse of cognitive consciousness, each Thought, dies away
> and is replaced by another. The other, among things it knows, knows
> its own predecessor, and finding it "warm," . . . greets it, saying:
> "Thou art *mine,* and part of the same self with me." Each later
> Thought, knowing and including thus the thoughts which went

6. Extending the Cartesian *ergo sum* to include mind, soul, or spirit is justified because
Descartes uses soul as a synonym for mind and also points out that he "makes no distinction" between "the spirit or the soul of man" (n.d., pp. 110–11).

7. This illustrates one of the many meanings of the word *unconscious* — inability to observe
or experience directly. In this sense the congenitally blind are unconscious of the world of
color, and all of us are unconscious of the sound of Plato's voice. This is not to deny the
existence of color or say that Plato was mute.

before, is the final receptacle—and appropriating them is the final owner—of all that they contain and own. Each Thought is thus born an owner, and dies owned, transmitting whatever it realized as its Self to its own later proprietor. As Kant says, it is as if elastic balls were to have not only motion but knowledge of it, and a first ball were to transmit both up into *its* consciousness and passed them to a third, until the last ball held all that the other balls had held, and realized as its own. It is this trick which the nascent thought has of immediately taking up the expiring thought and "adopting" it, which is the foundation of the appropriation of most of the remoter constituents of the self.

The passing thought, James held, does no more than supply the "foundation" for what may develop into "the remoter constituents of the self." James failed to equate the passing thought with the "I" implicit in the Cartesian *cogito* or to find any "mind stuff" in the way of a *res cogitans* or "thinking thing."

Descartes had divorced this supposed *res cogitans* from the brain as a *res extensa,* as is evident from his contention "that the mind can work independently of the brain."[8] For him the brain, as a spatial constituent of the body, was subject to the laws of mechanics. But the mind, being a nonspatial entity, was free from mechanical restrictions and as "pure intelligence" could function independently of the brain. Accordingly, a noncorporeal mind had no commerce with a tridimensional brain. This applied to human beings but not to animals, for the *res cogitans* was exclusively human. In the Cartesian scheme animals were physiological automatons, the equivalent of machines, whose actions were governed by the laws of physics. Of course the human body also resembled a machine, but it was saved from mechanical automatism by the sovereign control of the *res cogitans.*

This Cartesian view of animals as biological machines was not equivalent to regarding them as insensitive objects. Descartes was familiar with gross

8. It is not indefensible to suggest that some mental activity takes place independently of brain changes—compare the idea of "functional" mental illness independent of brain pathology. Even where brain pathology is clearly linked to cognitive impairment, this correlation is not inevitable. For example, the psychiatrist Le Roy Levitt noted that there is a significant reduction in the number of brain cells in demented patients, then added: "Severe brain changes may be seen in patients who have had no dementia, however, indicating that there is not always a correlation between degree of anatomical change and degree of intellectual impairment" (1970, p. 211).

This finding is not isolated or recent. About one hundred years ago the great neurologist Hughlings Jackson, in a lecture entitled "The Diagnosis of Tumours of the Brain," had this to say (Jackson 1958, 2:279): "The generalization is that *destruction* of a considerable part of either the cerebrum or cerebellum (especially if that destruction be effected slowly) can occur without the production of striking symptoms of any sort—'mental' or 'physical.' "

anatomy and had dissected the eye and other organs. Consequently he did not think of sense organs as useless appendages. He knew that, through their linkage with the brain, they provided for visual, auditory, and other sensations. According to Descartes animals were not blind, deaf, anosmic machines; they were endowed with what Aristotle had termed a sensitive soul.

Descartes had followed Aristotle in making the *res cogitans,* a "thing which thinks," unique to man like the rational soul of Aristotle's psychology and in maintaining that "mind can work independently of the brain." Aristotle had failed to attribute sensation to the brain because wounded soldiers reported no sensations when their exposed brains were subjected to pressure.

That sensory nerves terminate in the brain was first established by Herophilus (fl. 300 B.C.), an Alexandrian anatomist, who thus corrected Aristotle by recognizing sensation as a brain function. Descartes accepted this correction in considering the sensitive soul a function of the animal's brain, with automatic response to sensory impressions like sights, sounds, and pains. Unlike man, however, animals were incapable of reflecting upon such impressions, for they lacked the requisite *res cogitans.* In his view animals were unthinking automatons but not insensitive or nonconscious.

Cartesianism: A Psychologist's Objections

This Cartesian view of mind has met objections from both psychologists and philosophers. Representative is E. B. Titchener (1867–1927). In his widely circulated textbook of 1917 he argued that popular psychology, in contrast to scientific psychology, is replete with "statements" stemming from the philosophy of Descartes. As he saw it (1917, p. 11):

> These statements all point to a view of mind which is not often expressed outright, in so many words, but which is very generally held; the view, namely, that mind is a living being, with all the qualities and powers that are possessed by material living beings; an immaterial animal, so to say, that dwells within the material animal; an inward man, manifesting itself in the behaviour of the outward man. A mind so conceived cannot fill space, because it is not material; but it has all the other properties of a living creature. It is free to act as it pleases, just as you are free to come or to go, to do this or to do that. It can influence the body, and be influenced by the body just as you may influence or be influenced by your friend.

These key principles of popular psychology are predominantly Cartesian; "what is common sense today was high Cartesian philosophy two centuries and a half ago" (p. 12).

In part Titchener objects to this commonsense psychology of Cartesian descent because it fails to explain how an inextended or nonspatial mind can influence an extended body—"for the very good reason that nobody knows." Furthermore, visual spatial illusions like the Müller-Lyer illusion[9] show that "mental experience" is as readily cast in spatial form as "physical experience." The free-will implications of the Cartesian tradition must also be rejected. Arguing that "mind is free to act as it pleases" rejects scientific psychology's implicit faith in the dependability of "the laws of mental experience."

For Titchener mental experience is not a realm drastically different from the physical. He objected to the doctrine that body can influence mind and mind can influence body and sponsored a different doctrine (p. 13):

> Our own position has been that mind and body, the subject-matter of psychology and the subject-matter of physiology, are simply two aspects of the same world of experience. They cannot influence each other, because they are not separate and independent things. For the same reason, however, wherever the two aspects appear, any change that occurs in the one will be accompanied by a corresponding change in the other. . . . This doctrine of the relation of mind to body is known as the doctrine of psychophysical parallelism: the common sense doctrine is that of interaction.

One may question the names Titchener assigned to the two doctrines. The rejected Cartesian or commonsense doctrine is correctly designated interactionism, but Titchener's preferred doctrine is more in accord with the "double-aspect theory" of the mind/body relation than with psychophysical parallelism. These doctrines are closely related, and some writers confuse them, yet their implicit metaphysical assumptions distinguish the two. The double-aspect theory implies an underlying identity of conscious events and concomitant brain events, making it a monistic theory. Parallelism, while not always defined as explicitly or even necessarily dualistic, has definitely been considered so by such leading parallelists as G. W. Leibniz (1646–1716) and G. T. Fechner (1801–87). Although Titchener calls himself a parallelist in the passage quoted, he seems to support the iden-

9. Most students of experimental psychology will recognize this illusion by sight if not by name. It takes this general form:

Line A is usually judged to be longer than line B, even though the lines are equal. The illusion is created when one compares *areas* rather than *lines*. Although the illusion has been known for many decades, it continues to engage the interest of investigators. Piaget, for example, refers to it on more than thirty pages of *The Mechanisms of Perception* (1969). Some of Piaget's conclusions about this illusion have been questioned by Pollack (1970).

tity hypothesis when he declares that "matter and mind . . . must be fundamentally the same thing" and that mind and body "are not separate and independent things," reinforcing this support by making them "two aspects of the same world." In doing so he echoes Spinoza (1632–77), whose early formulation of the identity hypothesis took this form: "The order and connection of ideas is the same as the order and connection of things." In the modern era the physicist C. F. V. Weizsäcker expressed Spinoza's double-aspect version of parallelism: "Body and soul are not two substances but one. They are man becoming aware of himself in two different ways."

Titchener's parallelism was also a monistic doctrine, since he did not conceive of mind and body as "separate and independent things," which led him to reject Cartesian interactionism and to cast doubt on the popular notion of a reciprocal causal influence by which mind affects body and vice versa.

More than five decades later, these issues continue to be debated. In a 1969 article David Krech called Titchener the sponsor of a "brainless psychology" who "from his noninteractionist, psychophysical-parallelistic position, would—and did—assert that the study of brain physiology . . . had little value for the psychologist." For this reason, Krech added, Titchener explained that his textbook "would omit any discussion of brain anatomy or physiology" (Krech 1969, p. 4).

Actually, Titchener had qualified that statement in his preface by saying that he had "no desire to minimize the importance" of the study of "nervous physiology" for the psychologist, but that he had "always held that the student should get his elementary knowledge of the nervous system, not from the psychologist, but from the physiologist; the teacher of psychology needs all the time at his disposal for his own science" (1917, p. viii). Moreover, Titchener keeps reminding the reader of the importance of the nervous system. Here are a few such reminders:

> The nervous system does not cause, but it does explain mind. . . . In a word, reference to the nervous system introduces into psychology just that unity and coherence which a strictly descriptive psychology cannot achieve. (p. 39)

> But is meaning always conscious meaning? Surely not: meaning may be carried in purely physiological terms. (p. 369)

> The explanation of association, like that of perception, must be sought in the nervous system. (pp. 377–78)

Krech appears to have overlooked the implications of these reminders when he disparaged Titchener's work as a "brainless psychology." It may be that he primarily objected to Titchener's parallelism, since he seemed to endorse interactionism: "Brain chemistry and brain morphology determine behavior, but brain chemistry and brain morphology are just as clearly determined by the behavior they determine!" (p. 6). This reference to behavior is not a denial or an evasion of the reality and importance of consciousness. In raising questions "about the nature and quality of consciousness" Krech says he means "*consciousness*—not some behavioristic ersatz" (p. 8). Though neurochemically more sophisticated than that of Descartes, his interactionism thus appears to provide for the Cartesian *cogito*.

Krech's stand did not settle the issue raised by Titchener's parallelism. For example, in a discussion of Krech's paper Peter Milner came close to defending Titchener against the "brainless psychology" charge by writing that "it is possible to be a good psychologist without knowing much about the real brain (not that anybody does). In fact, trying to keep up with the latest information about the brain is a full-time occupation; anyone who does so is not likely to have enough time left to think fruitfully about the mechanisms of behavior" (1969, p. 19).

Cartesianism: A Philosopher's Objections

Some thirty years after publication of Titchener's textbook, Gilbert Ryle, an Oxford philosopher, wrote *The Concept of Mind*. Like Titchener, he objected to the view of mind as an immaterial, nonspatial being housed in a spatial body, which he stigmatized as "Descartes' myth," devoting a whole chapter to the "absurdity" of treating mind as a "ghost" in the bodily machine (1949, pp. 11–24)—regarding the "I" of the Cartesian *cogito* as a disembodied spirit.

Whether Descartes would have endorsed this interpretation is hard to say. He might have objected to the spatial location suggested for the "I" or mind by placing the "ghost" *in* the machine, since he thought of mind as functioning "independently of the brain." Although he referred to the pineal body as "perhaps" the receiving station for sensory impressions, Descartes never actually designated it the "center" for mind. Ryle's Cartesian "ghost" was more of a free-floating "mind" devoid of specifiable commerce with the machinery of the body.

Ryle also objected to the concept of the body as a machine whose functions can all be explained by the laws of mechanics. "Men are not machines," he wrote, "not even ghost-ridden machines" (1949, p. 81).[10] He thus rejected both the Cartesian mind and the Cartesian body: the *res cogitans* and the *res extensa*. His objection to mechanical explication of

10. Objections to the machine as the ideal scientific model had already been voiced by Wolfgang Köhler (1887–1967) in his *Gestalt Psychology* (1929). Chapter 4, "Dynamics as Opposed to Machine Theory," presents an array of considerations of direct psychological relevance that, though different, supplement Ryle's basic thesis.

the latter went beyond Descartes's notions, and he warned against "a very popular fallacy" that "everything in Nature is subject to mechanical laws." He denied that living things—trees, animals, and men—are more or less complicated machines. Machines are built by assembling parts—bolts, wheels, wires, and camshafts—unlike living things, which emerge by differentiation from a growing seed or developing embryo. Inventing a new machine is thus not a process of copying nature (p. 82).

Ryle was more interested in the broad implications of this mechanistic fallacy than with its bearing on Cartesian neurophysiology; his critique of Cartesianism focused on the myth of "mind" as free-floating, and he was interested in exorcising the Cartesian "ghost" rather than finding it a congenial cerebral habitat. Ryle's objective was to expose the myth by accounting for the concepts of selves and thinkers in naturalistic, non-mystical terms. Another philosopher, A. G. Widgery, believed this objective was not realized, since "Ryle gives no satisfactory account of himself as the thinker of his own theories" (1970, p. 2). Let us thus consider Ryle's view of the self as thinker.

The Cartesian myth, Ryle indicated, had to do with the referent of "I" and what he called the word's "systematic elusiveness." He recognized both the popular and the technical aspects of the problem (p. 186):

> Not only theorists but also quite unsophisticated people, including young children, find perplexities in the notion of "I." Children sometimes puzzle their heads with such questions as, "What would it be like if I became you and you became me?" and "Where was I before I began?" Theologians have been exercised over the question "What is it in an individual which is saved or damned?" and philosophers have speculated whether "I" denotes a peculiar and separate substance and in what consists my indivisible and continuing identity.

The Self and Index Words

To dispose of some of these perplexities, Ryle pointed out that "I" belongs to a group of words sometimes designated *index* words, which indicate specific items, times, places, things, or episodes. In the sentence "I'll see you tomorrow," *tomorrow* is an index word. So is *you,* since it refers to a particular person, just as *tomorrow* refers to a particular time. As an index word "I" also has such a specific reference—the individual employing it. Whatever *he* regards as belonging to or related to *his* biography consequently falls within the scope of what "I" may designate. In this context "I" and "self" are synonymous, so that whatever pertains to self may also pertain to "I" or "me" and similar pronouns. Thus the concept of self may include *my* house, cousin, debts, clothes, glasses, doubts, hopes, children, bank balance, mistakes, honors, and anything else that *I* am willing to claim as *mine*. Such a random array of claimed possessions illustrates "the remoter constituents of the self" in the previously cited quotation by William James.

The mystery of the quest for some fixed entity presumably symbolized by "I" diminishes when we consider "I" as an index word. By such detailed consideration Ryle disposed of the Cartesian myth of a disembodied mind or self, elaborating on the views of George Frederick Stout (1860–1944), one of Ryle's philosophic predecessors at Oxford. Long before, Stout had objected to the Cartesian cleavage of mind and body and urged a more integrated view of the psychophysical relationship. His account of this relationship is reminiscent of Aristotle's concept of mind as embodied (Stout 1931, pp. 154–55):

Mind and body are not primarily apprehended as distinct *things;* mental processes are not taken apart from bodily in such wise as to raise questions concerning the way in which they are combined with each other. What we are primarily aware of is the individual unity of an embodied Self. It is this which is signified by the personal pronouns "I," "you," and "he." Consider the phrases: I see the moon, I hear a bird, I handle a knife, I walk from this place to that, I feel a wound, I am in prison. We cannot, at any rate without a radical change of meaning, substitute for the personal pronoun in these statements either "my body" or "my mind!" I cannot say "My body sees a bird" or "My mind sees a bird!" Such language does violence to Common Sense, though it may be appropriate to some materialistic or spiritualistic theory. I may indeed say "My body walks" or "My body handles a knife." But if I do so it is because I intend to indicate that it is not I but only body that is implicated. It is true also that there are cases in which "I" and "my body" may be used interchangeably. But when this is so, "I" has no longer its proper and primary, but only a transferred and derivative meaning. I may say indifferently that "I" or "my body" will sometime be mouldering in the grave. But I readily recognize that the dead and buried body will not really be I. I continue to speak of it as "I" or even as "my body" only because it is thought of as connected by a continuous history with my present individual experience as an embodied self.

Ryle may have had this last comment in mind when he considered the referents of the pronouns in the sentence, "Cremate me after I am gone" (Ryle 1949, p. 189). Here the "me" could be replaced by "my body" so as to read "Cremate my body after I am gone." However, it would be absurd to do the same for the "I" by having the sentence read "Cremate me after my body is gone." Rejecting the Cartesian myth thus does not limit the first-person pronoun to its function as an index word for body, as in phrases like "my stomach" or "my brain" or any other bodily organ. As Ryle makes clear, it sometimes functions this way, but in other instances it cannot. Thus someone with a bruised thumb can say "I'm in pain" or "My finger hurts." It would make sense for him to say "I was careless when I hit my thumb with the hammer," but it would be nonsense for him to say "My body was careless." Similarly, it would make sense for a lawyer to say "I argued with the judge" but it would be ridiculous for him to say "My mouth argued with the judge."

In the latter instance the lawyer is using "I" as an index word to point to those phases of his "individual experience" by which he established his professional status as a member of the bar. As such they merge with all personally significant experienced phases of the "continuous history" of his "embodied self"—events he might include in an autobiography.

Both Stout and Titchener were anti-Cartesian in their views. Moreover, in approaching a definition of mind both stressed the concept of experience: Stout conceived of "individual experience as an embodied self," while Titchener referred to the "laws of mental experience." As products of different psychological traditions, they thus independently arrived at the same conclusion by making experience an important criterion of mind or consciousness. Whether it is the most important one or the only one is a separate issue.

Criteria of Consciousness

We have seen that no single identifying characteristic or criterion of consciousness came to light. Consequently, it would make sense to talk about the phenomena rather than the phenomenon of consciousness. The manifold nature of the concept was evident centuries ago. Locke's *Essay Concerning Human Understanding* listed "perception, thinking, doubting, believing, reasoning, knowing, willing" as "actings of our own minds" of which we are conscious. In his textbook of 1886 John Dewey wrote about the *facts* of "psychical phenomena" and the *"forms"* of consciousness." The absence of a single differentiating criterion of consciousness was also implicit in his asserting that consciousness cannot be defined. In the 1950s Karl Lashley (1890–1958), an outstanding student of brain physiology, made this explicit at a symposium on *Brain Mechanisms and Intelligence* when he declared, "There is no one criterion of consciousness" (1954, p. 425).

Lashley stated that any definition of consciousness would have to be very general, as when we define a social organization like government.

Here too, he noted, the characteristics of the constituent parts—executive, judicial, and legislative agencies—are too varied to permit one all-embracing definition. No single agency or individual can be designated as *the government.* A satisfactory account of the nature of government must include criteria for the structure and function of each agency. The final accounts drafted by different political scientists might not be the same, since they might attribute varying importance to given agencies or criteria.

Accounts of the nature of mind or consciousness by different psychologists have also varied according to the aspect or criterion of mental life selected as dominating and made the hallmark of a particular psychological school or system. Thus systems have been based on the importance attributed to sensations or reflexes or wishes or perceptual patterns or the self or the inferiority complex or instincts or mental acts or redintegration or associations or variants of the foregoing. It is manifestly impossible to bring all these separate systems of psychology into one comprehensive system or to incorporate all their insights into a definition of psychology. Brown and Herrnstein expressed this as follows (1975, p. 3):

> We may as well have the scandal out at once and get it over with: "psychology" cannot be defined. Not properly anyway, not as most people understand defining. Neither can the professional subfields be defined. "Clinical psychology," "experimental psychology," "social psychology": they none of them can be defined.

Part of the difficulty of defining the subfields of psychology is that they are abstractions from psychology as a whole; hence explaining the subfields presupposes knowledge of the whole. The same is true for any one segment or criterion of mind: topics like sensation, memory, and olfaction are abstractions from mental life as experienced. The concept of consciousness is also an abstraction—a topic with such widespread implications that it calls for a separate chapter.

References

Aristotle. 1947. *De anima.* In *Introduction to Aristotle,* ed. C. R. McKeon, 145–240. New York: Modern Library.

Berkeley, G. 1910. *A new theory of vision and other select philosophical writings.* London: J. M. Dent.

Boring, E. G. 1950. *A history of experimental psychology.* New York: Appleton-Century-Crofts.

Brett, G. S. 1912, 1921. *A history of psychology.* 2 vols. London: George Allen and Unwin.

Brown, R., and Herrnstein, R. J. 1975. *Psychology.* Boston: Little, Brown.

Cassell's New Compact Latin-English English-Latin Dictionary. 1964. Comp. D. P. Simpson. New York: Funk and Wagnalls.

Chappell, V. C., ed. 1963. *The philosophy of David Hume.* New York: Modern Library.

Descartes, R. n.d. *Discourse on method* and *metaphysical meditations.* Trans. G. B. Rawlings. London: Walter Scott Publishing Company.

Dewey, J. 1893. *Psychology.* 3d ed. New York: Harper. First published 1886.

English, H. B., and English, A. C. 1958. *A comprehensive dictionary of psychological and psychoanalytical terms.* New York: Longmans, Green.

Jackson, J. H. 1958. *Selected writings of John Hughlings Jackson.* 2 vols. Ed. J. Taylor. New York: Basic Books.

James, W. 1890. *Principles of psychology.* Vol. 1. New York: Henry Holt.

Klemm, O. 1914. *A history of psychology.* Trans. E. C. Wilm and R. Pinter. New York: Charles Scribner's Sons.

Köhler, W. 1929. *Gestalt psychology.* New York: Liveright.

Krech, D. 1969. Does behavior really need a brain? In *William James: Unfinished business,* ed. R. B. MacLeod, 1–11. Washington, D.C.: American Psychological Association.

Lashley, K. S. 1954. Dynamic processes in perception. In *Brain mechanisms and consciousness,* 422–43. Springfield, Ill.: Charles C. Thomas.

Levitt, L. 1970. Dementia. In *Encyclopaedia Britannica,* 7:210–12.

Locke, J. 1901. *The philosophical works of John Locke.* Ed. J. A. St. John. Vol. 1. London: George Bell.

Milner, P. 1969. Do behaviorists really need a brain drain? In *William James: Unfinished business,* ed. R. B. MacLeod, 17–19. Washington, D.C.: American Psychological Association.

Perry, R. B. 1904. Conceptions and misconceptions of consciousness. *Psychological Review* 11:282–96.

Piaget, J. 1969. *The mechanisms of perception.* Trans. G. N. Seagrim. New York: Basic Books.

Plotinus. 1957. *The Enneads.* Trans. S. MacKenna. 2d ed., rev. B. S. Page. New York: Pantheon Books.

Pollack, R. H. 1970. Müller-Lyer illusion: Effect of age, lightness, contrast, and hue. *Science* 170:93–95.

Royce, J. R. 1982. Philosophic issues, Division 24, and the future. *American Psychologist* 37:258–66.

Ryle, G. 1949. *The concept of mind.* New York: Barnes and Noble.

Stout, G. F. 1931. *Mind and matter.* Cambridge: Cambridge University Press.

Strong, C. A. 1903. *Why the mind has a body.* New York: Macmillan.

Titchener, E. B. 1917. *A text-book of psychology.* New York: Macmillan.

Warren, H. C. 1934. *A dictionary of psychology.* Boston: Houghton Mifflin.

Wicklund, R. A. 1979. The influence of self-awareness on human behavior. *American Scientist* 67:187–93.

Widgery, A. G. 1970. Immortality. In *Encyclopaedia Britannica,* 12:1–2A.

2 / Abstractions and Consciousness as Experienced

There is a direct relation between language and conscious content in the sense that grammatical terms reflect modes of consciousness. Thus the adjectives "green" and "blue" suggest awareness of two colors. Similarly, the nouns "book" and "man" indicate awareness of two different entities. When used as index words in phrases like "this book" or "that man," such words stand for concrete experiences. In phrases like "the average book" or "the average man," however, they exemplify the abstract or the conceptualized and entail more mature thinking. Abstract thinking calls for more verbal skill than concrete thinking. A baby might think about a bottle, but no infant is apt to think of abstractions like heaviness or professionalism. Language is essential for abstract thinking; hence, like infants, animals do not deal with abstractions. This is an old observation; Carl Sagan noted that John Locke observed "beasts abstract not" (1977, p. 107). In this connection Sagan mentioned Washoe, the famous chimpanzee who had been taught the sign language of the deaf. He believed she could abstract, but this is questionable. She could make a sign for sweet food but had no sign for sweetness, and she had a word for hat but none for haberdashery. Her thinking, like that of a very young child, was concrete, not abstract.

The development of the young child's thinking is intimately associated with language development. Though a child may generalize in using new words, this is not the same as abstract thinking. When a child calls all bearded men "Grandpa" and all furry animals "doggy" he is placing *grandpa* in one category and *doggy* in another. These are instances of over-inclusion, not abstraction. Restriction of the words to a single man and a single kind of animal comes with more experience.

A child learns abstract terms gradually, after becoming familiar with concrete terms. Once he knows the word *conscious* he may in time deal with *consciousness* as an abstract term. A host of other words will instigate the gradual growth of such abstractions as honesty, furniture, mind, education, athletics, religion, time, corruption, space, or olfaction. Such concepts form the warp and woof on the loom of thinking as we daydream, spin yarns, read detective stories, argue with friends, or write term papers.

Abstractions perform a useful function;[1] they dispense with the need to list concrete examples to express general ideas. At the close of the previous paragraph I listed five examples. This was necessary because I could find no single word to designate the abstraction or concept involved. Even with a list of concrete examples, this unlabeled concept may be elusive or obscure. Once we have the needed abstract terms, thinking is free from the impediment of listing concrete examples. A word like *furniture* eliminates the need for referring to tables, beds, chairs, and wardrobes; they are all covered in an economist's report that strikes in the lumber industry will result in higher furniture prices. In similar fashion all breeds of dogs are included in a veterinarian's statement that dogs are susceptible to rabies. In understanding the economist's report and the veterinarian's statement, just how do we become *conscious* of the meaning of these abstract ideas of furniture or dogs in general or any other abstraction? A closely related question involves the way we move from the meaning of the abstract term to its application in a concrete situation. How do we make the transition from the idea of furniture to the cost of individual articles or from the idea of dogs in general to specific cases of rabies? Actually, both questions, involving transitions from the abstract to the concrete, have to do with thinking as a *conscious* process.

1. The function of abstractions is directly related to problem solving as contrasted with habitual or routine behavior. This is evident in the observations reported by Kurt Goldstein (1878–1965) of changes in the behavior of soldiers hospitalized with brain injuries. In general, they could handle familiar concrete situations such as striking a match or taking a drink. But when given an empty matchbox and asked to show how to strike a match, they could not do so. Similarly, they could not pretend to drink from an empty glass. In Goldstein's words, this revealed impairment "of the abstract attitude." He listed six ways the abstract attitude facilitates problem solving, thus attributing to it six broad functions (1944, p. 305): (1) voluntary initiation of a mental set; (2) deliberate *shifting* from one part to another of a problem situation; (3) keeping different aspects of a problem in mind at the same time; (4) perceiving the essential elements of a problem or analyzing a whole into its significant parts so they can be isolated; (5) detecting relevant factors with a view to planning the next step, which often involves formulating hypotheses, so that the thinker can dwell upon things that are theoretically or conceptually possible though not assured of concrete realization; (6) maintaining an objective or impersonal attack on a problem by keeping one's ego detached from it.

Goldstein and a colleague described special tests designed to detect impairment of the abstract attitude in Goldstein and Scheerer (1941).

The Transition from Abstract to Concrete Ideas

Once our attention is called to the phenomenon of ideational transitions, we can detect them in virtually any ordinary sentence. Not long ago I was confronted with this statement: "Tigers are native to India." The reference to tigers as a class constituted an abstraction from the totality of wild animals; but the meaning of the animals as a class was symbolized in my mind by a concrete image—a two-dimensional outline of a tiger. Of course, no one has ever experienced a two-dimensional tiger. A related experience is reading a geometric proposition that pertains to *all* triangles. To deal with the proposition we must either draw or have a mental image of a single triangle that serves as a concrete symbol of triangles in general. It will have to be given a definite form—scalene, equilateral, isosceles—but its particular angular characteristics do not stop it from representing all the triangles in the universe, including all that have previously existed and those yet to come into existence. The symbol is being treated as a three-sided figure devoid of angles, which obviously cannot exist in reality; hence the similarity to my two-dimensional tiger.

Once the meaning of the word *tiger* is aroused by the transition to the two-dimensional symbol, there will be an additional transition to impressions aroused by the word *India*. This could take the form of a vague image of the map of India, muscular tension as if pointing in the direction of India, mouthing the word *Ganges,* or a transient recollection of Calcutta—any fragment of experience with India that might serve as an effective symbol of the country.

There need be no *logical* relationship between the symbol and the country; any *psychological* linkage will serve. Transition to the meaning of very familiar words can occur immediately, without a symbolic intermediary. Thus a word like *shoe* might be understood without transitional images of a boot or a heel or the feel of leather. For readers of this page the meaning of $ probably will not require associated images of dollar bills or coins or wallets. After repeated experiences such images are no longer needed. The resulting process may be described as imageless thinking—it has been termed "conscious decay under habituation." This is familiar to people who have learned a foreign language. When one first reads a foreign language, French, for example, each word has to be translated into one's native tongue. Once some mastery is achieved, less and less translation is required. An "imageless" level of competence in French has been achieved when the student is able to think in French. In terms of my original sentence, the sight of *le tigre* will no longer call for the French-English dictionary.

The transition from a symbol to its referent is a shift from an experienced item to its meaning. The word *transition* describes such a shift as a transitive relation; the symbol points to or means or intends the symbolized concept as its object. This kind of objective reference was stressed as an inherent characteristic of consciousness in the system of psychology sponsored by Franz Brentano (1838–1917), which was especially concerned with *intentional* factors.

Consciousness and Intentionalism

Brentano's system is known as *act* psychology because of the importance it attributes to such acts as thinking or judging or loving. Such acts, in Brentano's view, reflect an essential characteristic of consciousness — the objective reference inherent in every conscious act. One is never conscious without being conscious *of* something. In thinking something is considered; in judging something is evaluated; in loving something is cared for and cherished. These acts involve a transitive relationship like the grammatical structure of transitive verbs. Verbs like "grasp," "open," and "hide" imply objects to be grasped, opened, and hidden. In terms of the transitive nature of consciousness, there are intentions to be carried out or goals to be achieved. Brentano has abstracted this intentional aspect of consciousness from the totality of mental events and analyzed it separately, as is evident in the prominence he accords it in his account of the meaning of psychical phenomena. The following passages from his book on empirical[2] psychology show this prominence (1874, pp. 115–16):

> Every psychical phenomenon is characterized by that which the scholastics of the Middle Ages called the *intentional* . . . inexistence of an object and what we, although not without altogether ambiguous expressions, would call the relationship to a content, the orientation toward an object (which is not to be understood as a reality), or immanent objectivity. Every psychical phenomenon contains something as object within itself, although not in the same way. . . . This *intentional* inexistence is exclusively peculiar to psychical phenomena. No physical phenomenon reveals anything like it. And so we can define psychical phenomena by saying they are such phenomena as *intentionally* contain an object within themselves. (Italics added.)

2. The title of Brentano's book should be translated *Psychology from the Empirical Standpoint*. The German for "empirical" is *empirisch*, not *empiristisch*, "empiristic." Although both words refer to experience, they have different meanings. To be empiristic is to regard mind as entirely a product of experience. Locke was empiristic in this sense. To be empirical is to explain mind in the light of experience as Kant tried to do. Brentano's psychology was empirical, not empiristic. For more detailed discussion of the difference see Boring (1950, pp. 304–8, 380).

The word *inexistence* has several meanings, but Brentano uses it to mean being inseparable, bound up with, or inherent, so that "intentional inexistence" as applied to mental phenomena makes intentionality an inherent characteristic of them—the objective reference inherent in every conscious or mental act. In Brentano's view the concept of mind presupposes objective reference. Flashing a card with *tiger* printed on it in front of a cow would presumably give rise to a visual sensation, but the cow would not be perceiving a word *qua* word. Brentano classified the cow's sensation as a physical, not a mental phenomenon—a bare, meaningless sensation devoid of objective reference. Like any inert physical item, it lacked symbolic intent—at least for the cow.

As Brentano employed the term, *intentionality* was broad in scope, applying to ideas, to real or fancied items, or to any experience deemed an object of thought. William James dealt with the concept in *The Meaning of Truth,* using the following example (1927, pp. 43–44):

> Suppose, to fix our ideas, that we take first a case of conceptual knowledge; and let it be our knowledge of the tigers in India, as we sit here. Exactly what do we *mean* by saying that we know the tigers? . . .
>
> Most men would answer that what we mean by knowing is having them, however absent in body, become in some way present to our thought; or that our knowledge of them is known as presence of our thought to them. A great mystery is usually made of this peculiar presence in absence; and the scholastic philosophy, which is only common sense grown pedantic, would explain it as a peculiar kind of existence, called intentional inexistence, of the tigers in our mind. At the very least, people would say that what we meant by knowing the tigers is mentally *pointing* towards them as we sit here.

Here James is explaining intentional inexistence in terms of *conceptual* knowledge, asking what it means to *know* the tigers in India in terms of our general ideas of tigers. His reference to "mentally pointing towards them" implies that knowing the tigers is an active process, which is in accord with the centrality of mental acts in Brentano's psychology. As an act, knowing is different from the passive reception of sensory impressions, as Aristotle noted when he called attention to the difference between having an experience and observing an experience.[3] Observation is a

---

3. As a close student of Aristotle, Brentano was undoubtedly mindful of this difference and its systematic implications. His familiarity with Aristotle is also reflected in his classifying sensations as physical phenomena, which is congruent with Aristotle's teaching that psychology is a branch of physics. For details see McKeon (1947, p. xxiv). Nor is this kind of classification absent today. In *Behavior and Conscious Experience* Kendon Smith wrote an introductory chapter in defense of physical monism and explained that "to say that con-

dynamic process incorporating such activities as attending, noting, discriminating, judging, comparing, and either liking or disliking or being indifferent. In Brentano's act psychology the last three activities were described as aspects of the psychical act—ideating, judging, and loving/hating. They were thus regarded as inseparable from the act and therefore indicative of the unity of mental life, given separate consideration only for descriptive convenience. For Brentano, cognition, feeling, and conation were not detached divisions of mind but were inherent in the constitution of the psychical act. Their inherence in the unity of mind is reminiscent of a passage in Aristotle's *De anima* (1947, p. 170): "If, then, there is something else which makes the soul one, this unifying agency would have the best right to the name of soul, and we shall have to repeat for it the question: Is it one or multipartite? If it is one, why not at once admit that 'the soul' is one?" The unity of mind implicit in Brentano's concept of mental acts is an elaboration of Aristotle's recognition of the unity of the soul. Despite, or possibly because of, the antiquity of the recognition, this unity of mind and consciousness continues to be overlooked, obscured by the idea of mind as multipartite.

The Unity of Mind and Consciousness

For Brentano a mental act—such as choosing a birthday gift for a friend—involves the three categories of classical psychology, thinking, feeling, and mentally pointing, all with reference to the intended recipient. What James called "mentally pointing" is like projection in that it attributes a feeling or characteristic or location to some remote object; here it reflects the intentional or *conative* aspect of choosing a gift. Trying to decide whether the gift is appropriate for the occasion reflects the *cognitive* aspect, and anticipating the friend's delight reflects the *affective* aspect. All three aspects are inherent in the act itself, and isolating them for separate examination entails abstraction, since they are embedded within the act. Such abstraction is necessary, for example, when cognition is to be investigated apart from conative and affective aspects of mental life or when these two aspects are subjected to the same treatment. It is then common to regard the aspect being segregated as having independent existence. The unity of mind is thus broken down into the departments of thinking, feeling, and willing—or ego, id, and superego.

The disintegration of mind implied by this transformation into cogni-

---

sciousness is physical . . . is to say, flatly and unequivocally, that sensations, perceptions, and ideas are absolutely nothing more than, nor less than, nor different from, changes in the very substance of the brain" (1969, p. 12).

tion, feeling, and conation is likely to increase as these three divisions are analyzed. A host of separate units of mind becomes enshrined in introductory psychology textbooks, and students are presented with separate chapters on sensation, perception, association, memory, intelligence, imagination, reasoning, motivation, instinct, emotion, personality, and so on. Each of these topics is subdivided into smaller units—vision, the optic chiasma, the law of effect, auditory theories, factor analysis, nonsense syllables, taste buds, projective tests, biofeedback, the Doppler effect, conditioned reactions, and hundreds of others. Each of these units has been isolated from some larger unit, which in turn came from a still more comprehensive unit; but their actual affiliation with the unity of mind is apt to be ignored, overlooked, forgotten, or never realized. Mind becomes a congeries of separate units, at best brought together into clusters of faculties such as attention, volition, vision, thinking, and emotion. The student fails to recognize what Brentano glimpsed as the unity of mind inherent in every psychical act, what the neurologist conceives of as the integrative action of the nervous system, and what the psychiatrist refers to as an integrated personality.

The Unity of the Person

One textbook that does not lose sight of the underlying unity beneath the multiplicity of details is the *General Psychology* of William Stern (1871–1938).[4] It views the human being as a *person,* not just an organism. From this standpoint the person—his mind, his consciousness, or the totality of his experience—is seen to be a *unitas multiplex,* or manifold unit. In the words of Stern (1938, p. 73), "This must be taken literally." All the elements, phases, factors, and other items of experience are integral "to the totality and not just superficially cemented to it." This means they are integral to the person; for the totality of experience is understood and evaluated not by "the unity of consciousness nor the organism in its mere vitality," but by "the *person himself* as an *unitas multiplex*" (p. 529).

Experience is thus subject to a variety of interpretations. But this appears to be overlooked by those psychotherapists who interpret the dream sym-

4. Stern belongs to the second generation of founding fathers of modern psychology; he was a contemporary of men like Ebbinghaus, Binet, Stumpf, Woodworth, McDougall, Warren, and Thorndike. He contributed to many fields of psychology. The term "intelligence quotient" was based upon his concept of "mental quotients." Auditory theory was influenced by his invention of tone variators, and forensic psychology benefited from his work on the reliability of testimony. Educational psychology was indebted to him for his investigations of child psychology. He even was among the first to subject driving safety to laboratory investigation.

bolism of their patients in accordance with "some *preconceived theory*" (p. 329):

> The immense variety of fanciful forms is then classified under one sole heading or within a very few domains of alleged primordial urges. Thus one and the same fantasy image may appear in orthodox psychoanalytic interpretation as a sexual symbol, while Individual Psychology views it as a symptom of overcompensation for an inferiority, and Jung's Analytical Psychology traces its roots in "racial memory," i.e., in basic experiences of far distant ancestry. Clinging to their simplifications, these several branches of depth psychology are in danger of overlooking the fact that the person is a unity in *multiplicity*, and of becoming blind to the varieties of imaginative meanings and symbols.

The "unity" Stern attributed to the person was not the unity of consciousness and mind; it came closer to meaning the unity of the self. But the meaning of person, as he understood it, was different from the ordinary meaning of self. It was also different from any of the eight or more dictionary definitions I find for the word "person." For Stern the "person" is to be defined as a "living whole, individual, unique, striving towards goals, self-contained and yet open to the surrounding world, and capable of having experience." To clarify this he added (p. 70):

> Into the totality of the person are interwoven both his physical and psychical aspects. Goal-directed activity is manifested in breathing as well as in thinking and striving. Independence of and exposure to the environment apply both to bodily functions and to conscious phenomena.
>
> The attribute "capable of having experience" is distinct from all the others in that it is *non-compulsory*. Every person *must* be at all times and in all respects a totality possessing life, individual uniqueness, goal-directed activity, independence of an openness to the world, *but not always consciousness*. Even at times when nothing is being "experienced" the person exists, while the loss of any one of the other attributes would suspend existence.

Brentano's intentionalism is manifestly reflected in the person's "striving towards goals" and being engaged in "goal-directed activity," but this is not an elaboration of Brentano's empirical psychology. Stern was incorporating the intentional factor into the separate science of *personalistics*, a science of the person "that studies him in his totality and psychophysical neutrality," thus promoting understanding of his physiology, sociology, pathology, and also psychology. Personalistics was one science and psychology a different one: "*Psychology is the science of the person as having experience or as capable of having experience"* (pp. 70–71; Stern's italics).

Stern did not define psychology as the science of consciousness, and, unlike personalistics, he did not consider it psychophysically neutral. In fact, he stated that all attributes of the person except "experiencing" are psychophysically neutral. Thus he refused to take a metaphysical stand on whether the person is ultimately a physical or a mental being or some other kind. But this did not apply to his view of psychology, since he made experience a sine qua non for that science yet exempted "experiencing" from the neutralist criterion. One might conjecture that he could not conceive of experiencing as divorced from some mentalistic criterion, but he did not explain why he regarded personalistics but not psychology as psychophysically neutral.

My conjecture about Stern's reason is based upon the assumption that, metaphysically, mind is either monistic or dualistic—either wholly physical or wholly mental or both physical and mental, with no other options. But this assumption may be questioned in view of a stand adopted by William James, which is relevant even though twentieth-century psychology has tended to disdain metaphysics.[5]

To the dilemma of choosing between a mental universe and a physical universe, James added the notion of a pluralistic universe. Pluralism was thus to replace the metaphysics of dualism. The significance of this for James's philosophy is clarified in Ralph Barton Perry's monumental biography of James (1935, pp. 583–98). For psychology there is one "alternative" that, according to Perry, "would be the most consistent with James's theory that *mind is a peculiar type of relationship among terms which in themselves are neither physical nor mental"* (p. 592; italics added).

For James this relationship was intrinsic to experience rather than a phase of consciousness. Stern in effect followed this precedent in his definition of psychology by stressing "having experience" and ignoring the phenomenon of being conscious. The phrase "having experience" is a translation of *erleben,* which has a connotation different from that of *erfahren,* another German word meaning to have experience. The nouns corresponding to these two German verbs would be *Erlebnis* and *Erfahrung,* for which there are no precise English equivalents. In general, there are two broad

5. It is difficult for the psychologist to eschew metaphysics completely. He is dealing with metaphysics whenever he employs terms like physicalism or mentalism or prefers monism to dualism or vice versa. Boring, writing about the "faith" of a "hard-headed monist," revealed his metaphysical preference thus (1933, p. 14): "While there is no possibility of disproving or proving dualism, the exposition of the present book is based on the assumption that it is scientifically more useful to consider that all psychological data are of the same kind and that consciousness is a physiological event." Seymour Kety expressed a dualistic faith years later by writing that "consciousness cannot be explained in terms of physics and chemistry, that consciousness is qualitatively different from matter and energy" (1952, p. 14).

kinds of experience: direct personal involvement and indirect or vicarious involvement. Experiences of the first kind are *Erlebnisse;* experiences of the second kind are *Erfahrungen.* Undergoing an appendectomy would be an *Erlebnis,* while reading about the operation would constitute an *Erfahrung.* The congenitally blind can never experience color as an *Erlebnis,* since their knowledge of color must be limited to *Erfahrungen* through the reports of sighted people. The essential difference is between knowledge *about* something and personal acquaintance *with* something.

Stern's rejection of consciousness in favor of experience (*Erlebnis*) was not exceptional in definitions of psychology. This emphasis on experience had already given rise to Brentano's empirical psychology and to Wundt's statement that psychology is the study of "immediate experience," both views being first published in 1874. Though contrary definitions of psychology were also advanced,[6] experience was favored over consciousness by some influential early twentieth century psychologists, such as James and Titchener. This is evident in Titchener's definition of mind as "the sum-total of human experience considered as dependent upon the experiencing person" (1917, p. 9). James puts it just as clearly in a series of articles brought together in *Essays in Radical Empiricism.* Although some were of more philosophical than psychological importance, one raises a crucial question about the concept of consciousness. James asked whether consciousness was fact or fiction in the essay's provocative title, "Does 'Consciousness' Exist?"

James gave a negative answer, contending that consciousness does not exist. This essay had first appeared in 1904 as a journal article (James 1938a) and James noted that for seven or eight years he had been telling his students about the nonexistence of consciousness and had "tried to give them its pragmatic equivalent in realities of experience." He had thus introduced his students to his concept of *radical empiricism,* which he explained in another journal article first published in the same year (1938b, p. 42):

> To be radical, an empiricism must neither admit into its construc-
> tions any element that is not directly experienced, nor exclude from
> them any element that is directly experienced. For such a philosophy,
> *the relations that connect experiences must themselves be experienced*
> *relations, and any kind of relation experienced must be accounted*

6. In their *Elements of Physiological Psychology* Ladd and Woodworth wrote, "We shall . . . consider psychology as that science which has for its primary subject of investigation all the phenomena of human consciousness, or of the sentient life of man. If the term 'sentience' be employed as preferable to consciousness, it must be understood as equivalent to consciousness in the broader sense of the latter word" (1911, p. 2). A second illustration is the opening sentence from J. R. Kantor's *Principles of Psychology:* "The domain of psychology comprises the phenomena which we may call conscious or psychological reactions" (1924, p. 1).

as "real" as anything else in the system. Elements may indeed be redistributed, the original placing of things getting corrected, but a real place must be found for every kind of thing experienced, whether term or relation, in the final philosophic arrangement.

As the title of the essay indicates, this kind of empiricism had to do with "a world of pure experience," not a world of pure consciousness. Moreover, unless *every item* of experience is given due consideration, it does not exemplify *radical* empiricism. Since language reflects experience, James stressed the significance of *all* parts of speech—not just nouns and verbs, but prepositions and conjunctions and pronouns. Conjunctions connect words, phrases, and sentences in various ways. Words like *or, and,* and *with* are coordinating conjunctions; *because, if, as,* and *however* are subordinating ones. There are also correlative conjunctions like *both . . . and* and *either . . . or.* James emphasizes their importance with italics: "Radical empiricism, as I understand it, *does full justice to conjunctive relations.*" Such relations range from the most peripheral or external to the most central and intimate (1938b, p. 45):

> The organization of the Self as a system of memories, purposes, strivings, fulfilments or disappointments, is incidental to this most intimate of all relations, the terms of which seem in many cases actually to compenetrate and suffuse each other's being.
>
> Philosophy has always turned on grammatical particles. With, near, next, like, from, towards, against, because, for, through, my— these words designate types of conjunctive relation arranged in a roughly ascending order of intimacy and inclusiveness.

To explain what took place in a given experience we employ a vocabulary of conjunctive relations that indicates the transitions, frustrations, dependencies, and other interactions of the events—the vocabulary James called "grammatical particles." These words express how our experiences are *known* as experienced relations. When someone reports, "I stayed with my friend through the night because of his asthma," the words *with, my, through, because,* and *his* refer to experiences within the total experience of staying with a sick friend. These component experiences add to our knowledge of the total experience. They are items of information rather than bits of consciousness, and they exemplify what James regarded as the most distinctive of our experiences (1938a, p. 25):

> *The peculiarity of our experiences, that they not only are, but are known, which their "conscious" quality is invoked to explain, is better explained by their relations—these relations themselves being experiences—to one another.*

James was regarding experience as different from consciousness; his radical empiricism shows that his contemporaries who were defining psychology as the science of experience also considered them different. Although it makes sense to report having an experience, it would be absurd to report having a consciousness. But isn't it also absurd to contend that consciousness does not exist? James anticipated this question early in his essay (1938a, pp. 3–4):

> To deny plumply that "consciousness" exists seems so absurd on the face of it—for undeniably "thoughts" do exist—that I fear some readers will follow me no farther. Let me then immediately explain that I mean only to deny that the word stands for an entity but to insist most emphatically that it does stand for a function. There is, I mean, no aboriginal stuff or quality of being, contrasted with that of which material objects are made; but there is a function in experience which thoughts perform, and for the performance of which this quality of being is involved. That function is *knowing*.

In recognizing *knowing* as the chief function of thinking, James anticipated the view of mind that became current decades later with the emergence of cybernetics. In noting that consciousness is not some "aboriginal stuff" he foreshadowed a concept of mind introduced by the philosopher Abraham Kaplan in connection with cybernetics (1956, p. 1308):

> The analysis of mind and individual personality as a structure of certain information processes renders obsolete not only the "mind substance" of the idealist, but mechanistic materialism as well. *Mind is a patterning of information and not spirit, matter, or energy.* (Italics added.)

This is not the equivalent of regarding consciousness as a patterning of information. In this context mind and consciousness have different meanings. Viewed as a patterning of information, mind stands for a process, not an entity; in this respect it is like consciousness as viewed by James. James was explicit in denying that consciousness stands for an entity, a denial that merits more than passing mention.

Consciousness Not an Entity

If the word *entity* is given the customary interpretation of some concrete object or external reality, then saying that consciousness is not an entity is calling attention to the obvious, since no one is likely to regard consciousness as a thing with independent existence. Such hypostatization often occurs when people think about the unconscious, and it also is applied to consciousness, though less frequently. Those unfamiliar with loss of consciousness as a technical problem might construe it in this way; they are likely to regard the return of consciousness after a knockout as the restoring of a vanished entity. But even those familiar with brain physiology and kindred technical issues may think, or at least write, of consciousness as an entity, as in the following excerpt from *Hypnosis and Related States,* by Gill and Brenman, in which consciousness becomes an "apparatus" (1961, p. 188):

> We must introduce here the concept of consciousness as an apparatus of the ego. We mean of course consciousness as it operates in the secondary process where it is brought about by attention cathexis and not as in the primary process in which drive cathexis is responsible for the quality consciousness. . . . Freud called consciousness a "supcrordinate sense organ," which makes it quite clear that he considered it an ego apparatus. The term "consciousness" is used both for the apparatus and for the result of the functioning of this apparatus as it employs attention cathexis. Consciousness seems to be equivalent to attention since "attention" may likewise be used to designate an apparatus or the result of the functioning of that apparatus.

Since these authors do not appear mindful of the teaching that consciousness is not an entity, which James presented, it appears that he was not calling attention to the obvious.

As I mentioned earlier, the essay in which James denied the existence of consciousness was published in 1904. When his *Principles of Psychology* appeared in 1890 no question was raised about the existence of consciousness; his famous chapter on the "stream of thought" is replete with allusions to consciousness. The same is true of the chapter on "the consciousness of self." Yet in the 1904 essay he wrote, "For twenty years past I have mistrusted 'consciousness' as an entity" (1938a, p. 3), so he must have entertained such misgivings while writing these two chapters. Why he failed to give them overt expression is a separate question.

That James was setting the stage for his subsequent treatment of the issue is suggested by his avoidance of terms that describe consciousness as static or substantial or having "thinghood." Consciousness, he pointed out, is not "chopped up in bits" (1890, p. 239):

> Such words as "chain" or "train" do not describe it fitly as it presents itself in the first instance. It is nothing jointed; it flows. A "river" or a "stream" are the metaphors by which it is most naturally described. *In talking of it hereafter, let us call it the stream of thought, of consciousness, or of subjective life.*

The metaphor of a river or stream reflected his recognition of consciousness as a *process,* not a thing. Moreover, in writing about "Thought's stream" he italicized what was to be highlighted in the essay (1890, p. 271): *"Human thought . . . is cognitive or possesses the function of knowing."*

The phrase "function of knowing" was repeated in the essay. The *existence* of thoughts was positively affirmed in the essay, and was not denied in the *Principles*. Both in the book and in the essay, thoughts as existents were recognized. The continuity of thought or ideation gave rise to James's metaphor of the stream of consciousness. Note that in employing the word *consciousness* James had abstracted something from thoughts as existents and was dealing with the idea as with any common abstraction—like heaviness, stoniness, or sweetness. These common expressions do not stand for entities; they are abstractions from concrete objects such as weights, stones, or lumps of sugar.

Treating abstractions as concrete entities, as A. N. Whitehead (1861–1947) noted, is apt to be a source "of great confusion." He called it the *fallacy of misplaced concreteness*. It is the "error of mistaking the abstract for the concrete" (1948, p. 52). James was calling attention to this error when he stated that consciousness is not an entity. It is rather common in psychology, occurring whenever abstractions such as intelligence or imagination or volition are treated as independent, circumscribed, autonomous agencies or faculties. Traditional warnings about the mistakes of faculty psychology referred to the fallacy of misplaced concreteness.

James called attention to another mistake when he contended that consciousness "does not denote a special stuff or way of being" (1938a, p. 25), saying that experience is not made of consciousness and thus depriving experience of conscious existence.

The Stuff of Experience

A phrase like "conscious existence" sounds odd, and its meaning is obscure and ambiguous. It might refer to existence of which somebody is aware in contrast to unobserved existence. It even suggests that existence in the abstract is aware of itself. James, who first employed the phrase, used it in a discussion of the "stuff" of experience, anticipating objections to his denial of the existence of consciousness (1938a, pp. 26–27):

> First of all, this will be asked: "If experience has not 'conscious' existence, if it be not partly made of 'consciousness,' of what then is it made? Matter we know, and thought we know, and conscious content we know, but neutral and simple 'pure experience' is something we know not at all. Say *what* it consists of—for it must consist of something—or be willing to give up!"
>
> To this challenge the reply is easy. Although for fluency's sake I myself spoke early in this article of a stuff of pure experience, I have now to say that there is no *general* stuff of which experience at large is made. There are as many stuffs as there are "natures" in the things

experienced. If you ask what any one bit of pure experience is made of, the answer is always the same: "It is made of *that,* of just what appears, of space, of intensity, of flatness, brownness, heaviness, or what not." . . . Experience is not only a collective name for all these sensible natures, and save for time and space (and, if you like, for "being") there appears no universal element of which all things are made.

Experience as James conceived of it was an elaboration of some phases of British empiricism. James acknowledged this by stating that the thesis he was defending "does little more" than clarify and "carry out" the method Locke and Berkeley "were the first to use" (1938a, pp. 10–11). Both men raised questions about the "stuff" of our ideas. Locke derived all ideas from sensation or reflection. He noted that there were simple, passively aroused ideas and also complex ideas due to "acts of the mind" as well as ideas involving a single sense, such as color, and ideas of space and motion that involved several senses. Locke defined the word *idea* as "whatsoever is the *object* of the understanding when a man thinks." Applied to external objects, this makes ideas the result of sensory impressions. Berkeley identified sensory impressions with all being or reality by making existence contingent upon perceptibility—"to be is to be perceived." According to James, Berkeley was thus saying that "what common sense means by realities is exactly what the philosopher means by ideas."

Locke and Berkeley believed ideation was directly dependent upon sentience. They anticipated James by maintaining that ideas or thoughts as experienced are constituents of sensory data rather than some product or stuff called consciousness. As James made explicit, there is no *general* physical or mental stuff of which experience is constituted. In the essay itself he held that the same is true for consciousness. This is evident in reference to such attributes of sensation as intensity, brownness, or heaviness. Each sense modality contributes something unique, enabling us to be *conscious* of lights, colors, sounds, noises, smells, pains, thirsts, tastes, hungers, throbbings, itches, and whatever else falls within the scope of the concept of sentience. The concept of sentience, like the concept of consciousness, is an abstraction; neither is an entity. Both are fictions or convenient inventions.

They are myths because they refer to something that can never actually occur, divorcing conscious content from the reality of sensory experience so that nothing remains but bare sensitivity—what all our sensory experiences have in common—the process of sensing or being conscious *of* something. We can no more eliminate this something and be conscious without being conscious of something than we can separate a dog's bark from the dog. We can talk about sentience or consciousness in the abstract only in the way we talk about an average bark or an average triangle or average wickedness. To consider these as things having real existence is to entertain a myth and indulge in the fallacy of misplaced concreteness, hazards of treating abstractions as concrete entities.[7] It was against such hazards that James and Whitehead both warned. James ended his essay with this statement about the "entity known . . . as consciousness" (1938a, p. 37): *"That entity is fictitious, while thoughts in the concrete are fully real. But thoughts in the concrete are made of the same stuff as things are"* (James's italics).

James noted the ambiguity implicit in common phrases that suggest something mental in one context and something physical in another. For example, does a phrase like "healthy thoughts" refer to the well-being of thoughts as mental or to thoughts about physical health? James also called attention to the difference between "wicked desires" and "desires for wickedness" as well as between "good impulses" and "impulses towards the good."

Ambiguity of the Mental/Physical Dichotomy

In a later essay, "The Place of Affectional Facts in a World of Pure Experience," James resumed his discussion of the "stuff" of experience and of the mind/matter antithesis (1938c, pp. 137–38): "There is no thought-stuff different from thing-stuff, I said [in the earlier essay]; but the same identical piece of 'pure experience' (which was the name I gave to the *materia prima* of everything) can stand alternately for a 'fact of consciousness' or for a physical reality, according as it is taken in one context or another."

Pure experience as *materia prima* or the unformed ground of being was thus deemed neither physical nor mental. Perry seems to have referred to this when he described James's theory of mind as "a peculiar type of relationship among terms which in themselves are neither physical or mental." Recall also that sensation in the abstract has been hard to classify in terms of the mental/physical dichotomy. Both Aristotle and Brentano regarded sensations as inherently physical. Locke, however, regarded some sensations as physical and others as mental. Those he called primary qualities, such as solidity, extension, and number, he deemed inherently characteristic of external objects and consequently physical, in contrast to such

7. James noted another hazard in dealing with abstractions in his *Meaning of Truth* (1927, chap. 13). He called this error "vicious abstractionism," the error of isolating a single characteristic of a situation and then regarding the situation as consisting only of that characteristic. James referred to concept formation based upon isolated characters, which, he said, resulted in "acting as if all the other characters from out of which the concept is abstracted were expunged" (p. 249). Regarding taxation as the sole function of government is an example of vicious abstractionism; conceiving of schizophrenia as nothing but confused thinking is another. Current studies of cognitive psychology are replete with additional examples.

secondary mental qualities as colors, sounds, and tastes, which he classified as mental because he deemed them more characteristic of mind. Other
thinkers rejected the distinction between primary and secondary qualities
of sensation and considered *all* sensations mental, either as Berkeleyan
percepts, as ingredients of conscious content, or sometimes as building
blocks of mind. Such varying psychophysical interpretations of the concept of sensation illustrate the ambiguity James found in his analysis of
pure experience, as he noted in his essay on "affectional facts" (1938c,
pp. 153–54):

> Our body is the palmary instance of the ambiguous. Sometimes
> I treat my body as a part of nature. Sometimes, again, I think of
> it as "mine," I sort it with "me," and then certain local changes and
> determinations in it pass for spiritual happenings. Its breathing is
> my "thinking," its sensorial adjustments are my "attention," its
> kinesthetic alterations are my "efforts," its visceral perturbations are
> my "emotions."
>
> The obstinate controversies that have arisen over such statements
> as these . . . prove how hard it is to decide by bare introspection
> what it is in experiences that shall make them either spiritual or mate-
> rial. It surely can be nothing intrinsic in the individual experience.
> It is their way of behaving towards each other, their system of rela-
> tions, their function; and all these things vary with the context in
> which we find it opportune to consider them.

A familiar instance of context influencing the interpretation of experience is dreaming. During the dream, its events are experienced as genuine
material objects or beings having three-dimensional existence — as real, not
imaginary. In extreme form such events constitute nightmares. Their imaginary or purely mental status is not recognized until the dreamer awakens
and perceives them in a different context.

This ambiguity can also involve the inverse of dreams, when genuine
sensory impressions are mistakenly regarded as imaginary. This was experimentally demonstrated at Cornell more than seventy years ago in a famous
study by C. W. Perky (1910). The children and adults who served as experimental subjects were tested individually. Each was seated alongside the
experimenter, directly in front of a screen made of smoked glass, and was
asked to focus on the screen while imagining some colored object suggested by the experimenter. Thus the subject was asked to imagine a red
tomato or a yellow banana and to describe it. The experimenter's two
assistants, hidden behind the screen, projected faint pictures of the object
on the screen. The subjects were unaware of the projection and took the
pictures to be products of their own imaginations. The physical picture
was judged to be a mental one.

The experimenter overlooked one factor when instructing the subjects to imagine a banana; he did not tell them what position the fruit was to assume—vertical or horizontal or oblique. The projected banana was always horizontal. Subjects who chanced to imagine a vertical banana were mystified by what they took to be a change in the imagined banana, but the change was not recognized as intrusion by a real picture. The Perky experiment clearly demonstrates James's point that it can "be so hard to tell, in a presented and recognized material object, what part comes in through the sense-organs and what part comes" from the mind.

Although Perky's laboratory study of imagination took place many years ago, it continues to influence experimental studies, as is brought out by Jerome Singer's citations of research on how the "Perky phenomenon" affects "subjects who were high and low in daydreaming" (1974, p. 418), discussed in his presentation of related experiments on man's fantasy life undertaken by Singer and his students at Yale. What Perky investigated at Cornell (as one of Titchener's students) thus influenced investigations at Yale many decades later,[8] an indirect influence of Titchener's thinking.

Titchener came to Cornell in the early 1890s and remained there until the 1920s, setting a pattern for scientific work in psychology for successive generations of graduate students. He was explicit in what he accepted and what he rejected in terms of psychology as science, and his ideas were opposed by some. He had much to say about the critical study of conscious phenomena, and his views and the opposition they aroused will be considered in the next chapter, serving as a foundation for discussion of differing views of mind, consciousness, and experience as related to such topics as adjustment, animal behavior, insight, and thinking.

References

Aristotle. 1947. De anima. In *Introduction to Aristotle,* ed. C. R. McKeon, 145–240. New York: Modern Library.
Boring, E. G. 1933. *The physical dimensions of consciousness.* New York: Century Company.

8. The Perky investigation has not been forgotten at Cornell: Ulric Neisser mentions it in *Cognition and Reality* (1976). The Cornell setting notwithstanding, Neisser takes a dim view not only of Perky's findings but also of the kind of introspection sponsored by Titchener, referring to it as "a sloppy tool" (p. 2) and calling the Perky experiment "seriously flawed" (pp. 129–30), since he notes that when awake we "almost always" can tell the difference between images and percepts. This is a questionable contention, however, since Perky did not hold that we "always" have difficulty with this sort of differentiation, and since the conditions of the Perky investigation were not of the kind "always" experienced in daily life but were exceptional, like those giving rise to mirages in the desert. Similar exceptional conditions account for double vision when the victim of retinal displacement cannot differentiate between a percept and its imaged duplicate.

————. 1950. *A history of experimental psychology.* 2d ed. New York: Appleton-Century-Crofts.

Brentano, F. 1874. *Psychologie vom empirischen Standpunkte.* Leipzig: Duncker und Humboldt.

Gill, M. M., and Brenman, M. 1961. *Hypnosis and related states: Psychoanalytic studies in regression.* New York: International Universities Press.

Goldstein, K. 1944. The significance of psychological research in schizophrenia. In *Contemporary psychopathology,* ed. S. S. Tompkins, 302–18. Cambridge: Harvard University Press.

Goldstein, K., and Scheerer, M. 1941. Abstract and concrete behavior: An experimental study with special tests. *Psychological Monographs* 53:1–115.

James, W. 1890. *Principles of psychology.* Vol. 1. New York: Henry Holt.

————. 1927. *The meaning of truth.* New York: Longmans, Green. First published 1909.

————. 1938a. Does "consciousness" exist? In *Essays in radical empiricism,* 1–38. New York: Longmans, Green. First published 1912.

————. 1938b. A world of pure experience. In *Essays in radical empiricism,* 39–91. New York: Longmans, Green. First published 1912.

————. 1938c. The place of affectional facts in a world of pure experience. In *Essays in radical empiricism,* 137–54. New York: Longmans, Green.

Kantor, J. R. 1924. *Principles of psychology.* New York: Alfred A. Knopf.

Kaplan, A. 1956. Sociology learns the language of mathematics. In *The world of mathematics,* ed. J. R. Newman, 2:1294–1313. New York: Simon and Schuster.

Kety, S. S. 1952. Consciousness and the metabolism of the brain. In *Problems of consciousness,* ed. H. A. Abramson, 11–75. New York: Josiah Macy, Jr., Foundation.

Ladd, G. T., and Woodworth, R. S. 1911. *Elements of physiological psychology.* New York: Charles Scribner's Sons.

McKeon, R. 1947. *Introduction to Aristotle.* New York: Modern Library.

Neisser, U. 1976. *Cognition and reality: Principles and implications of cognitive psychology.* San Francisco: W. H. Freeman.

Perky, C. W. 1910. An experimental study of imagination. *American Journal of Psychology* 21:422–52.

Perry, R. B. 1935. *The thought and character of William James.* Vol. 2. Boston: Little, Brown.

Sagan, C. 1977. *The dragons of Eden: Speculations on the evolution of human intelligence.* New York: Random House.

Singer, J. L. 1974. Daydreaming and the stream of thought. *American Scientist* 29:417–25.

Smith, K. 1969. *Behavior and conscious experience: A conceptual analysis.* Athens: Ohio University Press.

Stern, W. 1938. *General psychology from the personalistic standpoint.* Trans. H. D. Spoerl. New York: Macmillan.

Titchener, E. B. 1917. *A text-book of psychology.* New York: Macmillan.

Whitehead, A. N. 1948. *Science and the modern world.* New York: Mentor Books. First published 1925 by Macmillan.

3 / Consciousness and Scientific Psychology

Chapter 2 was in some ways more philosophical than psychological in orientation. James's articles were first published in philosophical journals, and they appeared in 1904, when James was professor of philosophy at Harvard. He had relinquished the title professor of psychology in 1897, five years after publishing a briefer version of the *Principles*. Thus it was as contributions to philosophy that James presented his defenses of radical empiricism and of pragmatism as well as his critique of consciousness as an entity. But these contributions were not without psychological relevance, nor was what Whitehead as philosopher had to say about the fallacy of misplaced concreteness. The previous chapter thus concerned consciousness and philosophical teachings; the present chapter will examine the concept of consciousness as influenced by scientific psychology.

As I noted in chapter 1, scientific psychology received its initial impetus as an official movement under academic auspices from Wilhelm Wundt at Leipzig in 1879. It was there that experimental psychology as a laboratory science got under way, and most courses in experimental psychology in American universities were started by men who had been Wundt's students. Though they all shared Wundt's faith in the promise of a real science of psychology, some of them deviated from Wundt's prospectus. But such deviation was little evidenced in the scientific psychology Titchener sponsored during his many years as director of the laboratory at Cornell University. He arrived there in 1892, the year the American Psychological Association was organized, and remained for thirty-five years, until his death in 1927. The doctoral candidates he trained and the scholarly articles and books he published established him as an outstanding interpreter of scientific psychology in accordance with Wundt's teachings on the nature and limits of laboratory psychology.

The importance of Titchener's interpretation and elaboration of Wundt's "new" scientific psychology is recognized in the tribute E. G. Boring (1886–1968) paid to both men in his classic *History of Experimental Psychology* (1950). The only picture in the book is the frontispiece, a photograph of a bronze plaque of Wundt cast in 1905 to celebrate the fiftieth anniversary of his medical degree. Of the many men Boring discussed in his *History*, he devoted the most space to Wundt, leaving no doubt about his eminence in the origins of experimental psychology. Yet the book is dedicated not to Wundt, but to Titchener (1950, pp. xi–xii):

> In dedicating this book to Edward Bradford Titchener, I am acknowledging my greatest intellectual debt. Whatever of merit in care, thoroughness, or perspective the book may have derives originally from him. Especially was it due to his influence that I gained the conviction that the gift of professional maturity comes only to the psychologist who knows the history of his science. In experimental psychology Titchener was the historian *par excellence*.

By 1905 Titchener had written four erudite volumes on the qualitative and quantitative aspects of laboratory psychology that deeply influenced early twentieth century sponsors of scientific psychology, both those who endorsed Titchener's views and those who reacted against them. His ideas on the nature and scope of scientific philosophy were not ignored during these first decades of American laboratory psychology. Let us then consider what he had to say about the concept of consciousness, since, as Boring noted, Titchener regarded "sensory consciousness as the *raison d'être* of psychology" (1950, p. 410).

Titchener's View of Psychology as Science

Titchener presented his views of psychology as science as early as 1896 in his *Outline of Psychology,* which was revised in later years and eventually appeared as *A Text-Book of Psychology,* the last edition being published in 1917. This volume brings out Titchener's views of scientific psychology as presented to the first generation of American laboratory psychologists, who were also interested in establishing psychology's status as a science.

Titchener opened his textbook with this definition: "A science consists of a large body of facts, which are related to one another, and are arranged under general laws" (1917, p. 1). He then used physics as an example of an established science in which definite observational data give rise to laws of motion, radiation, mechanics, and electricity and to other physical laws. As "observed," the facts must have been experienced or noticed by some physicist, and Titchener pointed out that "all the sciences have the same sort of subject-matter" in that they concern some "aspect of the world of human experience." The special sciences emerge from this general background of human experience. Observation of birds gave rise to ornithology, and ichthyology owes its origin to the systematic observation of fish. Thermodynamics emerged from experience with heat and cold, and experience with tones and noises led to the physics of sound and to acoustics as scientific specialties.

Though all sciences are rooted in human experience, they approach it from different viewpoints. Like the rest of us, the physicist experiences the sensory world of color, sound, time, space, pressure, solids, air, and liquids. But when he writes his physics textbook he ignores the sensory aspects of these experiences and writes about an impersonal world of vibration frequencies, energy changes, electronic orbits, and similar nonsensory concepts. As Titchener explains, he is writing about these derivatives of human experience "as independent of the experiencing person," so that from his viewpoint as a physicist the physical world "is neither warm nor cold, neither dark nor light, neither silent nor noisy" (p. 8). It is a conceptual rather than a perceptual world and as such can never be experienced in terms of the sensory immediacy of everyday observations.[1]

Titchener contrasted this conceptual physical standpoint with direct awareness of sensory impressions as experienced, which, he held, is the standpoint of psychology as the science of mind when mind is defined as "the sum-total of human experience considered as dependent upon the experiencing person" (p. 9). Titchener used the phrase "experiencing person" as functionally equivalent to an activated nervous system (p. 16):

> Mind thus becomes the sum-total of human experience considered as dependent upon a nervous system. And since human experience is always process, occurrence, and the dependent aspect of human experience is its mental aspect, we may say, more shortly, that mind is the sum-total of mental processes. All these words are significant. "Sum-total" implies that we are concerned with the whole world of experience, not with a limited portion of it; "mental" implies that we are concerned with experience under its dependent aspect, as conditioned by a nervous system; and "processes" implies that our subject-matter is a stream, a perpetual flux, and not a collection of unchanging objects.

1. Boring discussed this issue of the relation between physics and psychology in his *The Physical Dimensions of Consciousness*. He pointed out that it would be contrary to the facts of history to interpret this distinction between the perceptual world of psychology and the conceptual world of physics as meaning that physics is a derivative of psychology. In some ways, he indicated, psychology might also be viewed as "mediate" or conceptual. As he saw it, Titchener's view amounted to this: "Experience, instead of being prior to physical entities, like the nervous system, is now held to be dependent upon the experiencing individual, and the experiencing individual is, for all practical intents, the nervous system" (1963, p. 5).

Although Titchener defined mind in terms of "human experience" as a function of neural processes, he did not consider mind exclusively human. For him mind was not a Cartesian "thinking thing" independent of brain action and alien to the animal world. He maintained that higher animals have minds and that, just as we credit our fellow human beings with minds, so "we have no right to deny them to the higher animals" (p. 27).[2] As long as the structure of an animal's nervous system resembles ours, we are justified in granting that it has a mind, since in response to stimuli that "arouse certain feelings in us" the animal's behavior often indicates similar feelings.

Note that Titchener *infers* such feelings and does not define the animal's mind as "experience considered as dependent upon a nervous system." In his view the study of experience called for "introspective reports furnished by a number of different observers," and of course no animal can furnish such reports; hence animal psychology must be restricted to the study of behavior. The more closely an animal's nervous system approximated that of a human being the more confident Titchener was concerning its mental endowment, but he was ready to grant some degree of mind to any creature whose behavior seemed to be regulated by neural structures.

Whether he attributed the rudiments of mind to protozoans and other creatures lacking neural structures is not clear. He acknowledges that "it is difficult to limit mind to the animals that possess even a rudimentary nervous system" because simpler creatures manage to accomplish "practically everything that their superiors do by its assistance." As a result he finds that "the range of mind" appears "to be as wide as the range of animal life." It thus seems that protozoans fall within this range and might constitute a departure from Titchener's criterion of mind as dependent on neural activity. Although he failed to mention unicellular organisms, he did consider whether to extend the range of mind to include plants and decided that "we have no evidence of a plant-consciousness" even though "the development of the plant-world has evidently been governed by the same general laws of adaptation to environment that have been at work in the animal kingdom" (p. 28). In his opinion "plants . . . appear to be mindless" (p. 27).

By calling plants mindless Titchener meant they are neither conscious nor capable of having experience, thus alluding to mind, consciousness, and experience as related terms. Although he regarded mind and consciousness as almost identical in meaning, he did distinguish between them, referring to mind as "the sum-total of mental processes occurring in the life-

2. At the time Titchener wrote this there must have been some who did deny mind or consciousness to higher animals, but Titchener does not mention anyone by name. Had he been challenged he might have quoted Freud's 1915 article "The Unconscious": "To-day, our judgment is already in doubt on the question of consciousness in animals" (1950, p. 102).

time of an individual" and to consciousness as "the sum-total of mental processes occurring *now*" in the immediate present (p. 19).

He introduced no formal definition of *experience,* since the everyday meaning of the term evidently was satisfactory for his purpose. Thus it could refer either to mind or to consciousness, depending on the context. With respect to mind he used the term to mean the totality of events lived through or *experienced* in a lifetime; with respect to consciousness he limited it to the totality of momentary or ongoing experiences associated with neural functions. The latter qualification accounts for Titchener's willingness to attribute some semblance of mind to "insects and spiders and crustaceans," which "show a fairly high degree of nervous development" (p. 27), and his unwillingness to attribute mind or consciousness to plants. It seems fairly safe to say he would have regarded one-celled animals as akin to plants in being mindless, making the range of mind only wide enough to include animals that possess neural tissue.

Two Important Problems

Whether Titchener was justified in restricting consciousness or mind to animals with nervous systems depends on one's criterion for the presence of mind. How can one know whether a creature such as a hippopotamus or a snake or a moth has a mind or is conscious? A related problem involves how one applies one's criterion of consciousness to different animal phyla. At what stage in the course of biological evolution did mental processes first enter the phylogenetic scheme. And at what stage of ontogenetic development is consciousness to be ascribed to the organism? Titchener did not raise this question, but in terms of his basic thesis it seems he would have refused to attribute consciousness to the developing embryo before its nervous system emerged.

Titchener seemed to take it for granted that human beings may not require a criterion for the existence of mind, since each of us is directly cognizant of his own experience—"each one of us can have direct acquaintance only with a single mind, namely, with his own" (p. 25)—though we have no immediate access to the minds of others. Titchener faced this egocentric predicament bluntly, wondering how it is possible to develop a scientific psychology if its data are limited to what a single individual "knows at first-hand," even though his observations are reported under laboratory control. He asked, "How can psychology be anything more than a body of personal beliefs and individual opinions?" How can we escape from our egocentric bondage or assure ourselves that we are not alone in being conscious—that other people share our kinds of experience, have minds like ours, and are conscious in the way we find ourselves conscious?

Titchener disposed of the predicament by calling attention to the fundamental similarities of anatomy among human beings. We all have similar sense organs, hence we feel justified in assuming similar sensory experiences. Moreover, the very existence of language supports the belief that our fellow human beings have minds. Titchener asked, "Would a man invent language in order to talk to himself?" He went on to answer this (pp. 26–27):

> Language implies that there are more minds than one. And would the use of a common speech be possible if minds were not essentially alike? Men differ in their command of language, as they differ in complexion, or in liability to disease; but the general use of language testifies to a fundamental likeness of mental constitution in us all.

Unlike Descartes, Titchener did not regard mind as exclusively human. He endorsed the scientific legitimacy of animal psychology and comparative psychology and cited references to them both (p. 44). However, since animals lack language and cannot supply introspective reports, one must ask, "How are we to decide whether the animal before us does or does not possess mind?" (p. 32). He considered it important to distinguish reflex movements from those under conscious control, since he regarded reflexes as reactions to stimuli "received" both "mindlessly and mechanically."

Adjustment as a Criterion of Mind

One criterion for distinguishing between mindful and mindless behavior is the concept of adjustment. By this criterion Titchener assumes the existence of mind if an animal copes with novel problem situations rather "rapidly" (p. 32). This is reminiscent of a famous definition of intelligence formulated by William Stern in his *General Psychology* (1938, p. 309): "Intelligence is the personal capacity to meet new demands by making appropriate use of thought as a means." This modifies an earlier definition from his *Intelligence Testing* (1914) that closely approximates the criterion of mind under consideration. There intelligence is defined as "a general capacity of an individual consciously to adjust his thinking to new requirements. It is general mental adaptability to new problems and conditions of life." Both definitions involve the challenge of a problem situation, and both make solving the problem a function of mind, one by referring to "thought as a means" and the other by referring to "mental adaptability."

Reflexes, by contrast, do not entail thought and are elicited by fixed or stereotyped stimuli rather than under novel conditions. They are unlearned mechanical reactions, either segmental like the pupillary reflex or more diffuse like the startle reflex, that operate right from the start, independent of experience. This applies even to such a complex reflex mechanism as swallowing. Newborn puppies, kittens, or babies do not have to learn how to swallow, though they learn many things about food as they grow older—to discriminate between the edible and the inedible, the solid and the liquid, and the desirable and the undesirable. Such capacity for discrimination may also be a criterion of mind, since all learned adjustments involve perception of differences or changes in quality, quantity, location, and direction.

This prompts animal psychologists to place a premium on discrimination in their study of animal mind. Countless experiments have called for various species to distinguish triangles from circles, true paths from blind alleys, electric shocks from buzzers, right turns from left turns, high notes from low notes, sugar from saccharin, or long paths from short ones.

Often many trials are needed before the requisite discrimination is established, and this might not meet Titchener's criterion, since he called for a *rapid* adjustment to the problem situation. He may have been distinguishing between insightful or reasoned solutions to a problem and chance solutions achieved through impulsive, unplanned maneuvering. The way one of Thorndike's monkeys escaped from a problem box to reach food may be contrasted with the way one of Köhler's apes managed to bring food into its cage. In the first case the monkey succeeded only after unsystematic pushing, pulling, and shaking of bars, strings, and projections until quite by chance the door of the cage opened. The monkey showed no understanding of the mechanical principles involved, and on subsequent trials it kept up the same futile maneuvers. Eliminating the extraneous motions took a long time, so that learning to escape from the box was a gradual process; hence it was argued that the monkey learns by "monkeying," not by thinking.

In the other case, described in Köhler's *Mentality of Apes* (1925), a different pattern of learning came to light. The title's allusion to "mentality" suggests more than a description of animal *behavior;* Köhler inferred animal *mind* from the animal's behavior when confronted by a problem. In Köhler's experiments food was placed outside the cage, and sticks that could be fitted together to make a pole long enough to reach the food were placed inside.

Such experimental settings made it possible for the animals to achieve solutions without aimless trials. Sultan, a chimpanzee, initially tried to reach a banana by extending one stick through the bars but could not reach the fruit. Next he pushed the stick toward the fruit as far as he could, then used a second stick to push the first one. He thus touched the banana but could not bring it into the cage. For a time Sultan turned away and stopped struggling with the problem. But more than an hour later he began playing with the sticks, which Köhler had returned to the cage. In the course of this playful manipulation he chanced to fit the ends together to make one long stick. As soon as he had done this, he dashed to the side of the cage and with his new tool was able to obtain the food. Köhler held that Sultan had perceived the relation between the lengthened stick and the remote banana and thus had "adjusted" to the problem situation. As a cognitive operation this kind of perception was said to involve *insight*. By implication, "adjustments" or solutions through insight were deemed more indicative of mind than those attained through what came to be designated *trial and error*. This may amount to arguing that the one kind of solution requires more consciousness than the other. To evaluate such an argument we must examine the two concepts more carefully.

These concepts were introduced into psychology at different times. Insight as understood by Köhler belongs to the tradition of Gestalt psychology, which had its official beginnings about 1912. Insight is thus a twentieth-century concept. The antithetical concept of trial and error is of nineteenth-century origin and belongs to the tradition of association psychology. Let us examine the older concept before continuing with the more recent one.

Trial and Error as a Concept

The phrase *trial and error* was first employed[3] by the Scottish associationist Alexander Bain (1818–1903) in a volume entitled *The Senses and the Intellect,* first published in 1855. In a chapter called "Constructive Association" he applied the concept of trial and error both to the mastery of a motor skill such as swimming and to the acquisition of the verbal skills needed for accurate linguistic expression.

Bain noted that the beginning swimmer comes to his first lesson already able to exercise voluntary control over his arm and leg muscles in such everyday tasks as dressing, walking, writing, and lifting. To swim he must acquire a new combination of these muscular adjustments. Through persistent effort he stumbles upon the "happy combination" of required movements and can then proceed to practice these movements. The "happy combination" is one that will keep him afloat and is the "effect" he was seeking in trying out different patterns of movement. Bain went into some detail about each of these steps, then summarized them (1868, p. 572): "In

3. Bain introduced the phrase in the 1860s. Howard C. Warren's *Dictionary of Psychology* erroneously states (1934, p. 382): "The term was first used by Lloyd Morgan in 1894. The procedure was (more properly) named by Thorndike the method of trial, error, and accidental success."

the full detail of Constructiveness, we shall have to exemplify these three main conditions: — namely, (1) a previous command of the elements entering into the combination; (2) a sense of the effect to be produced; and (3) a voluntary process of trial and error continued until the desired effect is actually produced."

In comparable fashion Bain analyzed the process of achieving linguistic control according to his concept of trial and error. As he saw it, it is also by constructive association that a speaker or writer finds the right combination of words to express what he means (1868, p. 574):

It would thus appear, that the first condition of verbal combinations for the expression of meaning, is a sufficient abundance of already formed combinations to choose from; in other words, the effect depends on the previous acquisitions, and on the association forces whereby old forms are revived for the new occasion. If a complex meaning has to be expressed, every part of this meaning will revive by contiguity and similarity, some former idea of an identical or like nature, and the language therewith associated; and out of the mixed assemblage of foregone phrases, the volition must combine a whole into the requisite unity, by trial and error. The more abundant and choice the material supplied from the past by the forces of intellectual recovery, the better will be the combination that it is possible for the mind to form by the selecting effort. . . . In all difficult operations for purposes or ends, the rule of "trial and error" is the grand and final resort.

These pioneer accounts of trial-and-error learning of motor and linguistic skills were written some decades before experimental psychology came into existence; hence Bain could not base his accounts on the kind of experimental data Thorndike and Köhler cited to support their interpretations of problem solving.

However, Bain anticipated Thorndike's law of effect, by which responses with satisfying effects tend to be more closely linked to their antecedent stimuli than are responses with annoying effects. Bain had used the word *effect* in connection with trial-and-error behavior, and both he and Thorndike alluded to *hedonic* effects — Bain's *happy* combination and Thorndike's *satisfying* outcome.

By implication, such hedonic effects are not unconscious, but conscious. Bain's swimmer recognized the correct stroke and was elated at his success. Presumably Thorndike's monkey was also aware of reaching the satisfying goal object. Awareness is implicit in Thorndike's law of satisfying and annoying effects for the same reason that ordinary behavior control by rewards and punishments presupposes such awareness. "Blind" trial-and-error maneuvering culminates in recognition of success once one stumbles on the "happy combination" or rewarded goal, but such recognition is not the kind of awareness Köhler attributed to Sultan's insight.

Köhler's Concept of Insight

Köhler had first introduced the concept of insight as a factor in animal behavior in his *The Mentality of Apes* (1925), in which Sultan appeared as a paragon of insight. Köhler reported that Sultan and the other apes solved experimental problems without trial-and-error maneuvering, instead using what appeared to be more intelligent or thoughtful activity. Köhler related such activity to the principles of Gestalt psychology in his *Gestalt Psychology* (1929), devoting the last chapter to the concept of insight. He explained that his use of the term *insight* in the 1925 volume had been regrettably misinterpreted—some readers thought he was endowing the ape with some "mysterious" cognitive ability called *insight*. Köhler insisted this was not so. Instead, he was using the word to mean the understanding of simple cause-and-effect connections. As examples he cited understanding of another's enjoyment of a cold drink on a hot day, an experimenter's annoyance when laboratory apparatus fails, and a parent's joy at a baby's first smile. In these instances of insight people observe connections between antecedents and consequents—they note the effects of given causes.

Köhler was referring not to complex relations like the causes of market fluctuations or malaria, but to simple ones like learning that fire burns and dogs bark. No prolonged research is needed to establish such relations; the burned child may dread the flame after a single experience. A connection of this sort, Köhler noted, is what is meant by the German *verständlicher Zusammenhang,* "understandable relationship"—the burned child perceives or "understands" fire to be the cause of pain. Such understanding or insight is not restricted to human beings, for animals react to carrots and sticks as causes of reward and punishment. A dog cringing at a menacing stick apparently recognizes it as the instrument of pain.

This perception of causality, Köhler pointed out, is different from the inductive operation David Hume described as the "constant conjunction" of successive events giving rise to "a customary association of ideas." For Hume, establishing a causal relation requires many experiences. This is what Köhler denied. After a single experience a child may know that ice is cold, water is wet, and candy is sweet, with no need for repeated trials to identify the "causes" of such sensations.[4] These associations are not

4. How children come to understand the nature of causality is a more complex affair than is suggested by these simple examples, as Jean Piaget pointed out more than fifty years ago in *The Child's Conception of Causality* (1930). It has been a recurrent theme through the

produced by inductive reasoning or by repeated exposure to Hume's temporal contiguities. Instead there is a direct apprehension of the connection between an object and a sensory impression that, Köhler maintained, constitutes insight.

This is tantamount to arguing that perceiving causal relations involves insight. Support for this contention is found in the work of Albert Michotte (1881–1965), a Belgian psychologist who spent more than thirty years studying causality as a psychological problem. He worked out ingenious experimental approaches to the problem and reported the results in considerable detail in *The Perception of Causality* (1963). That insight may be essential to the perception of causality was made clear by two of Michotte's observations—a nail being driven into a plank and bread being sliced. In watching such operations, Michotte wrote, one can "see" one object "acting" on another and "producing" certain effects. In this connection he asked (1963, p. 15), "when we observe these operations, is our perception limited to the impression of two movements spatially and temporally co-ordinated, such as the advance of the knife and the cutting of the bread? Or rather do we directly perceive the action as such—do we see the knife actually cut the bread? The answer does not seem to me to admit of any doubt."

Michotte cited these examples not only as instances of direct impressions of causality, but also as illustrations of Köhler's explanation of insight. He mentioned Köhler's chapter on insight and gave the concept additional recognition by stressing the word *see* in his allusions to *seeing* "the knife actually cut the bread" and *seeing* the nail being acted on by the hammer.

This made insight a function of perceptibility and helped account for the contrast between two modes of problem solving: insightful solutions and trial-and-error solutions. Thorndike's monkeys in the problem box could not use insight because the locking devices were not completely visible and there was no way to perceive the relation between the visible bolt and the concealed releasing mechanism. As in a mystery story where even the brilliant detective cannot find the hidden jewels by deduction or by insight but must resort to trial-and-error searching for a trapdoor, sliding panel, or hollow brick, both monkey and detective "adjust" to the situation by using trial and error.

Insight versus Trial and Error

"Adjustments" attributed to insight have generally been regarded as more

years in his investigations of children's mental development. A summary of these later investigations, written in collaboration with Bärbel Inhelder, has been published as *The Psychology of the Child* (1969).

"intelligent" than those achieved by trial and error. Sultan's success notwithstanding, insight has also been regarded as characteristic of human behavior. Of course Sultan's insight was not described as the equivalent of a mature human's abstract thinking; it was more like the thinking of a young child. As R. B. Cattell noted in analyzing the concept of intelligence (1970, p. 346): "The capacity of animals, even of higher apes, to perceive complex relationships is far below that of adult man, and seldom exceeds the level of a three-year old child, yet it is of the same nature as the intelligence of man. Blind trial-and-error behaviour, the very antithesis of intelligence, is common in animal behaviour."

Cattell included an account of Sultan's "insight" in using the lengthened stick to reach food, but he noted that such insight does not appear to be common among animals. In particular, he pointed out, the complex tricks of circus animals, though they seem insightful, are actually "the result of prolonged, blind, trial-and-error learning."

One may question whether this antithesis between intelligence and "blind trial-and-error behaviour" constitutes such a complete dichotomy. Trial-and-error behavior may not be altogether blind and stupidly impulsive, and intelligent behavior may not be altogether insightful. Although the antithesis is a helpful abstraction, it is not an accurate means of classifying concrete behaviors. It is less like the division between odd and even numbers than like the division between liberals and conservatives — not a mutually exclusive polarity. A person may be liberal in politics and conservative in religion, and a freethinker in religion may be conservative in other respects. To appreciate this analogy we need to consider the concept of "error" in this context.

Are All "Errors" Wrong?

On its first trial in an ordinary maze the experimental animal — say a dehydrated rat in quest of water — seems to scamper along the alleys in random fashion. By convention the experimenter considers the true path the shortest route from the entrance to the reward compartment. Deviations from this path by entrance into blind alleys are scored as errors. They are errors in terms of the experimenter's knowledge of the maze pattern, but are they errors in terms of the animal's first exploratory tour of the maze? Are they wrong moves from the standpoint of a thirsty animal in quest of water? Can a false trail be recognized as false without traversing it? It might be argued, however, that repeated traversals of the same blind alley are certainly errors. They are failures to perceive the move as wrong and hence show lack of insight.

Still, even this last judgment may not be correct in all instances. In some common human situations repeating seemingly futile moves turns out to be justified. In searching for a missing book, a fourth or fifth inspection of the same shelf brings the missing volume to light. Repeated inspections of the same row of books does not necessarily indicate stupidity; instead of lack of insight, we are more likely to ascribe the error to oversight. May not the rat's repeated entrances into the same cul-de-sac be like our repeated inspection of the same shelf?

Another example of the ambiguity of "error" within the context of trial-and-error behavior is a toxicologist investigating a case of suspected poisoning. He tests the victim's gastric contents or blood successively for strychnine, arsenic, potassium, cyanide, oxalic acid, and several mercury compounds. If all these tests prove negative, are they errors? The murderer, who knows what poison he used, might call them errors, since they fail to solve the problem, but they are not errors from the chemist's viewpoint. Each poison he tests for must be eliminated as a *possible* toxic agent, like an animal's initial exploration of a blind alley. What if the chemist repeats some of these negative tests? Is such repeated testing foolish and erroneous? Not necessarily, since a second test sometimes fails to confirm the first negative result. Our toxicologist might decide to repeat one of the mercury tests and be rewarded by a definite positive reaction.

This chemical analogy does not mean that chemists and rats solve their problems in the same way or that the rat in the maze, like the chemist in his laboratory, has a systematic plan of exploration. But interpreting trial and error as impulsive random activity until an animal finds water or food in the maze fails to explain how over repeated trials the animal *learns* to get to the reward compartment by the *shortest* route. How are the blind alleys and longer routes eliminated? They certainly have to be explored at least once before they can be rejected as delaying speedy attainment of the goal. As initial maneuvers, they are leads to be tested rather than blunders.

Many years ago Ladd and Woodworth called attention to this aspect of the learning process. After describing many experiments using mazes and puzzle boxes, they concluded (1911, p. 550):

> In the experiments already described, the method by which the animal learns to master a maze or a puzzle box has been called learning by "trial and error." We prefer to call it "learning by varied reaction through selection of successful variants." Without variation of reaction, the cat would continue trying to squeeze between the bars toward the food, just as iron filings tend along lines of force toward a magnet from which, perhaps, they are separated by a sheet of paper. On the other hand, without some sort of selection from among the varied reactions, no progressive shortening of the whole time of reaction would occur.

The "progressive shortening" of the time means gradual elimination of maladaptive movements or change in patterns of behavior that results in "adjustment" to the problem. This elimination is not a stereotyped mechanical affair like the movements of a marble released by the plunger of the marble game. The marble never "learns" to roll into a particular hole, and despite innumerable trials there is no reduction in time of rolling from one end of the board to the other, no preference for a special "goal," and no emerging "pattern" of movement. There is plenty of "varied reaction" as the marble chances to bounce against obstructing nails, but no "selection" of specific variants. If there were such selection, the marble would be learning, and *learning by varied reaction through selection of successful variants.* This formulation supplies a more accurate description of the nature of learning commonly attributed to trial and error. For *error* it substitutes the concept of *varied reaction,* recognizing exploratory as opposed to mistaken maneuvers.

Unfortunately, the suggested formulation is too long for easy communication. Furthermore, the phrase *trial-and-error learning* is too firmly established in our professional and everyday vocabularies to be dislodged just by calling attention to its technical shortcomings. It may be possible, however, to change the connotation of "error" so it will be understood to mean "wrong" only from the standpoint of one who already knows the correct move or the right answer. I shall continue to use the phrase, but by *error* I mean *varied* reaction rather than *stupid* reaction.

Is Trial and Error Planless?

Trial-and-error behavior is not necessarily stupid even when used by a rat in a maze; at least it is not altogether at variance with the demands of the problem to be solved. A hungry or thirsty animal in quest of food or water explores the maze in seemingly random or planless fashion, but its exploring is both sensible and appropriate. Were the animal to run in circles in one alley, go to sleep in another, or just scratch itself, such actions would be senseless, inappropriate, and stupid as possible "trials." The "trial" part of trial and error is not an aimless selection from among all the actions of which the animal is capable. The trials are not the equivalent of panic behavior or the convulsions of an epileptic seizure. The trials in the course of "adjustment" to a learning situation consist of a series of actions more or less relevant to the exigencies of the situation. In the maze rats explore the alleys by running, and in the problem box cats try to escape by clawing, squeezing between the slats, and pulling at strings suspended from pulleys. Köhler's apes, before the moment of insight, had tried to reach the food with one of the nonjoined sticks.

The difference between solutions attributed to insight and those attributed to trial and error is not sharply differentiated. Insight is often, if not usually, preceded by trial-and-error operations, and trial and error reflects at least minimal insight in the sense of some apprehension of what the situation demands. Trial-and-error behavior is not altogether planless.

In a relatively simple laboratory study in 1935, Wayne Dennis explored this question: Is a rat's exploration of a maze just a product of chance impulsiveness, or is it governed by what in human affairs would be called sensible choices? To get the answer, Dennis used a Y-shaped maze, containing no reward, and examined what effect exploring one of the arms in an initial trial had upon the next trial. As soon as it had explored one of the arms, the animal was brought back to the starting point for a second trial. This constituted the test for that day. After two days the test was repeated. Each rat being tested was subjected to twelve pairs of trials spaced at intervals of forty-eight hours.

If the first choice had no influence on the succeeding one, the second choice should have been the same as the first in about 50 percent of the trials, in accordance with chance probability as in tossing coins. However, Dennis found that most second choices *differed* from the first choice. If the left arm had been explored in the first trial, the right arm was likely to be explored in the second trial and vice versa. In 82 percent of the cases the animals explored the portion of the maze not chosen in the preceding trial. In only 18 percent was the second trial a repetition of the first.

The animals acted as if they remembered exploring one arm of the Y and leaving the other unexplored. Since the maze contained no reward, neither branch served as a goal, and the animals were not deprived of food or water to induce goal-seeking behavior.

What, then, did induce rats to explore? The statistical outcome suggests it was not random or chance behavior. It might be that an animal analogue to human curiosity about new surroundings led the animals to traverse all parts of the maze trying to learn something. The animals acted as if they wanted to find out what was in the unexplored parts of the maze. In making the second choice different from the first they seemed to remember or *know* that they had already explored one arm of the maze. By acting in the light of such knowledge the animals were exhibiting an implicit or incipient plan of action and discriminating between explored and unexplored portions of the maze. They were aware or *conscious* of a difference in direction as they reached the junction. Although seeing this difference does not constitute insight, it does suggest that trial-and-error behavior is not *blind,* the conclusion Cattell reached: "Blind trial-and-error behaviour, the very antithesis of intelligence, is common in animal behaviour."

Trial and Error Can Lead to Insight

Trial-and-error behavior is not stupid in the sense of being inappropriate, irrational, or altogether at variance with the demands of the problem situation. It is not "the very antithesis of intelligence." If intelligent behavior is equated with insightful behavior, then trial and error might be held to be congruent with intelligent behavior rather than opposed. Sultan had manipulated sticks by trial and error before using them insightfully. He had even tried to retrieve the banana by pushing one stick toward the fruit, then using a second stick to push the first one. Another part of his trial-and-error experience was finding out that the bamboo sticks were hollow, which, we may presume, gave rise to the "trial" of bringing together the ends of the two sticks. This "trial" was not undertaken when he was first confronted with the problem situation and thus seemed to be unrelated to the problem. It was more of a playful maneuver, like a baby's playing with two spoons. It was this maneuver that resulted in insight, not insight that prompted the maneuver. When the lengthened stick suddenly appeared, Sultan rushed to the scene of the problem to do with the one long stick what he had failed to accomplish with the two short ones, as if he recognized the joined sticks as a useful instrument, not a mere plaything. This recognition constituted insight that had emerged from his trial-and-error experience. Without the trial and error, it seems safe to say, Sultan would not have been able to supply Köhler with this particular example of insight.

That trial and error can lead to insight was also demonstrated by a series of experiments reported by H. F. Harlow in 1949. A peanut was hidden under one of two objects that a monkey could easily reach. The objects differed in color, size, or shape, and the experimenter used a screen to prevent the animal from seeing which object the peanut had been hidden under. Assume that on the first trial the peanut was concealed under the round green cover and there was nothing under the triangular red cover. Locating the peanut was a matter of chance: choosing green meant success and choosing red meant failure. Whatever the monkey's choice, the trial was terminated and the screen was replaced while another peanut was concealed. The screen was then removed so the monkey could choose a second time. This procedure was continued, with the peanut always placed under the round green cover, though from time to time the positions of the red and green covers were reversed. By such reversals the monkey learned to disregard the position of the covers. The series of trials ended when the monkey consistently chose the green cover irrespective of its location with respect to the red cover.

Harlow devised a vast number of such problems involving discrimination between objects of different kinds, colors, shapes, and sizes. He mentions using 344 different pairs of objects. Eight monkeys had to deal with this series, with each given 50 trials on the first 32 problems, 6 trials on the next 200 problems, and 9 trials on the last 112 problems. The results, presented as learning curves, show obvious improvement from one block of trials to the next, and, as Harlow noted, the curves for the last series of problems resemble the kind of curve regarded as indicating "insightful learning" in human problem solving. The monkeys had apparently learned what to expect and how to cope with the successive series of problems (1949, pp. 53, 56):

> The monkeys *learn how to learn* individual problems with a mini-mum of errors. It is this *learning how to learn a kind of problem* that we designate by the term *learning set*. . . . Before the forma-tion of a discrimination learning set, a single training trial produces negligible gain; after the formation of a discrimination learning set, *a single training trial constitutes problem solution.* These data clearly show that *animals can gradually learn insight.*[5]

Additional support for Harlow's last conclusion was supplied by con-fronting the monkeys with problems requiring them to reverse established discriminations. Harlow introduced a series of 112 such problems, but let us continue to consider discrimination between the red and green covers. By hypothesis, the monkey had formed the habit of looking for the peanut under the green cover. Could this habit be broken? Harlow now placed the peanut under the red cover so that raising the green one brought no reinforcement. In the early trials of the new series, the monkey favored the green cover, in line with its established habit. When it failed to find the peanut in the accustomed place it hesitated briefly, then lifted the red cover and found the reward. For a while the monkey continued to look under both covers, but with more trials it selected the red cover imme-diately and no longer reacted to the green cover. The old habit had been broken and a new one instituted. Like the old habit, this new one had been established by trial and error, not by insight.

Since the objects differed in size and shape as well as in color, it was easy to confront the monkey with the 112 discrimination problems. With repeated exposure to reversals, the shift from the old response to the new one took place more promptly. After enough practice the monkey made the shift immediately following the first absence of the expected reward. Without hesitating or examining both covers, it turned at once to the hitherto unrewarded one, as if it had discovered the principle governing the changed location of an anticipated reward. This discovery or insight

---

5. Harlow also cited data showing that young children exhibited comparable learning sets resulting in insight and that "after the first day or two of training" they "did as well or better" than the monkeys. These children ranged in age from two to five and in IQ from 109 to 151.

eliminated the need for a trial-and-error search by providing an appropriate learning set, but the insight developed out of a series of trial-and-error experiences. Yet whether this constitutes genuine insight depends on how the concept is interpreted.

Is Animal Insight Really Insight?

The concept of insight has several meanings, and not all apply to the insight attributed to animals. We can eliminate the psychiatric usage, as in statements that a patient lacks insight because he fails to recognize his delusions and phobias as abnormal. We can also rule out the related nonpsychiatric usage of insight as a synonym for self-knowledge in the sense of sound judgment of one's own talents, abilities, reputation, handicaps, and personality traits. Neither of these usages has anything to do with the insight of Köhler's Sultan or Harlow's monkeys except to the extent that all usages connote seeing into or knowing something, as expressed in the literal meaning of *in*sight or the equivalent German word *Einsicht.* As Köhler applied it to Gestalt psychology, *Einsicht* implied a sudden apprehension of what moves would reach a goal or solve a problem. Sultan's sudden use of the lengthened stick to reach the banana illustrates this meaning, as does a chess player's suddenly realizing what move will win the game. In neither instance is the correct move the accidental result of trial and error. As insight or *Einsicht,* it involves a more definitely cognitive appreciation of what the problem demands. This cognitive aspect of insight is made explicit in the French term *connaissance intuitive,* "intuitive knowledge."

One could say a chess master has an "intuitive knowledge" of the game in the sense of having an inherent talent like that of the "born mathematician" or "born composer." He has insight into brilliant moves just as a mathematical genius has insight into abstruse numerical or spatial abstractions and the musical genius has insight into new tonal relations.

Can Sultan be said to have exhibited this kind of intuitive knowledge? Was his insight like the insight of a chess master or that of a Newton or a Mozart? Was Köhler crediting Sultan with human insight?[6] R. S. Woodworth (1869–1962) questioned the validity of doing so (1940, p. 299):

6. According to E. R. Hilgard, the insight experiments of the Gestalt psychologists were so interpreted by many educators and others at the time (1956, p. 224): "Therefore the return to a more balanced view, represented by the insight experiments, gave new hope to teachers and others who saw thinking and understanding returned to respectability. Insight was not a new discovery—it was a return to a conception laymen had never abandoned. Nobody uninfluenced by peculiar doctrines would ever have denied insight as a fact—yet it took Köhler to restore it as a fact in American psychology."

Shall we regard this dramatic incident as the typical case of learning and conclude that all learning is learned by insight? In other experiments even chimpanzees—yes, even men—show a melancholy lack of understanding of some mechanical device and still acquire a practical mastery of it. The word *insight* is too strong. We humans, in this modern age, learn to manage automobiles and radios without having more than the vaguest insight into their mechanism. No one has complete insight into any concrete thing. . . . The child who "sees" that pushing the wall switch turns on the ceiling light must be allowed to have "insight" though he has not the faintest idea of the wiring or of the nature of an electric circuit.

By putting "insight" in quotation marks Woodworth was indicating that the child's reaction to the light switch is not genuine insight and also advising caution in drawing inferences from Sultan's "dramatic incident." As an example of insight, it is not "typical" of chimpanzee learning, for more complex mechanical problems are not necessarily solved through insight. An ape can ride a bicycle without understanding the mechanical principles involved. His "practical mastery" of the task would not enable him to deal with a breakdown of the steering mechanism. Sultan might not have known what to do if Köhler had plugged the hollow end of the stick with a wad of paper so that one stick would no longer fit into the other. If so, then, as Woodworth implied, even the nontypical "dramatic incident" would not have constituted full-fledged insightful learning.

Moreover, he says, such full-fledged insight is absent from much of human learning. We learn to use a microscope without understanding just how it makes the invisible visible, and we learn to make hard-boiled eggs without understanding colloids. Similarly, we can write checks without knowing the social and mechanical transactions the checks undergo as they pass through the clearinghouse and return to us. Though we talk familiarly about eating and breathing, most of us are ignorant of the physiology of digestion and respiration. Merely knowing how to eat and how to breathe is not the equivalent of having insight into the processes involved. This is why Woodworth regarded *insight* as too strong a word to describe our practical efficiency in handling ignition keys, television dials, restaurant menus, and checking accounts. We have "insight" rather than insight. We need a better way to express the difference than Woodworth's quotation marks, but technical psychology has not yet found satisfactory designations for the two concepts.

Foresight and Hindsight

Woodworth may have tried to find such a pair of words. Immediately after objecting to the careless use of the word *insight,* he pointed out that animals sometimes show *foresight* and at other times show *hindsight.* He noted that Sultan showed foresight when he rushed to the site of the banana once he had fitted the two sticks together, but in recalling its location he was using hindsight. Similarly, Harlow's monkeys, after being trained to react to a particular color, showed hindsight by acting as though they remembered that on previous trials the peanut was under the green cover, and their immediate removal of the green cover suggests anticipation of the reward. Such anticipation or expectation[7] indicates foresight. As foresight this is not as dramatic as Sultan's first use of the joined sticks, since ideally, as Woodworth noted, foresight connotes seeing the route to a goal before trying it out. Seeing the route as correct after trying it would thus constitute hindsight. However, such perception, whether foresight or hindsight, is hardly genuine insight, for it involves apprehension of spatial relations rather than sophisticated understanding of scientific principles. This is true of much of human learning and very likely of all instances of animal learning. To avoid misunderstanding, Woodworth advises, it might be better to avoid the term *insight* (1940, p. 300):

> Because insight usually implies some penetration into the true nature of things, we had better avoid the word and speak simply of learning by observation. Even this word is rather too strong, as it suggests deliberate effort to observe. All we mean is that the animal, through the use of his senses, gets acquainted with the usable characteristics of the situation. In the case of foresight the animal, inspecting the field of operations, perceives a way to the goal, as he can when the way is direct and unobstructed. Very often, however, the usable characteristics of a situation cannot be discerned by mere inspection, and then trial and error are necessary and observation consists largely in hindsight.

In granting animals foresight and hindsight Woodworth was recognizing their sensitivity to their surroundings and their ability to profit from it. His reference to the animal's making "use of his senses" implies that the animal is aware of sights, sounds, smells, pains, or pressures as given sensory receptors are stimulated. He alludes to the animal's becoming acquainted, or inspecting, or discerning, or in general being able to observe, but these modes of awareness or observation are not to be equated with sophisticated human efforts to solve problems. Woodworth did not consider animal observations functions of a Cartesian *res cogitans,* and he

---

7. Attributing expectation to a monkey would not strain the credibility of many animal psychologists, since as far back as the 1930s E.C. Tolman had already attributed "cognitive expectations" to rats as well as monkeys (1932, p. 77).

thus warned against interpreting *observation* to mean that animals make a "deliberate effort to observe."

In effect he was endowing animals with Lockean sensations but not Lockean reflections. Their foresight and hindsight are not the equivalents of human efforts to plan for remote contingencies or to survey the past. Animal foresight is limited to more immediate problems characterized by "direct and unobstructed" perceptibility of "a way to the goal." This is very different from the kind of human foresight that makes us buy fire extinguishers, burglar alarms, or insurance policies. As a cognitive operation this kind of planning involves insight into long-range possibilities far more complex than that by which Sultan perceived a relation between the lengthened stick and the banana.

Moreover, these future possibilities cannot be presented to the animal by concrete objects or symbols in the here and now. Presenting them requires language; man's sophisticated foresight is made possible by calendars, libraries, and the whole vast educational enterprise that depends on language symbols. Their lack of language symbols also deprives animals of the long-range hindsight of ancestral experience as transmitted by social tradition and recorded history. Because of this language barrier animal consciousness will always differ from human consciousness; the insight of Sultan will never equal the wisdom of Solomon. Whether this is a difference in kind or in degree continues to be an unsettled question.[8]

Cognition and Language

Some of this difference between animal and human consciousness is due to animals' inability to talk — they cannot express experience either through

8. Those who sponsor a humanistic psychology tend to view it as an unbridgeable qualitative difference. Often they contrast humanism with behaviorism or humanistic psychology with animal psychology. It is an ongoing contemporary controversy, as reflected in the special symposium on "Psychology and Humanism" in the April 1971 issue of the *Humanist*. (See the antibehaviorism article by F. W. Matson and the probehaviorism articles by K. MacCorquodale and by W. F. Day.) The controversy started before humanistic psychology had emerged as a distinct movement or "third force" in psychology. It engaged those who were dubious about animal psychology because of its alleged remoteness from important and distinctively human problems as well as those who saw it as genuine scientific preparation for dealing with more complex human problems.

By the 1940s this controversy culminated in two provocative articles. Gordon Allport, in "Scientific Models and Human Morals" (1947), argued that studies of animal behavior fail to promote understanding of human nature, since animals cannot deal with symbols, though they can respond to words, gestures, and noises of a trainer as *signals*. John P. Seward, in "The Sign of a Symbol: A Reply to Professor Allport," subjected this argument to critical analysis in defending this thesis: "The conative and cognitive processes of humans and other species belong on a continuum, varying only in complexity" (1948, p. 293).

inner speech or by talking to others. And because of the close relation between cognition and language, indicated by the high correlations between scores on vocabulary tests and measures of intelligence, they can never be creatures of intellect. This reciprocal influence of intellectual development and speech development was recognized long before statistical correlations were discovered. According to August Messer, Plato came close to identifying the two kinds of development; he quotes Plato as having held that "thought and speech are one and the same"[9] (1908, p. 101). Reasoning or critical thinking thus grows out of and merges with the capacity to give adequate symbolic expression to ideation as it is experienced. People rely on notes, diagrams, outlines, equations, and similar overt means of symbolization when confronted by problems too complex or difficult for covert reflection. To cope with Euclid's theorems the student needs drawings, letters of the alphabet, and the vocabulary of geometry to make implicit meanings explicit and visible on writing tablets and blackboards. Aristotle said the scope of thought is "potentially whatever is thinkable," and when the potential thoughts become actual their "characters may be said to be on a writing-tablet" (McKeon 1947, p. 220).

The "characters" Aristotle mentioned may include all graphic modes of symbolization, any written "character" that represents a thought or an idea — not only words, but also pictures, maps, blueprints, and signs like %, +, and $. Thinking is aided by such "characters" or symbols, which express our ideas and intentions as do talking, nodding, pointing, shrugging, and similar symbolic actions in conversation. "Silent thinking" is inhibited or incipient conversation with ourselves; Alexander Bain referred to it as "restrained speaking or acting" (1894, p. 358). Years later (1924) John B. Watson (1878–1958) provided for thinking in his behavioristic psychology by treating it as a laryngeal rather than a cerebral process. He identified thinking with the activation of laryngeal mechanisms and thus made talking the equivalent of thinking. Watson was not refusing to credit the congenital deaf-mute with ability to think, for one thus afflicted could think provided he had learned to "talk" with his fingers in sign language.

This behavioristic identification of thinking with talking is descriptively accurate to the extent that talking gives symbolic expression to an antecedent or concomitant cognitive process. When it does not, verbalization does not indicate thinking. There are times when ritual prayers amount to thoughtless vocalization. The student of a foreign language can reel off conjugations not only without thinking about their meanings, but while he is conscious of thoughts alien to the words he utters. Mechanical, parroted verbalization is not to be identified with thinking. Neither is the

9. "Gedanke und Rede sind dasselbe."

aphasic patient incapable of thinking because, like the stutterer, he lacks control of his laryngeal mechanisms.

Thus on occasion thinking may be independent of verbalization, just as verbalization may be independent of thinking. Nevertheless, in general there is a close association between use of language symbols and cognitive efficiency. Without such symbols thinking, planning, analyzing, and similar components of the life of reason are not likely to emerge, as Titchener brought out (1917, p. 522):

> Thought requires symbols; language is a system of symbols; and we have no reason to suppose that, in the history of mind, it supervened upon or took the place of any previous system. Thought and language, in other words, appear to have grown up side by side; each implies the other; and in this sense it is true to say that there is no thought without words; reasoning and language are two aspects of the same phase of mental development. The old conundrum: Why don't the animals talk? Because they have nothing to say—contains a sound psychology; if the animals thought, they would talk; since they do not talk, they do not either think.

In the latter conclusion Titchener was saying that thinking that is contingent upon the use of language is unique to human beings and as a cognitive process is alien to animal psychology. Of course Titchener did not arrive at this conclusion by conducting animal experiments. Unlike Köhler, he never confronted animals with learning problems that might elicit thinking; but this does not invalidate his conclusion. He might have regarded the thinking implicit in Sultan's "insight" as different from the distinctively human thinking revealed in the language of Socrates or Newton or even the average healthy schoolboy. If so, he would have been anticipating Harlow's conclusion (1959, p. 478): "The monkey possesses learning capacities far in excess of any other infrahuman primate, abilities comparable to those of low-level human imbeciles. The monkey's learning capabilities can give us little or no information concerning human language, and only incomplete information relating to thinking."

Harlow wrote this before the days of chimpanzees like Washoe, Nim, and Lana or Koko the gorilla, who were trained in the American Sign Language (ASL) of the deaf. Another chimpanzee, Sarah, was trained to respond to plastic signs. Some investigators claimed they could carry on conversations with their animal subjects and interpreted this as the use of language by animals. They did not regard the chirping of birds and the barking of dogs as language, but they considered the ASL signing to be symbolic communication. Two or more signs used together were deemed sentences.

Within the past few years, however, these interpretations have been called into question. Terrace and his colleagues asked, "Can an ape create a sentence?" and found little affirmative evidence. They concluded that apes "show no unequivocal evidence of mastering the conversational, semantic, or syntactic organization of language" (1979, p. 901). Similarly, Savage-Rumbaugh, Rumbaugh, and Boysen asked, "Do apes use language?" but could "find no definite demonstration that Washoe, Sarah, Lana, Koko, or Nim used symbols representationally" (1980, p. 55). In a third study of these investigations, Appleton (1976) raised a different issue, their bearing on animal consciousness. He stressed a "basic difference between our consciousness and that of animals" in that, unlike animals, we are conscious of history, of religion, and of death. Human consciousness in this sense is a product of language as spoken and written, but Washoe and the other animals never learned to talk or to write. Their performances do not appear very different from what Harlow attributed to his monkeys.

Thus animal and human consciousness are different in kind, not just in degree. Viewed in historical perspective, this may be considered a twentieth-century confirmation of the human distinctiveness of Aristotle's rational soul, the Cartesian *res cogitans,* and the Lockean reflection. The significance of such distinctiveness for certain phases of consciousness may escape casual observation. Some of these phases were not brought to light until the early 1900s, when psychologists began to subject thinking as a conscious process to deliberate observation under controlled conditions, thus enriching our understanding of human thinking.

Thinking as a Conscious Process

As I noted in chapter 1, Locke used the term *reflection* to include "all the different actings of our own minds" ordinarily referred to as "perception, thinking, doubting, believing, reasoning, knowing," and willing. Though hardly a rigorous definition, this is a good example of a casual allusion to a psychological term, for it fails to make clear just what differentiates these operations from one another. Is thinking independent of reasoning, or is it just an aspect of reasoning? Is not thinking involved in all the "different actings of our own minds" so that thinking is really not different from Locke's reflection? If so, then the various aspects of cognition such as judging, questioning, imagining, and conceiving are really modes of thinking or of consciousness. Accordingly, thinking as a process meets the more pervasive criteria for consciousness.

I have already noted the close relation between thinking and language that has led some writers to define thinking as the manipulation of language symbols. Such a definition is too restrictive, since thinking is not limited to verbal symbols. Virtually any experienced item may function as a symbol if it stands for, represents, points to, or is a reminder of something else. Thus pain may point to tooth decay, a dry throat may symbolize thirst, the sound of a bell may mean dinner, a fire, a telephone call, or recess, a picture of John Bull may induce thoughts of England, and a whiff of perfume may remind one of a romance of long ago. These are all nonverbal symbols that instigate thinking. The symbols being manipulated may be public or private: the picture of John Bull would be a public symbol, but my dry throat would be private.

Items of experience are traditionally referred to as *mental content*. All experiences constitute mental content, but they function as symbols only if they point to something beyond themselves. Pain merely experienced as pain is mental content, but it may not symbolize anything to the victim even though his physician knows it is a sign of gallbladder disease. Once the patient learns what the pain signifies, he can recognize it as a symptom of gallbladder trouble. It has now become symbolic mental content and the patient can say, "I know what this pain means." In more technical language he might say, "I understand what the pain as a sign signifies." And in still more technical language he might say, "This pain is a good example of *transcendent reference,* since for me it now points to something beyond itself: a damaged gallbladder."

All mental content becomes such transcendent reference as soon as it functions as a symbol. An infant seeing the printed word *fire,* unlike its father, would not think of flames, smoke, and danger. For the infant the word would be bare mental content, but for the father it would be a symbol, enabling him to deal *mentally* with various implications of fire. Thus his reverie might include the hazards of smoking in bed, fire insurance, spontaneous combustion, fire-resistant textiles, playing with matches, and the location of fire hydrants.

I emphasized the word *mentally* to call attention to the elementary but important distinction between having an object in mind and direct perception of the object. Thinking about a fire hydrant is different from watching a fire hose being attached to a hydrant. James said that knowing the tigers in India consisted of "mentally *pointing* towards them as we sit here." This is the same as having an *idea* of or *thinking* of the animals in the jungle or in a zoo. Pointing one's finger at animals in a cage as one explains that they are tigers is not pointing mentally.

Using pencil and paper to add the numbers 8, 5, 3, and 9 is not "doing *mental* arithmetic," though it is a mental operation in that it requires recognition of the numerical symbols. The transcendent reference of 8 is different from that of 5, and 3 points to a different amount than does 9. Adding 8 real items like marbles or matches to 5 more items would be less of a mental operation than adding the written symbols, since dealing with the visible items is less ideational than dealing with their more abstract symbolic surrogates. Dealing with abstractions involves more thought than dealing with concrete objects.

Cognition entails a continuum of change from the concrete and representational at one extreme to the highly abstract and nonrepresentational at the other. A photograph of sugar lumps is more concrete and representational than the chemical formula $C_{12}H_{22}O_{11}$. The photograph stands for actual lumps more immediately and manifestly than does the chemical formula. But both point to or mean or *intend* sugar as once experienced. This brings up a troublesome question in the psychology of thinking: To think of something, must we experience its image or likeness, or may thinking be imageless?

The Question of Imageless Thought

It is easily shown that in thinking about something we often experience a "mental picture" of that thing. In looking at the word *sugar* we may see a *visual* image of a white cube, or remember a sweet *taste*, or imagine a crunching *sound*, or possibly have the *muscular* or kinesthetic feeling of manipulating sugar tongs. Words like *imaginal* or *imaginary* thus apply to all sense modalities, not just sight. The congenitally blind, though they cannot experience visual images, may develop a rich fantasy life in terms of their intact receptor mechanisms. Like sighted individuals, they may talk about their "mental pictures"—in imagination they can reproduce the sound of a bugle, the fragrance of perfume, or the feel of velvet. When employed in this way the phrase "mental picture" is enlarged to include all sense modalities.

Such allusions to mental pictures are common in popular psychology. They are implicit when someone says, "Can you picture this happening to me?" But this approach to thinking is not to be devalued just because of its popular acceptance. Fundamentally it reflects the influential psychological tradition of associationism, in which thinking arouses mental pictures or images. Without such images ordinary words would be as meaningless as an unfamiliar foreign language. This traditional associational teaching was endorsed by most psychologists until early in this century, when the German psychologist Oswald Külpe (1862–1915) challenged it because, as quoted by Müller-Freienfels (1931, p. 56):

> Definite problems induced me to occupy myself with the subject of thinking. It struck me that one could think of the objects of the external world, such as material bodies, or metaphysical objects, such as the ideas of Plato or the monads of Leibniz, in immediate fashion without having to form images of them. From this I concluded not

only that thinking must be a particular mode of mental activity, but also that it must stand in an altogether different relationship to its objects from sensations or images.

At the time, Külpe was lecturing at the University of Würzburg, where he and his students investigated thought processes using techniques and interpretations at variance with traditional associationist doctrine. Their conclusions are commonly known as the views of the Würzburg school, and their teaching became known as the doctrine of *imageless* thinking. The new doctrine did not completely reject the old, but rather added to or modified it. Külpe called into question the notion that thinking must *always* have its object clothed in images. He and his students reported instances in which the thinker was aware of the thought's object without any associated imagery—they reported unclothed or naked thoughts.

The idea of an invisible God might illustrate such imageless thought. The biblical injunction to "have no other gods before me" comes close to urging an imageless thought of God, since it is followed by this commandment: "Thou shalt not make unto thee a graven image; nor the form of anything that is in heaven above, or that is in the earth beneath, or that is in the water under the earth." With image and form ruled out, the word *God* cannot symbolize any tangible, visible, or definite entity subject to direct inspection. Its meaning is more elusive than that of words indicating physical objects like gloves, apples, or pins, which can be pointed to and pictured or looked at. To Külpe and his students such objects were *anschaulich,* or capable of being looked at in terms of their sensory characteristics. Thoughts refractory to such inspection were designated *unanschaulich,* not amenable to inspection, and thinking of this kind was called *unanschauliches Denken,* translated as "imageless thinking," connoting thoughts not amenable to scrutiny as well as thoughts devoid of specifiable images.

Some experimental support for the reality of imageless thinking was supplied in 1915 by T. V. Moore, who reduced the problem to this basic question: To grasp the meaning of a word, is arousal of relevant imagery indispensable? His experimental subjects reacted to a series of words presented singly with two sets of instructions. According to one set, they were to signal as soon as the word aroused an image; according to the other set they were to signal the instant they understood the word's meaning. They signaled by activating a telegraph key, so the time of each reaction was readily recorded. If meaning depends on imagery, it should take longer to understand a meaning word than to become aware of imagery: imagery ought to precede meaning. But this outcome was not realized. Moore found that eight of his nine subjects required more time for arousal of imagery, averaging a full second compared with half a second for apprehending a word's meaning.

However, neither Moore's findings nor those reported by Külpe's students at Würzburg or by other investigators[10] settled the controversy over imageless thought, which was never decisively resolved. Some questioned the Würzburg findings because in reduplicating the experiments they found imagery of some sort, apparently overlooked because it bore no *logical* relationship to the thought in question. They noted that often imagery, along with other sensory content, is *psychologically* even though not logically expressive of the object of thinking. The meaning of *dictionary* may be understood at once without a visual image of the dictionary page, fleeting ideas of Webster, or any other *logical* associate of experiences with dictionaries. But if an early experience was with a musty dictionary in grandfather's attic, then hearing the word might arouse fragmentary images of grandfather's pipe, the ladder leading to the attic, or a vague olfactory image of a musty odor. Asked how we think of the word, we might fail to mention these bits of mental content since they are so remote from the expected associates of the concept; hence our report of an "imageless" thought. For those mindful of the *psychological* relevance of such logically irrelevant associates, however, analysis of the meaning as experienced might never be altogether imageless.

Though the question of imageless thought remained unresolved, the work of the Würzburg school was not in vain. Hitherto neglected or overlooked aspects of the thought process were discovered in the course of studies they initiated or stimulated in laboratories in other countries. The distinction between logical and psychological relationships is one such discovery. And investigations of the psychology of judgment and reasoning brought about the discovery of what came to be called *conscious attitudes*.

Conscious Attitudes: Their Nature and Variety

Consider the experience of an essay examination in some academic subject. In our initial hasty survey of the questions we are conscious that some are easy and others are difficult, and we are confident about answering the former and doubtful about the latter. As we write answers to individual questions we may feel that some point we are about to introduce is not really relevant, that another theme would take too much time, and that still another would clash with the examiner's favorite theory. While we write we may experience shifts of attitude as we are delayed in finishing or else successfully complete the task. We may complete an answer

10. For example, Binet of France confirmed the existence of *pensées sans images*. Woodworth confirmed their occurrence in his own thinking and in that of his subjects at Columbia.

but feel we have failed to dispose of possible objections to our conclusions. We may be unable to recall some name we need, though we know we would recognize it if we heard it. Such knowing that we know something is a conscious attitude, as are the attitudes exemplified by feelings of ease, difficulty, confidence, doubt, irrelevance, delay, or impending success or failure.

These are but a few of the examples offered by those who introduced the term *conscious attitude*.[11] Others include viewing a situation seriously or playfully or approvingly or considering it significant or trivial, and so on and on. The number of possible attitudes is vast. According to members of the Würzburg school, attitudes are concomitants of the thought process but are not experienced in the form of definite images or sensations— they are imageless accompaniments, just as meaning was found to be imageless. But here too the distinction between logically and psychologically relevant imagery merits some consideration. More important, however, is that our understanding of conscious processes is enriched by recognition of these innumerable conscious attitudes. Superficial allusions to mind as a fusion of thinking, feeling, and willing fail to reveal such richness of conscious detail.

Many of the conscious attitudes influence thinking. Awareness of a digression or a clarifying illustration may direct the stream of thinking. In addition to conscious attitudes, Külpe's followers called attention to two related directive factors: the *Aufgabe,* or *mental set,* and the *determining tendency. Aufgabe* means task or lesson or exercise; as a psychological term it designates the effect of specific instructions on the resulting sequence of ideas. Thus when confronted with the numbers 20 and 4 a subject will reply 24 or 80 or 16 depending on whether he had been assigned the *Aufgabe* to add or multiply or subtract. In association tests, experimenters introduce such directive mental sets by calling for particular kinds of responses to stimulus words. The task may call for synonyms or antonyms or subordinates or foreign-language equivalents or correct spelling. In all such instances the assigned task tends to delimit the ideas likely to be aroused by the stimulus words. If accepted by the subject, a given task initiates *intention* to respond in a particular manner. This is the difference between free and controlled association. In controlled association the intention to respond in accordance with the assigned *Aufgabe* guides the ideational sequence. Specific instructions can also regulate muscular activity. When a sprinter is told to "get set," he makes muscular adjustments so he can react quickly to the starter's pistol. His tense crouch is the manifestation of the aroused determining tendency.

11. This is a translation of the term first introduced by Külpe's students, *Bewusstseinslage.* The latter is a fusion of *Bewusstsein,* "consciousness," and *Lage,* "condition, state, or attitude."

These ideas about determining tendencies, controlled associations, *Aufgaben,* and conscious attitudes as directive factors in thinking are some of the most positive findings of the Würzburg school and compensate for the failure to settle the question of imageless thinking. Külpe's followers showed that thinking is not a passive process by which ideas present themselves more or less spontaneously as determined by the laws of association, with the "thinker" a mere spectator of the sequence.

In place of such a spectator theory of thinking, Külpe and his students introduced a more dynamic *activity* theory, presenting thinking as governed by goal-directed intentions of the thinker. This emphasis on an *active* associationism is reflected in Külpe's statement about the role of self as active thinker (Saupe 1931, p. 21):[12]

> The self occupies the throne and administers executive acts. [Das Ich sitzt auf dem Thron und vollzieht Regierungstakte.] It notices, perceives, and takes account of what enters its realm. It occupies itself with these matters and consults with its experienced ministers: the principles and norms of its State, its acquired knowledge and insights, and the accidental needs of the present. On this basis it resolves upon a course of action with respect to the intruder — whether to disregard him, to use him or to take action against him.

Külpe's metaphor attributing such administrative functions to the self is reminiscent of the functions Freud attributed to the censor. Both men, working independently, thus called attention to a *regulative* factor in the dynamics of ideation. Thinking, in their view, was not a passive process in which a detached observer took note of events occurring on the stage of consciousness. Rather, the thinker was like a stage manager actively shaping the events. This metaphor is useful in explaining motivated thinking or goal-directed ideation; specific thoughts act upon us, and we react to them with approval or disapproval, clarity or confusion, conflict or resolution, and kindred acts of judgment and discrimination in the course[13] of thinking through a given problem. The role of conscious attitudes in regulating the dynamics of thinking is not to be underestimated. This also applies to *Aufgaben,* determining tendencies, and other findings of the Würzburg psychologists.

12. Messer quoted the original German in his account of the Würzburg findings in the volume edited by Saupe.

13. The *course* of such thinking, or what James called the "*stream* of consciousness," is not quite like a river flowing toward a fixed destination. As J. L. Singer made evident a few years ago, aside from its allusion to "the seeming continuity of thought" this metaphor of a stream fails to encompass the vicissitudes of thinking as an "inner experience." Singer called particular attention to the significance of daydreaming as a cognitive process related to reflective thinking.

Importance of the Würzburg Findings

It is unfortunate that the research of the Würzburg psychologists has been so exclusively identified with the question of imageless thinking. They themselves did not use the word *imageless,* which has no precise German equivalent, and there is no precise English equivalent for their *unanschauliches Denken.* Incidentally, in place of *imageless thinking* Woodworth once suggested *nonsensory thinking* as closer to the meaning of the German phrase. Had Woodworth's phrase been adopted, the Würzburg findings might have received more critical appreciation. Regrettably, their importance is all too often underestimated because of the mistaken notion that the Würzburg psychologists were concerned solely with images as indispensable to thinking as an ideational process.

A contemporary example of such disparagement of the Würzburg findings is in Robert Ornstein's *The Psychology of Consciousness,* in a passage dealing with the "limitations" of introspection (1972, pp. 4–5):

This and other limitations soon led to a sterility in the contents of psychology. Controversies of only academic import (in the worst sense of the term) arose, due to the limitations placed on inquiry. One, for instance, concerned whether "thoughts without images" could or could not occur. The concerns of psychologists drifted further away from the original ones.

By the "original ones" Ornstein meant the concerns of those who had started out to make psychology the study of consciousness. He held that the introspective study of consciousness advocated by Titchener "led to a sterility in the contents of psychology," a devaluation of Titchener's psychology in striking contrast to Boring's tribute cited at the beginning of this chapter. It is hard to reconcile such disparagement with the research Titchener instigated, the systematic psychology he developed, the critical thinking he provoked, and the doctoral students he trained.

Since the question of "thoughts without image" was subordinate to the more comprehensive question of the nature and dynamics of thinking, the work of the Würzburg psychologists is not to be stigmatized as having "led to a sterility in the contents of psychology." On the contrary, their work on the directive influence of determining tendencies and of mental sets or *Aufgaben* enriched psychology, as did their discovery of conscious attitudes as variegated concomitants of thinking. Ornstein fails to mention any of these findings, but they are intrinsic to thinking as a conscious process and ought to be included in a book on the psychology of consciousness. Their importance as mental processes is not contingent on whether imageless thoughts prove to be fact or fiction. In fact, neither their existence nor their significance was questioned by Titchener and others who considered imageless thinking more fiction than fact. In discussing the stand taken by a German colleague, Titchener acknowledged that the function of given mental processes can be examined independent of their association with the doctrine of imageless thinking (1929, p. 227): "He inclines toward the acceptance of imageless thinking: but, again, every function must on his view have some sort of correlated content. The experimental data regarding imageless thought do not here concern us."

During the years when the Würzburg psychologists were conducting their investigations, some psychologists in the United States were studying the functions of conscious phenomena, seeking to answer the question discussed in the next chapter: What is the function of consciousness?

References

Allport, G. W. 1947. Scientific models and human morals. *Psychological Review* 54:182–92.

Appleton, T. 1976. Consciousness in animals. *Zygon* 3:337–45.

Bain, A. 1868. *The senses and the intellect.* 3d ed. London: Longmans, Green.

———. 1894. *The senses and the intellect.* 4th ed. New York: D. Appleton.

Boring, E. G. 1950. *A history of experimental psychology.* 2d ed. New York: Appleton-Century-Crofts.

———. 1963. *The physical dimensions of consciousness.* New York: Dover Publications. First published 1933.

Cattell, R. B. 1970. Intelligence. In *Encyclopaedia Britannica,* 12:345–47.

Day, W. F. 1971. Humanistic psychology and contemporary behaviorism. *Humanist* 31:13–16.

Dennis, W. 1935. A comparison of the rat's first and second explorations of a maze unit. *American Journal of Psychology* 47:488–90.

Freud, S. 1950. The unconscious. In *Collected papers,* 4:98–136. London: Hogarth Press. Originally published 1915.

Harlow, H. F. 1949. The formation of learning sets. *Psychological Review* 56:51–65.

———. 1959. The development of learning in the rhesus monkey. *American Scientist* 47:457–79.

Hilgard, E. R. 1956. *Theories of learning.* 2d ed. New York: Appleton-Century-Crofts.

Köhler, W. 1925. *The mentality of apes.* New York: Harcourt, Brace.

———. 1947. *Gestalt psychology.* New York: Liveright. Originally published 1929.

Ladd, G. T., and Woodworth, R. S. 1911. *Elements of physiological psychology.* New York: Charles Scribner's Sons.

MacCorquodale, K. 1971. Behaviorism is a humanism. *Humanist* 31:12–13.

McKeon, R., ed. 1947. *Introduction to Aristotle.* New York: Modern Library.

Matson, F. W. 1971. Humanistic theory: The third revolution in psychology. *Humanist* 31:7–11.

Messer, A. 1908. *Empfindung und Denken.* Leipzig: Quelle und Meyer.

Michotte, A. 1963. *The perception of causality.* Trans. T. R. Miles and Elaine Miles. New York: Basic Books.

Moore, T. V. 1915. The temporal relations of meaning and imagery. *Psychological Review* 22:177–225.

Müller-Freienfels, R. 1931. *Die Hauptrichtungen der gegenwärtigen Psychologie.* Leipzig: Quelle und Meyer.

Ornstein, R. E. 1972. *The psychology of consciousness.* San Francisco: W. H. Freeman.

Piaget, J. 1930. *The child's conception of causality.* Trans. Marjorie Gabain. London: Routledge and Kegan Paul.

Piaget, J., and Inhelder, B. 1969. *The psychology of the child.* Trans. Helen Weaver. New York: Basic Books.

Saupe, E., ed. 1931. *Einführung in die neuere Psychologie.* Osterwieck-Harz: A. W. Zickfeldt.

Savage-Rumbaugh, E. S.; Rumbaugh, D. M.; and Boysen, D. 1980. Do apes use language? *American Scientist* 68:49–61.

Seward, J. P. 1948. The sign of a symbol: A reply to Professor Allport. *Psychological Review* 55:277–96.

Singer, J. L. 1975. Navigating the stream of consciousness: Research in daydreaming and related inner experience. *American Psychologist* 30:727–38.

Stern, W. 1914. *The psychological methods of testing intelligence.* Trans. G. M. Whipple. Baltimore: Warwick and York.

———. 1938. *General psychology from the personalistic standpoint.* Trans. H. D. Spoerl. New York: Macmillan.

Terrace, H. S.; Petitto, L. A.; Sanders, R. J.; and Bever, T. G. 1979. Can an ape create a sentence? *Science* 206:891–902.

Titchener, E. B. 1917. *A text-book of psychology.* New York: Macmillan.

———. 1929. *Systematic psychology: Prolegomena.* New York: Macmillan.

Tolman, E. C. 1932. *Purposive behavior in animals and men.* New York: Century.

Warren, H. C. 1934. *A dictionary of psychology.* Boston: Houghton Mifflin.

Watson, J. B. 1924. The place of kinaesthetic, visceral, and laryngeal organization in thinking. *Psychological Review* 31:339–47.

Woodworth, R. S. 1906. Imageless thought. *Journal of Philosophy* 3:701–7.

———. 1940. *Psychology.* 4th ed. New York: Henry Holt.

4 / The Function of Consciousness

The preceding chapters on the criteria of consciousness *described* different components or aspects of mental life, alluding to reflection, sensation, the self, index words, awareness, insight, learning, trial and error, intelligence, conscious attitudes, foresight, determining tendencies, and other terms presumably indicative of the "anatomy" of mind. To continue this metaphor, very little was said about the "physiology" of mind in the sense of the functions of these components of mental life. The function of a feature like visual sensations or foresight might seem obvious, like the function of the mitral valve or the semicircular canals or some other anatomical structure. Accordingly, asking about the function of consciousness might appear fatuous, like asking what good it is to hear, to reason, to remember, to be motivated, and to be endowed with other characteristics that fall within the scope of consciousness, or like questioning the value of intelligence or understanding or mental health.

But these are not foolish questions to be disposed of by facile, self-evident answers. They have been taken seriously as critical scientific issues, and they embody troublesome metaphysical implications. I shall thus undertake a brief historical review.

The Automaton Theory in Historical Perspective

William James provided an illuminating introduction to the history of these issues in a chapter devoted to the "automaton theory" (1890, vol. 1, chap. 5). According to this theory, all modes of behavior can be accounted for as functions of the organism's neuromuscular mechanisms, an idea, James indicated, that has affiliations with Descartes's views on animal behavior. As I explained in chapter 1 (p. 12), Descartes considered animals mindless automatons governed by reflex mechanisms.[1] However, in James's words, this Cartesian "opinion that beasts have no consciousness at all was of course too paradoxical to maintain itself long as anything more than a curious item in the history of philosophy." It was more than two hundred years after Descartes before James's opinion, extended to apply to men as well as animals, won the endorsement of eminent scientists. This happened about 1870, and James quoted two of these scientists to illustrate the nature of their endorsement. His quotation from the biologist T. H. Huxley (1825–95) concludes as follows (James 1890, 1:131):

> It seems to me that in men, as in brutes, there is no proof that any state of consciousness is the cause of change in the motion of the matter of the organism. If these positions are well based, it follows that our mental conditions are simply the symbols in consciousness of the changes which take place automatically in the organism; and that, to take an extreme illustration, the feeling we call volition is not the cause of a voluntary act, but the symbol of that state of the brain which is the immediate cause of that act. We are conscious automata.

The second writer James quoted was the famous mathematician and philosopher W. K. Clifford (1845–79).[2] Like Huxley, he questioned the causal efficacy of so-called volitional consciousness. In particular he asked whether it would be correct to say that a man was impelled to run because he felt cold, and he introduced a striking exposition of one theory of the mind/body relation (James 1890, 1:132):

> When . . . we ask: "What is the physical link between the ingoing message from chilled skin and the outgoing message which moves the leg?" and the answer is, "A man's will," we have as much right to be amused as if we had asked our friend with the picture what pigment was used in painting the cannon in the foreground, and received the answer, "Wrought iron." It will be found excellent practice in the mental operations required by this doctrine to imagine a train, the fore part of which is an engine and three carriages linked with iron couplings, and the hind part three other carriages linked with iron couplings; the bond between the two parts being made up of the sentiments of amity subsisting between the stoker and the guard.

1. Descartes did not use *reflex* as a technical expression, but he did grasp the concept of reflex action. As Garrison noted, in 1649 Descartes gave "the first experiment in reflex action — the familiar one of making a person bat his eyes by aiming a mock blow at them — with the correct explanation of the phenomenon" (1929, p. 258).

2. It was Clifford who coined the phrase "mind-stuff," familiar to all students of James as "The Mind-Stuff Theory," chapter 6 of the *Principles*.

Both Huxley and Clifford thus regarded consciousness as an incidental by-product of brain activity, having as little to do with the outcome of such activity as the noise from a sawmill has to do with the transformation of logs into boards. This theory of the mind/body relation came to be called *epiphenomenalism*. According to this theory, though conscious phenomena may be correlated with neural processes, they do not influence them. As *mental* phenomena, they cannot cause changes in the *physical* realm of the nervous system. The epiphenomenalists were implying that brain activity causes conscious phenomena but that such phenomena do not cause anything, making them virtually superfluous, noncausal by-products of brain metabolism. If they are devoid of causal efficacy, it is as foolish to ask about their function as it would be to ask the function of wet tire marks on pavement.

James indicated that Huxley and Clifford's sponsorship of epiphenomenalism in the "conscious automaton theory" made it appear that mental events do not belong to the world of physical science—that the mental and the physical are different and independent forms of existence—thus creating an ideational chasm. This is like viewing psychiatry and neurology as independent and autonomous medical specialities, especially if psychiatric considerations are regarded as irrelevant intrusions into the neurologist's scientific thinking. This dichotomy is what James had in mind when he wrote (1890, 1:134–35):

> When talking of nervous tremors and bodily actions, we may feel secure against intrusion from an irrelevant mental world. When, on the other hand, we speak of feelings, we may with equal consistency use terms always of one denomination, and never be annoyed by what Aristotle calls "slipping into another kind." The desire on the part of men educated in laboratories not to have their physical reasonings mixed up with such incommensurable factors as feelings is certainly very strong. I have heard a most intelligent biologist say: "It is high time for scientific men to protest against the recognition of any such thing as consciousness in a scientific investigation." In a word, feeling constitutes the "unscientific" half of existence, and any one who enjoys calling himself a "scientist" will be too happy to purchase an untrammelled homogeneity of terms in the studies of his predilection, at the slight cost of admitting a dualism which, in the same breath that it allows to mind an independent status of being, banishes it to a limbo of causal inertness, from whence no intrusion or interruption on its part need ever be feared.

As interpreted by James, the biologist's protest against recognizing consciousness as a scientific concept was not the same as denying the existence of mind. Mind and consciousness, as synonymous terms, were to be banished from the realm of scientific, but not nonscientific, discourse. Exiled to the latter realm, they might influence folklore and the world of faith and fiction, but not science viewed as an impersonal world of causes and effects accounting for the behavior of living creatures — animals as well as men.

Watson's Denial of Consciousness

The biologist's protest might appear to anticipate the behavioristic protest J. B. Watson lodged against the introspective analyses of conscious content prevalent about 1912, more than twenty years after James cited the biologist's opinion. Introspective analyses under laboratory conditions had come to be accepted by followers of Wundt as essential to promoting psychology as science. Titchener was then the leading follower of this tradition in America, and he and his students tacitly endorsed the concept of consciousness in their meticulous descriptions of conscious content as introspectively observed under controlled conditions.

Now Watson objected not only to introspection as an observational process, but also to the concept of consciousness implicit in such a process. He criticized introspection as too subjective and too unreliable to merit endorsement as a scientific operation.[3] Moreover, using introspection to report conscious content must have struck him as futile, since he explicitly questioned the existence of consciousness.[4] In his contribution to a sym-

3. Wundt and his followers were mindful of the need for caution in making introspective observations; like Watson, they recognized the chances of error especially in reporting the "higher thought processes," and so Wundt had restricted introspection to simpler mental processes. Yet for certain kinds of scientific data introspective observations continue to be indispensable. For example, chemists studying odoriferous substances use reports by laboratory observers of the quality of smells experienced when chemicals are presented in the olfactometer. (See Friedman and Miller 1971 on odor incongruity.)

Introspective reports also continue to be required for certain psychological investigations. In a study of spatial recognition of rotated "three-dimensional objects" Shepard and Metzler had to rely on such reports, though they granted that "introspective reports must be interpreted with caution" (1971, p. 701).

4. I allude to an *explicit* statement on the existence of consciousness because not all students of behaviorism have come across Watson's statement to this effect. In his survey of behaviorist theory D. E. Broadhurst indicated that Watson's denial of consciousness had escaped him, and in discussing Watson's plan to study human behavior Broadhurst had this to say (1961, p. 24): "Just as the rat is observed to turn into one alley of a maze rather than another, so one can study the movements of human beings and compare the results of experiments on them with those on other species. In neither case is there any need to drag in conscious experience. This attitude has sometimes been regarded as a denial of the reality of consciousness, but it is hard to find any statement by Watson which goes so far. All he said was that science, being a public process, must ignore private awareness and deal only with those data which are available to everyone."

posium entitled *The Unconscious* he disposed of both the mind/body problem and the problem of consciousness in one sentence (1927, p. 94): "If the behaviorists are right in their contention that there is no observable mind-body problem and no observable separate entity called mind—then there can be no such thing as consciousness and its subdivision."

Watson's position as a behaviorist was not identical with the stand taken by James's biologist. For the biologist, consciousness was a by-product of brain metabolism and exercised no reciprocal causal influence on brain functions; hence there was no need to consider it in scientific discourse. But this was not the same as denying the existence either of conscious phenomena or of a mind/body relation. The biologist was thus an epiphenomenalist and a supporter of the conscious automaton theory. On the other hand, in denying consciousness Watson obviated the need for epiphenomenalism or any other psychophysical theory: "there is no observable mind-body problem." Once he eliminated mind, nothing was left to observe but the body's behavior. Thus Watson might be said to have rejected the conscious automaton theory in favor of an automaton theory.

If so, then he was doing for man what Descartes had prescribed for animals. With introspective observations ruled out of scientific court, there was no way to demonstrate the existence of a Cartesian *cogito,* and thus Watson studied man as a behaving rather than a thinking organism. He failed to recognize a "dividing line between man and brute," as he made clear in his first published behaviorist manifesto (1913, p. 158):

> Psychology as the behaviorist views it is a purely objective experimental branch of natural science. Its theoretical goal is the prediction and control of behavior. Introspection forms no essential part of its methods, nor is the scientific value of its data dependent upon the readiness with which they lend themselves to interpretation in terms of consciousness. The behaviorist, in his efforts to get a unitary scheme of animal response, recognizes no dividing line between man and brute. The behavior of man, with all of its refinement and complexity, forms only a part of the behaviorist's total scheme of investigation.

In this 1913 paper Watson did not actually deny the existence of consciousness as he did in the 1926 symposium. Nevertheless, he was explicit in his misgivings about attempts "to reason by analogy from human conscious processes to the conscious processes in animals, and *vice versa,*" and he stated that the time seemed to have arrived "when psychology must discard all reference to consciousness; when it need no longer delude itself into thinking that it is making mental states the object of observation."

Watson failed to emancipate himself from a subjective or "mentalistic" descriptive vocabulary. When he alluded to "thinking" or to "reason by analogy" or to self-delusion he was not referring to overt behavior like running, jumping, blinking, salivating, cringing, or whatever reactions laboratory animals exhibit in experimental situations. To refer to thinking at all is to acknowledge a process not readily amenable to objective demonstration. In his later writings Watson referred to thinking as *covert* behavior involving the subvocal activation of the speech mechanism, making it a laryngeal rather than a cerebral process and almost identifying talking with thinking. As I indicated on pages 61–64, such identification must be qualified to allow for the frequent instances of thoughtless verbalization.

Some researchers attempted experimental tests of Watson's thesis regarding subvocal thinking. In some experiments,[5] they attached recording instruments to the tongue or larynx or both while the subjects solved problems or thought about specified topics. There was no dearth of recorded subvocal activity, but it lacked uniformity and consistency; the same thoughts or ideas involved very different changes in the speech mechanism. Furthermore, some investigators always found some activation of the speech organs in thinking, while others found it in some subjects but by no means in all. Finally, thinking was sometimes reported in the absence of laryngeal and associated speech movements.

In view of these negative findings, Watson might have considered the organism thoughtless as well as nonconscious in accordance with the automaton theory; but this did not happen. His acceptance of thinking as a reality was derived from his prebehavioristic experiences as a thinking person, not from prior observations of changes in the throat musculature of men and animals. At no time did he equate the tongue movements of animals with any cognitive process, thus implying that thinking or reasoning was a distinctively human accomplishment. Despite the behaviorist manifesto, the ghost of the Cartesian *cogito* had not been completely exorcised; it survived in the verbalizations Watson accepted as identical with what we ordinarily call thinking. This acceptance implied that a conscious process was involved in such laryngeal activation, since Watson had discussed the nature of "the unverbalized in human behavior" (1924). By this he meant that what had come to be attributed to unconscious mental influences belonged more properly to processes not amenable to verbal expression, which made the unverbalized the equivalent of

---

5. A representative example of such an experimental undertaking is to be found in A. M. Thorson's study of internal speech as related to tongue movements, reported in 1925. During the same decade a related study of "silent thinking" was reported by Ruth Clark.

the unconscious and the verbalized the behaviorist equivalent of consciousness. This left man a talking automaton rather than a conscious automaton.

Clifford and Watson as Collaborators

This distinction between a conscious and an unconscious automaton may not be momentous. If conscious phenomena are mere by-products of brain action, then, as Huxley and Clifford maintained, they have no bearing on the behavioral consequences of brain action. In terms of Clifford's simile, they are like the proposal that the friendship between engineer and conductor connects the railroad cars in place of the iron coupling. When he denied conscious phenomena Watson agreed with Clifford in recognizing what he took to be the real connections between behavior and instigating stimuli or causes. Watson and Clifford, had they been contemporaries, might have collaborated in psychological studies, since both questioned the scientific value of conscious content reported through introspection. Such content, they would have argued, has no bearing on the neural circuits and reflex connections that account for the actions of men and the behavior of animals. To understand what men and animals do under given conditions, one must know how stimuli impinging on receptors come to influence activated effectors. Without the linkage of neural pathways such activation could not take place.

In the previous chapter I mentioned the pupillary reflex as an instance of an unlearned mechanical reaction; here let us consider briefly the neurological mechanism involved. Contraction of the pupil in bright light is a function of neural circuits rather than a consequence of antecedent awareness of the brightness per se, since such pupillary contraction can be elicited from a comatose patient, who cannot be aware of a light flashed in his eye. As an unlearned, involuntary response, the pupillary contraction will not take place any more promptly or efficiently when the patient regains consciousness, so it appears to result from light as a physical phenomenon, not an experienced sensation. Awareness of light as a sensation has no causal influence on the neural structures mediating the contraction; they operate independently of such awareness, and the operation of the reflex mechanism can be understood without assuming it is controlled by some concealed or *unconscious* sensation of brightness.

This also applies to other reflex or automatonlike body functions such as respiration and circulation. As physiological processes they too can be understood in terms of relevant neural and biochemical controls. No unconscious mind need be invoked to explain why the comatose patient's lungs and heart remain active despite the lapse of consciousness. These organs function even in babies born without a brain cortex — a condition known as *anencephaly*.[6] If, as appears to be a neurological axiom, the cortex is the anatomical sine qua non for mind, then these brainless babies, never having been conscious, are not comatose. This holds if the term *comatose* is restricted to conditions involving the loss of consciousness. These babies, by hypothesis, never had any consciousness to lose; hence their organic functions cannot be regarded as controlled by a dormant consciousness.

Clifford or Watson might ask, If such complex metabolic changes as those involved in digestion, respiration, and circulation proceed efficiently without conscious controls, why posit such regulation of any complex bodily activity? Watson, who actually denied the existence of consciousness, obviously saw no need for such controls. Like the earlier conscious automatists, he saw consciousness as a superfluous encumbrance to the scientific study of human and animal behavior. Watson might perhaps have written, "Even if consciousness existed, that would not influence my behaviorist experiments. I would proceed as if events traditionally described as conscious were unrelated to the problems I am trying to solve."

The behaviorist manifesto can be seen as challenging traditional psychology to demonstrate how its preoccupation with conscious content enhances scientific understanding of human affairs and leads to more dependable prediction and control of behavior. It asks precisely what functions consciousness serves. Would there be any difference in behavior between a robot endowed with consciousness and a robot without it?

Long before the behaviorist manifesto, William James anticipated this challenge by listing reasons to reject the automaton theory. After devoting several pages to "reasons for the theory," he concluded that "the automaton-theory . . . as it is now urged . . . is an *unwarrantable impertinence in the present state of psychology*" (1890, 1:138), and he then devoted the next few pages to "reasons against the theory."

Consciousness and Causal Efficacy

A basic reason for rejecting the automaton theory, James argued, is that

6. Even the complex conjugate rapid eye movement (REM) associated with dreaming in normal persons has been observed in anencephalics, suggesting that such eye movement is a function of an inherent oculomotor mechanism whose activation does not depend on cortical impulses. If dreaming as a conscious process is a function of the brain cortex, then this REM cannot be a sign of dreaming. Snyder discusses the issue in connection with a survey of investigations of dreaming and REM. Among other findings he mentions "the unmistakable occurrence of REMS even in those children born with a most tragic form of brain anomaly, anencephaly" (1967, p. 66).

it treats consciousness as a superfluous by-product of brain action, presumed to have no influence on the organism's behavior and thus no causal efficacy. James contended, "we ought to continue to talk in psychology as if consciousness had causal efficacy."

James introduced various arguments to support his contention that phenomena of consciousness have a direct influence on the organism's behavior. That he should need to do this may strike contemporary readers as incomprehensible. The post-Freudian generation has become accustomed to talk about the *un*conscious as a cause of behavior. If this assumption is seen as based on solid "scientific" foundations, then having to prove that the conscious is a cause of behavior might well appear absurd — like proving that expiration depends on inspiration or that a square has more corners than a triangle. But in the 1880s, when James was writing this chapter, the concept of mind as unconscious, though already current, had not yet become widely accepted as a fashionable scientific doctrine. Thus demonstrating the causal efficacy of consciousness was not deemed unnecessary — proving what nobody questions and everybody knows. With the advent of behaviorism the very concept of consciousness was being questioned, so James was not dealing with self-evident issues. In terms of later psychological developments, he might have been anticipating the need to prove the causal efficacy of consciousness before the notion of a dynamic unconscious could merit serious consideration.

Since he was writing when the doctrine of evolution was still intellectually exciting, James introduced his defense of causal efficacy by noting that consciousness might be biologically significant in the struggle for survival, and he called attention to a common belief that the complexity and intensity of consciousness increase with advances in evolutionary development. A man's consciousness, he wrote, "must exceed that of an oyster." From the evolutionary viewpoint this increase in consciousness is comparable to the increase in organic complexity that is presumed to help the animal survive. James was asking whether the biological advantages attributed to superadded body structures might not also come from superadded psychological processes. If so, he argued, they should be most serviceable when they compensate for shortcomings of the body organs with which they are most intimately associated. Since consciousness seems to increase with increases in neural organization, it is hardly likely that it has no role in the biological scheme.

James assigned consciousness a role as what he called a *selecting agency*. Unlike the lower nervous centers with their relatively fixed reflex adjustments, the brain centers cope with a vast array of impressions beyond the capacity of simple reflex mechanisms. Unlike basal ganglia and the spinal cord, the cerebral hemispheres are in unstable equilibrium. James stressed instability as one of "the defects of the nervous system in those animals whose consciousness seems most highly developed." Neural segments, like spinal reflexes, have few things to do and do them efficiently, but the hemispheres have so many tasks that with their "hair-trigger organization" they are "as likely to do the crazy as the sane thing at any given moment" (1890, 1:140). The business of consciousness is thus to prevent "crazy" actions by selecting modes of behavior congruent with attaining goals that benefit the organism, so that, as he expressed it, each act of consciousness appears to be a *fighter for ends*. He thus credited consciousness with a "teleological function" in the sense that it had ends to realize or purposes to accomplish. This entailed recognizing direct control over the neural currents governing the muscles involved in goal-directed action. Just how consciousness exercises such control, James granted, is an unsolved problem,[7] but he was convinced it did. This helpful occurrence argues against the automaton theory, James concluded, and he wrote: "it is enough for my purpose to have shown that it may not uselessly exist, and that the matter is less simple than the brain-automatists hold." He might also have written that belief in the causal efficacy of consciousness was justified because of its "teleological function."

7. Though there have been impressive advances in brain research since William James, the problem remains unsolved. Wilder Penfield (1891–1976), a noted neurosurgeon, referred to this at a symposium on consciousness and brain mechanisms. In an article reviewing his own experimental investigations and clinical observations, he said (1954, p. 304): "How it may be that ganglionic activity is transformed into thinking and how it is that thought is converted into the neuronal activity of conscious voluntary action we have no knowledge. Here is the fundamental problem. Here physiology and psychology come face to face."

Penfield's conclusion is substantially in agreement with that reached by Seymour Kety as cited in chapter 2, that "consciousness cannot be explained in terms of physics and chemistry, that consciousness is qualitatively different from matter and energy." Later in the same report Kety elaborated upon this (1952, p. 23): "Even if it is admitted that consciousness cannot be explained by matter and energy, we know from experience that consciousness can be altered by matter and energy. For example, if, while looking at this green table cloth I put a red lens before my eye, the sensation of greenness becomes a sensation of black. I take a drug, and the sensation of greenness may change in another way, or the table may no longer be a long straight table. I stop the circulation to my brain or remove glucose from my blood and profound changes in consciousness occur. Whatever consciousness is, it can be altered by matter and energy."

This last sentence, though recognizing that electrochemical processes can influence consciousness, is entirely consistent with Kety's earlier contention that consciousness cannot be explained in the language of physics and chemistry. These conclusions of Penfield and Kety were published in the 1950s, and some might question their relevance for the 1980s. But consider this from O. Hobart Mowrer's 1976 paper "How Does the Mind Work?" (p. 851): "More or less successful attempts to establish the locus of certain types of mental activity in the brain have been in progress for a long time, but we still do not know how the electromechanical activities of the nervous system become transferred into, or mediate, consciousness."

Concerning Functional Psychology

Early in this century the function of consciousness as considered by James became the central concern of an emerging school of psychology. Since its leaders were associated with the University of Chicago, it was first known as the Chicago school of functional psychology; later it was called simply the functionalist school. This systematic movement, reflected the thinking and leadership of, among others,[8] James Rowland Angell (1869–1949), who had studied with James during the early 1890s. Angell's account of the major tenets of the school is a convenient digest. Published in 1907 as "The Province of Functional Psychology," a paper presented the year before as Angell's presidential address to the American Psychological Association, it may be read with profit by the modern student.[9]

Angell did not regard the functionalist viewpoint as altogether novel in the history of psychology. Its basic biological orientation came from the teachings of Aristotle and their elaboration by Darwin and those influenced by him. Although he made no explicit reference to James, Angell doubtless expected his sophisticated audience to recognize his indebtedness for psychological interpretations of this biological orientation. Like James, he stressed the causal efficacy of consciousness by noting that it regulated behavior. As a functionalist, he was impelled "to regard consciousness as primarily and intrinsically a control phenomenon." Just as behavior might be considered the fundamental category of a functional biology, "so control would perhaps serve as the most fundamental category in functional psychology."

As this emphasis on control suggests, Angell was contrasting the "province" of functional psychology with that of structural psychology, and contrasting his own psychology with Titchener's. The contrast between the concepts of structure and function parallels that between anatomy and physiology. As Boring pointed out, Titchener had first noted the significance of these concepts for psychology (1950, p. 555) and had called attention to the parallel between three biological and three psychological viewpoints. In biology he noted three fields of study: *taxonomy,* the classification of organisms by structural resemblances; *physiology,* the study of the functions of cells, tissues, and organs; and *ontogeny,* the study of

8. John Dewey was one of these leaders, as was the social psychologist George Herbert Mead (1863–1931). How they and their students influenced psychology by their sponsorship and interpretation of functionalism is summarized in Boring's *History of Experimental Psychology* (1950, pp. 552–59) and, from a different perspective, in Hilgard's *Theories of Learning* (1956, pp. 328–67).

9. It has been reprinted in its entirety in a book of readings compiled and edited by Wayne Dennis (1948, pp. 439–56). A less complete version is in a book of readings edited by R. J. Herrnstein and E. G. Boring (1965, pp. 499–507).

individual development from birth to maturity. The three psychological counterparts to these biological viewpoints are those of structural, functional, and genetic psychology.

With considerable justification, Titchener had held that functional psychology is a very much older field than is structural psychology. Because of the relative newness of the latter field, Titchener was in favor of promoting its development before undertaking further studies of functional problems, as one might study anatomy before engaging in physiological studies, lest one consider the function of an organ while ignorant of its structure. One must know that a structure exists or *is* before one inquires into its function, or what it *is for.* In terms of the structure of mental content, as Boring indicated, Titchener deemed it advisable "to cultivate the *Is* in order to know enough about it to deal properly with the *Is-for.* Titchener was not against functional psychology. He actually gave it status, but he thought that it had had too much attention and ought to wait" (Boring 1950, p. 555).

Angell's Critique of Structuralism

Though Titchener, in Boring's words, "was not against functional psychology," Angell appears to have been against some features of structural psychology.[10] He had misgivings about whether the two kinds of psychology were analogous to the biological structure/function distinction between anatomy and physiology. When the structuralist analyzes a "moment of consciousness" into its constituent mental contents, he is not really producing the psychological equivalent of an anatomical dissection. The dissected anatomical "contents"—nerves, muscle fibers, ligaments, blood vessels—can be treated as definite and separate existents. They can be photographed, held up for demonstration, or preserved on slides or in bottles. No such relative permanence applies to the results of psychological analysis: sensations, images, feelings, ideas, and similar mental contents vanish in the very process of being observed. They lack existence as fixed, manipulable entities that can be treated as an anatomist treats dissected skeleton. As mental contents, in Angell's words, they "are evanescent and fleeting" and thus different "from the relatively permanent elements of anatomy." He added the following comment that bears on some questionable psychoanalytic interpretations (1907, p. 65):

10. In his advocacy of functionalism Angell did not intend to repudiate all that was being taught in the name of structuralism or to treat findings from the Leipzig and Cornell laboratories as pseudopsychology. He acknowledged his regard for such findings, saying: "I consider extremely useful the analysis of mental life into its elementary forms," and "I regard much of the actual work of my structuralist friends with the highest respect and confidence."

No matter how much we may talk of the preservation of physical dispositions, nor how many metaphors we may summon to characterize the storage of ideas in some *hypothetical deposit chamber of memory,* the obstinate fact remains that *when we are not experiencing a sensation or an idea it is, strictly speaking, nonexistent.* (Emphasis added.)

Angell's reference to "some hypothetical deposit chamber" is another way of alluding to an unconscious mind. Although his criticism was aimed at the introspective analyses of the structuralists, it also applies to those contemporary psychoanalytic thinkers who conceive of the unconscious as a "deposit chamber" harboring dynamic psychic entities in the form of balked desires striving for gratification.

This kind of thinking entails an inherent weakness that may not be obvious at first glance — Whitehead's fallacy of misplaced concreteness (see chap. 2), which Whitehead saw as a source of "great confusion." A more familiar form of this is the fallacy of reification, where processes are treated as things and abstractions as entities. Unless they avoid this fallacy, people may find themselves giving serious consideration to foolish questions. They may wonder about the customary habitat of a golfer's swing, a batter's home run, or a pianist's glissando as if the swing, home run, and glissando had independent existence as "things" separated from the club, bat, and piano.

Another of Angell's criticisms of structuralism concerns the accuracy of introspective reports that the *same* bit of mental content recurs as "the same sensation or the same idea." Angell maintained that "we not only have no guarantee that our second edition is really a replica of the first, we have a good bit of presumptive evidence that . . . the original is not and never can be literally duplicated." In terms of the home run example, this means that no two home runs are ever precise duplicates even when the same player uses the same bat against the same pitcher. Too many variables are involved for all of them to be reproduced. The flight of the ball is influenced by the force of the batter's swing and by the direction of the wind. Sometimes the ball lands in the stands and at other times it clears the fence. In rounding the bases the runner may not go at exactly the same speed each time. Although no two home runs are "structurally" the same, however, they all serve the same "function" of adding one run to the score of the batter's team. They are identical in function, though only similar in structure.

In the same way, we may experience similar but never identical ideas, perceptions, wishes, or other "mental contents," all abstractions from the perpetual flux of conscious processes. Referring to them as separate existences is more a matter of convenience than of descriptive accuracy, like comparing individual ocean waves as if they were units like marbles. Strictly speaking, we can never experience a single isolated wave or two identical waves. Titchener seems to have had an analogy of this sort in mind in discussing the abstract status of the structuralists' descriptive units. In his *Experimental Psychology,* first published in 1901, several pages are devoted to this issue (Titchener 1927, pp. 128–30), and they seem to anticipate a later objection that structuralism considered mind a collection or mosaic of psychic elements, irreducible particles of sensation. Titchener wrote, in italics, *"mind is not a mere mosaic of sensation-bits,"* then later stated that "we never have a perception." In elaborating upon this he described "consciousness" as a "shifting tangle of processes, themselves inconstant, and the perception is a little bit of pattern raveled out from the tangle and artificially fixed for scientific scrutiny."

Here we have a clear instance of Angell's objection to the contention that structuralism attempts to dissect the "anatomy of consciousness." Titchener recognized conscious processes as "shifting" and "inconstant" and thus devoid of fixed components. Because of this, *"stream* of consciousness" is a more revealing description than *"anatomy* of consciousness." Unlike an organism, consciousness as a stream cannot be divided into separate parts. To try, Titchener implied, would be unnatural. He saw something *artificial* in efforts to find *fixed* patterns in the "tangle" of conscious processes, as though he recognized the structuralists' "mental elements" as artifacts that did not exist in the actual course of conscious events. They are artifacts in the same way that the syllables into which the phonetician divides words lack separate existence for a speaker using words in spontaneous discourse. As phonetic analysis may be useful for certain purposes despite the artificial status of syllabic elements, so, Titchener said, analysis into mental elements may be useful in "scientific scrutiny" even though the elements are recognized as artifacts. Since Titchener recognized this, his structuralism may not have been irreconcilable with Angell's functionalism.[11]

Functionalism Opposed to Elementalism

Functionalism, as Angell interpreted it, had little use for the artifacts of mental elements: as the supposed building blocks of consciousness, they lack the separate existence and permanence of anatomical units. Yesterday's ideas and feelings are gone, never to return. Their seeming recur-

---

11. His structuralism was not as opposed to the basic teaching of Gestalt psychology as is sometimes believed. Some ten years before that school emerged he had voiced this basic teaching: "Mind is not a mere mosaic of sensation-bits."

rence in the stream of experience is not duplication any more than today's weariness is the *same* weariness experienced last year. Processes can be similar but never identical, and the context in which they are embedded and from which they are abstracted is always different. Their component "elements" are bound to be different just as no two traffic jams are identical because the "component" vehicles are different.

Let me illustrate one meaning of function as developed by Angell. Being trapped in a traffic jam on the way to an appointment is frustrating and may arouse anger. Other frustrating situations may also precipitate anger, from mild irritation to rage and overt aggressiveness. Though precipitating situations may vary widely, their functions as causes of anger are the same. Thus an identical function is activated when a neighbor's radio keeps us awake, when an important document fails to arrive, when a traffic judge rules against us, or—in brief—whenever an aroused desire is balked by extraneous interference. According to the frustration-aggression hypothesis,[12] all such patterns of causation serve an identical function; they all *function* as frustrating happenings. Even though they are all structurally different and may never recur in the identical form or as exactly the same experienced ideas, they share a common function. As Angell wrote (1907, p. 66):

> We may never have twice exactly the same idea viewed from the side of sensuous structure and composition. But there seems nothing whatever to prevent our having as often as we will contents of consciousness which mean the same thing. They function in one and the same practical way, however discrepant their momentary texture. The situation is rudely analogous to the biological case where very different structures may under different conditions be called on to perform identical functions, and the matter naturally harks back for its earliest analogy to the instance of protoplasm where functions seem very tentatively and imperfectly differentiated. Not only then are general functions like memory persistent, but special functions such as the memory of particular events are persistent and largely independent of the specific conscious contents called upon from time to time to subserve the functions.

That memory is "largely independent of the specific conscious contents" means that our recall of a given experience does not necessarily reactivate conscious events identical to those of the instigating experience. In recalling what somebody said we may forget the precise wording yet remember the meaning or substance. Such freedom from original wording is commonplace in everyday casual interchange of ideas. William Stern, in discussing

---

12. For a systematic discussion of this hypothesis see Dollard et al. (1939).

memory in his textbook of general psychology (1948, p. 205), cited a French linguist who had written about the language development of his bilingual child. His wife was German, and their son was exposed to both French and German from very early infancy. Mother and nursemaid always talked to the child in German, while the father spoke French exclusively. When the boy was not yet three the father told him to leave the cold room and go to the nursemaid, saying, "Ne restes pas ici, il fait trop froid," "don't stay here, it is too cold." When the child reached the nursemaid he transformed the admonition into this factual report: "Papas Zimmer ist zu kalt," "Papa's room is too cold." None of the words except "too cold" were translated into German. The German mental content was thus different from the original French mental content; but despite this drastic *structural* difference, the *function* of language as a medium of communication was not impaired. The lad's memory of his father's admonition was "independent of the specific conscious contents."

Functionalism's View of the Mind/Body Distinction

This episode of the bilingual child reveals another aspect of functionalism's specific interest in consciousness. Angell might have related the episode to functionalism's disposition of the mind/body relation, arguing that the child had to understand the meaning of his father's telling him to leave the cold room and go to the nursemaid. That he was conscious of the import of the instruction is shown by the way his German reflected the substance of his father's French as opposed to its literal meaning. His consciousness of his father's meaning, Angell might have said, was not a mere by-product of changes induced in the presumed language centers of the youngster's brain. As a functionalist Angell would have opposed such an interpretation, for he definitely rejected the automaton theory, saying that the functional psychologist was not committed to any particular psychophysical theory but must "of necessity set his face against any epiphenomenalist view."

Although all functionalists rejected epiphenomenalism, they were under no constraint to endorse the same mind/body theory provided they chose one that explicitly recognized the functional significance of consciousness. For Angell such recognition did not imply any particular metaphysical belief. He regarded "the mind-body relation as capable of treatment in psychology as a methodological distinction rather than a metaphysically existential one," thus implying that one could make scientific headway without understanding the ultimate nature of the problems being investigated. Physicists did not have to settle on a metaphysically satisfying definition of matter before solving specific problems. Optics could be studied apart from the metaphysical implications of proposed definitions of light, and electrical phenomena were successfully investigated before the nature of electricity was understood. Biologists developed botany and zoology by appropriate methods of study without first defining the basic difference between a plant and an animal or the ultimate difference between life and death.

In short, Angell implied, psychologists have ample scientific precedent for investigating mind as distinguished from body without first answering metaphysical questions concerning the ultimate difference between mind and body. The difference accounts for the existence of both psychology and physiology, each with its own methods of investigation—a methodological rather than a metaphysical distinction.

Consciousness as a Control Phenomenon

To avoid futile metaphysical debates, Angell urged attention to circumstances that give rise to the manifestation of mind or consciousness as contrasted with circumstances that evoke only the nonconscious or entirely physiological. This kind of knowledge, he held, "is on a level with all scientific and practical information" by specifying "the circumstances under which certain sorts of results will appear." By means of this knowledge the functionalist could describe "the genetic conditions under which the mind-body differentiation first makes itself felt in the experience of the individual"—he could ask how and when one first becomes conscious of being conscious. Once this stage was reached, the reflective functionalist generally came to grips with a basic issue as he considered the biological "utilities of consciousness," since he viewed mind as "primarily engaged in mediating between the environment and the needs of the organism." Mind or consciousness was thus brought into operation by the organism's need to master difficulties and to gain control over threats to its welfare. Angell stated this most explicitly (1907, p. 88):

> The functionalist's most intimate persuasion leads him to regard consciousness as primarily and intrinsically a control phenomenon. Just as behavior may be regarded as the most distinctly basic category of general biology in its functional phase so control would perhaps serve as the most fundamental category in functional psychology, the special forms and differentiations of consciousness simply constituting particular phases of the general process of control.

Functional psychology was foreshadowed by James when he repudiated the automaton theory and recognized the biological role of consciousness as a "selecting agency" and a "fighter for ends" when the "instable" organism is confronted with problems too novel for the reflexes or instincts. Having studied under James at Harvard, Angell was familiar with this stand and used it as a point of departure for his survey of the province of functional psychology. At the time — about 1907 — he could assume that those who heard or read his address were also familiar with James's *Principles* and would note his debt to James for the foundations of functionalism as a biologically oriented system of psychology. In his address Angell called attention to a rapprochement between biology and psychology: "We find nowadays both psychologists and biologists who treat consciousness as substantially synonymous with adaptive reactions to novel situations" (p. 71).

The "nowadays" was an allusion to the post-Darwinian period when "both psychologists and biologists" were accustomed to consider many of their professional problems as related to the doctrine of evolution. Angell's sentence implied that consciousness plays a role in evolution by providing for "adaptive reactions" to the strange, the unusual, or the unexpected. He could have elaborated by noting the intrusion or intensification of awareness in troublesome situations. Lost in a strange city, the perplexed tourist is vividly conscious of his predicament as he consults his map and gets his bearings. Returning to his hotel, he may not be aware of walking as he glances at shop windows, watches other pedestrians, and thinks about his schedule for the day. But if he stumbles, he will instantly be conscious of the need to regain his equilibrium. And if a long stretch of the sidewalk is littered with debris, he may need to concentrate on walking until he reaches unobstructed terrain where walking can again become an autonomous operation, leaving consciousness free for new contingencies.

All autonomous or quasi-reflex activities such as walking and breathing may function less efficiently when they are the object of attention. Becoming self-conscious about them is apt to disrupt their coordination. The victim of stage fright may stumble as he walks across the platform and may have trouble regulating his breathing as he becomes conscious of his constricted throat. Wondering about the position of his tongue as he starts his speech is likely to interfere with his articulation.

Becoming conscious of the components of any thoroughly mastered complex activity tends to disrupt the mastery. It would be unwise for the centipede to pause to decide which leg should take the next step. From the viewpoint of functional psychology, it would be a misapplication of a mental process to direct it to the automatism of locomotion. Once consciousness has established control of a novel situation, further control should be relinquished in the interests of efficiency, for overcontrol as well as undercontrol can interfere with optimal performance. This follows from Angell's basic functionalist thesis: "If one takes the position . . . that consciousness is constantly at work building up habits out of coordinations imperfectly under control; and that as speedily as control is gained the mental direction tends to automatism, it is only a step to carry the inference forward that consciousness immanently considered is *per se* accommodation to the novel" (p. 72).

As Angell noted, this conclusion constitutes a biological as well as a psychological generalization, since it is a "common belief" among biologists that consciousness is involved whenever "real organic accommodation to the novel" is taking place. However, once accommodative reaction has become habitual consciousness is no longer involved. What had been a voluntary or intentional reaction has become involuntary automatism. Let us consider a final aspect of this transition from consciousness to automatism.

Concluding Comments

Angell alluded to this aspect when he asked whether "conscious processes have been the precursors of our present instinctive equipment." He was asking whether our reflexes as native automatisms, viewed in the light of phylogenetic history, are products of whatever initially called for conscious adjustment to the novel. Having raised the question, Angell claimed he lacked the necessary "facts of heredity" to answer it. He disposed of the issue by noting that "many of our leaders answer strongly in the affirmative, and such an answer evidently harmonizes with the general view" of functionalism. There was no need for him to elaborate upon the issue, since the affirmative answer was familiar to psychologists of the period.

Among these "leaders," Angell may have been thinking of James and Wundt. James, with his emphasis on the causal efficacy of conscious processes, was certainly a precursor of functionalism. His long chapter on instinct (1890, vol. 2, chap. 24) was known to those Angell was addressing, so he had no need to explain his allusion to "our present instinctive equipment." At the time, it was taken for granted that man's life of action has its biological roots in instinct. In his 1905 textbook *Elements of Psychology*, for example, E. L. Thorndike (1874–1949) said this about human instincts (pp. 190–91):

> Too little is known about the extent to which human behavior is based upon instincts to allow their enumeration. But even with our present lack of knowledge the list of demonstrated instincts is a long one. It takes Professor James thirty-seven pages to list and describe them. *Probably the list will grow with further study, since many actions which common sense credits to acquisition are really*

the gift of nature. E.g., standing alone, walking and retrieving (getting an object and bringing it back) appear in babies who are given no incitement or assistance. The manifestations of grief,— puckering the lips, drawing down the face and a prolonged wail,— appear in babies at the stimulus of harsh speech or ugly looks, although such speech or looks have never been followed by any unpleasant consequence. The more carefully mental development is investigated, the more we find human life everywhere rooted in instincts. (Italics added.)

Thorndike's prediction concerning the probable discovery of new human instincts was not realized. As will be brought out in the next chapter, by the 1920s some psychologists believed that the total number had been reduced almost to the vanishing point.

A commonly overlooked or forgotten observation Thorndike made about instinct has to do with his being among the first to perceive functional psychology as a dramatic psychology. His textbook was divided into three parts, the third called "Dynamic Psychology." In the text itself he explained (1920, p. 184), "The science of the mind in action is called Dynamic Psychology," and he appended this footnote: "By some writers it is called *functional* psychology." By thus equating functional and dynamic psychology he was bringing the motivational implications of consciousness into sharper focus. He envisaged dynamic functionalism as shaped by two great sets of influences (p. 186): "(1) The power of nature, manifested in instincts and capacities. (2) The power of nurture, manifested in habits and acquired powers."

The dynamic viewpoint Thorndike attributed to the functionalists was not unique to them. Structuralists like Wundt and Titchener were also mindful of the impulsive aspects of consciousness. Thorndike was the first to describe these aspects as dynamic, but the dynamic nature of consciousness had already been recognized by James. And before James, philosophers like Spinoza and Schopenhauer had developed what Aristotle had called man's appetitive soul into a central feature of their philosophies. Finally, Wundt had made voluntarism, with its appetitive connotation, central to his systematic psychology.

References

Angell, J. R. 1907. The province of functional psychology. *Psychological Review* 14:61–69.

Boring, E. G. 1950. *A history of experimental psychology*. 2d ed. New York: Appleton-Century-Crofts.

Broadhurst, D. E. 1961. *Behaviour: A survey of twentieth century theory in behaviouristic psychology*. New York: Basic Books.

Clark, R. 1922. An experimental study of silent thinking. *Archives of Psychology,* no. 48, 1–101.

Dennis, W., ed. 1948. *Readings in the history of psychology.* New York: Appleton-Century-Crofts.

Dollard, J.; Doob, L. W.; Miller, N. E.; Mowrer, O. H.; and Sears, R. R. 1939. *Frustration and aggression.* New Haven: Yale University Press.

Friedman, L., and Miller, J. G. 1971. Odor incongruity and chirality. *Science* 172: 1044–46.

Garrison, F. H. 1929. *An introduction to the history of medicine.* 4th ed. Philadelphia: W. B. Saunders. Reprinted 1960.

Herrnstein, R. J., and Boring, E. G., eds. 1965. *A source book in the history of psychology.* Cambridge: Harvard University Press.

Hilgard, E. R. 1956. *Theories of learning.* 2d ed. New York: Appleton-Century-Crofts.

James, W. 1890. *Principles of psychology.* Vols. 1 and 2. Henry Holt.

Kety, S. S. 1952. Consciousness and the metabolism of the brain. In *Problems of consciousness,* ed. H. A. Abramson, 11–75. New York: Josiah Macy, Jr., Foundation.

Mowrer, O. H. 1976. How does the mind work? *American Psychologist* 31:843–57.

Penfield, W. 1954. Studies of the cerebral cortex of man. In *Brain mechanisms and consciousness,* 284–309. Springfield, Ill.: Charles C. Thomas.

Shepard, R. N., and Metzler, J. 1971. Mental rotation of three-dimensional objects. *Science,* 171:701–3.

Snyder, F. 1967. In quest of dreaming. In *Experimental studies of dreaming,* ed. H. A. Witkin and H. B. Lewis, 3–75. New York: Random House.

Stern, W. 1938. *General psychology from the personalistic standpoint.* Trans. H. D. Spoerl. New York: Macmillan.

Thorndike, E. L. 1920. *The elements of psychology.* New York: A. G. Seiler. First published 1905.

Thorson, A. M. 1925. The relation of tongue movements to internal speech. *Journal of Experimental Psychology* 8:1–32.

Titchener, E. B. 1927. *Experimental psychology, student's manual.* Vol. 1. New York: Macmillan.

Watson, J. B. 1913. Psychology as the behaviorist views it. *Psychological Review* 20:158–77.

———. 1924. The unverbalized in human behavior. *Psychological Review* 31:273–80.

———. 1927. The unconscious of the behaviorist. In *The unconscious: A symposium,* 91–113. New York: A. A. Knopf.

5 / Consciousness as Dynamic Psychology

The title of this chapter is a reminder of the dynamic implications of functionalism. According to Thorndike (1920, p. 184), functional psychology is "the science of mind in action"—consciousness coping with problems. Thorndike seems to have been the first to call this a "dynamic psychology." Ten chapters of his 1905 textbook are devoted to what he regarded as aspects of dynamic psychology; the other eleven deal with descriptive and physiological psychology. In his treatment of dynamic psychology he did not limit himself to members of the functionalist school. James, Wundt, and Titchener are mentioned in the text, and British, Italian, and French writers are cited in the references. Incidentally, Freud's name is conspicuously absent from the references, for Freud's writings were not yet widely known in the United States. Thus dynamic psychology had come into being independent of the dynamism attributed to the Freudian wish or to what is sometimes called Freud's dynamic psychiatry. The implications of this independence will be discussed later.

James had already called attention to consciousness as dynamic in his opposition to the automaton theory of the epiphenomenalists, thus endowing consciousness with causal efficacy and recognizing it as a "selecting agency" and a "fighter for ends." This, he stated, gave it a "teleological function." At the time he had not yet written the essay in which he explicitly denied the existence of consciousness as an entity. In the interest of clear thinking, let us bear in mind the significance of this denial. As an abstraction, to paraphrase Whitehead, consciousness has no concrete existence. The underlying concept, as both James and Whitehead would undoubtedly have acknowledged, goes back to Spinoza, who contended that intellect has no existence apart from individual ideas. Nor does volition exist apart from individual acts. In a famous statement, quoted by H. A. Wolfson,[1]

1. Wolfson's *Philosophy of Spinoza* (1934) is replete with quotations and interpretations of psychological import.

Spinoza succinctly expressed this (1934, 2:168): "The intellect and will . . . are related to this or that idea or volition as rockiness is related to this or that rock, or as man is related to Peter and Paul."

In thus bracketing intellect and will, Spinoza foreshadowed the recognition of volitional aspects of ideation that came into prominence early in psychology's emergence as a scientific enterprise, demonstrated by the central role voluntarism came to play in Wundt's psychology.

Wundt's Voluntarism

Although Wundt is sometimes thought of as a structuralist because of his interest in analyzing mental content into its presumed elementary components, he took a voluntarist view of the organization of mental life. He did not believe that volition is a separate faculty or power. The popular idea that resistance to temptation springs from willpower has nothing in common with Wundt's voluntarism. For Wundt "willpower" belonged to faculty psychology, which he repudiated as alien to a scientific psychology. Describing mind as an aggregation of autonomous powers or faculties like volition or memory leads to a series of tautological propositions: we are said to carry out intentions through a faculty of volition or to remember a lesson through a faculty of memory. Wundt was not the first to repudiate this kind of psychology. Several decades earlier faculty psychology had been criticized by J. F. Herbart (1776–1841), known for his "scientific pedagogy" as well as for his pre-Freudian accounts of the dynamics of ideas as they rise above or are kept below the threshold of consciousness. Moreover, well over a hundred years before Herbart, John Locke had already criticized belief in an independent faculty of volition: "We may as properly say that the singing faculty sings and the dancing faculty dances as that the will chooses."

What we choose, therefore, cannot be a function of an independent agency called volition. Our choices are determined by our desires, needs, longings, hungers, yearnings, and similar changing impulses associated with wishing, a word derived from the Latin *volo,* "I wish"—the basis of the concept of voluntarism.

In terms of this root meaning, Wundt's voluntaristic psychology becomes a dynamic psychology in which desire is as important as sensation for understanding experience. This was evident in his views on the conative aspects of feeling and emotion (1897, pp. 14–15):

> Voluntaristic psychology does not by any means assert that volition is the only real form of psychosis, but merely that, with its closely related feelings and emotions, it is just as essential a component of psychological experience as sensations and ideas. . . . In fact,

immediate experience shows that there are no ideas which do not arouse in us feelings and impulses of different intensities and, on the other hand, that a feeling or volition is impossible which does not refer to some ideated object.

The phrase "feeling or volition" reflects Wundt's recognition of a factor the two processes have in common — an intentional or conative orientation. When we will or wish for something, the aroused desire involves feeling or emotion, and we tend to strive for certain results. Thus annoyance leads to a wish and endeavor to get rid of the irritant. Feelings of tenderness for a helpless infant are accompanied by impulses to protect, nurture, and comfort. When we experience anger we desire to injure, and when we are afraid we desire to flee or hide. Wundt considered such a voluntaristic or conative factor an invariable concomitant of our feelings and emotions.

Wundt did not regard feelings as qualitatively different from emotions — the difference was in degree rather than kind, ranging over a continuum of intensity. He saw feelings as incipient emotions and emotions as intense feelings. Degrees of fear can be viewed as a series of transitions from vague uneasiness to definite apprehension to acute fear to devastating terror to running amok in panic. Each such transition increases impulsiveness or the urge to take action. These transitions, as viewed by Wundt, would thus constitute a series of volitional processes: "a feeling may be thought of as the beginning of a volition" (1897, p. 185).

Motivation: Impulsive and Ideational Aspects

As a voluntarist Wundt thus recognized the impulsive or motivational aspects of feelings and emotions along with their ideational aspects. Awareness of a fearsome situation constitutes the ideational aspect, and the impulse to flee is the motivational aspect. All volitional acts, Wundt wrote, involve such combinations of ideation and feeling (1897, pp. 185–86):

> These combinations of ideas and feelings which in our subjective apprehension of the volition are the immediate antecedents of the act, are called *motives* of volition. Every motive may be divided into an ideational and an affective component. The first we may call the *moving reason,* the second the *impelling force* of action. . . . The reason for a criminal murder may be theft, removal of an enemy, of some such idea, the impelling force the feeling of want, hate, revenge or envy.

In analyzing motivation into ideational and impulsive aspects Wundt reflected Schopenhauer's contention that the function of the intellect is to help the will achieve its ends.[2] This primacy of will or motivation had been known in Germany since Schopenhauer's *The World as Will and Idea* was published in 1819. In turn Schopenhauer reflected the thinking of Spinoza, whose psychology was also voluntaristic in its emphasis upon man's "basic endeavor" or *conatus* or "striving." He referred to this "basic conatus" in his *Ethics:* "Desire is the very essence of man." Schopenhauer endorsed the voluntarism implicit in Spinoza's "basic conatus" in the following quotation (Edman 1928, p. 93):

> Spinoza says that if a stone which has been projected through the air had consciousness,[3] it would believe that it was moving of its own will. I add to this only that the stone would be right. The impulse given it is for the stone what the motive is for me, and what in the case of the stone appears as cohesion, gravitation, rigidity, is in its nature the same as that which I recognize in myself as will, and what the stone also, if knowledge were given to it, would recognize as will.

Spinoza foreshadowed later psychological developments in other ways. He denied that will and intellect were independent faculties or psychological entities and held that "there is no will apart from the individual volitions, just as there is no intellect apart from the individual ideas" (Wolfson 1934, 2:172). This anticipated the indictment of faculty psychology lodged by men like Herbart and Wundt some two centuries later. He also anticipated their voluntarism when he concluded that "the will and intellect are one and the same" (Wolfson 1934, 2:170). They are the same to the extent that a volition constitutes a desire for some ideated goal and, unless hindered by opposing ideas, results in action of some sort. Generations of psychologists long after Spinoza expressed this observation in the theory

2. About a hundred years after Schopenhauer had thus subordinated intellect to volition E. J. Kempf arrived at the same conclusion. In his 1918 monograph on the influence of autonomic functions on personality he subordinated the cerebrospinal to the autonomic nervous system by maintaining that behavior is *motivated* by the latter and executed by the former.

3. This example of the falling stone contains one of the first accounts of unconscious motivation. This is clear from a letter Spinoza wrote in 1674 (Ratner 1927, p. 204): "The permanence of the stone's motion is constrained, not necessarily because it must be defined by the impulsion of an external cause. What is true of the stone is true of an individual . . . inasmuch as every individual thing is necessarily determined by some external cause to exist and operate in a fixed and determinate manner. Further conceive, I beg, that a stone, while continuing in motion, should be capable of thinking and knowing, and it is endeavoring, as far as it can, to continue to move. Such a stone, being conscious merely of its own endeavor and at all indifferent, would believe itself to be completely free, and would think that it continued in motion solely because of its own *wish*. This is that human freedom, which all boast that they possess, and which consists solely in the fact, that *men are conscious of their own desire, but are ignorant of the causes whereby that desire has been determined*" (italics added).

of ideomotor action. As a theory—particularly as presented by James—it seems to encompass Spinoza's *conatus*, Schopenhauer's *will*, and Wundt's *voluntarism*.

The Theory of Ideomotor Action

According to James, whenever the idea of a movement is *immediately* and *unhesitatingly* followed by its execution, ideomotor action is involved. There is no intervening act or power of will between the idea and its performance (1890, 2:522):

> All sorts of neuro-muscular processes come between, of course, but we know absolutely nothing of them. We think the act, and it is done; and that is all that introspection tells us of the matter. . . . Whilst talking I become conscious of a pin on the floor, or of some dust on my sleeve. Without interrupting the conversation I brush away the dust or pick up the pin. I make no express resolve, but the mere perception of the object and the fleeting notion of the act seem of themselves to bring the latter about.

James went on to explain that such ideomotor sequences are common. They take place unless inhibited by conflicting ideas. Thus a soldier standing at attention is not likely to react to dust on his sleeve or a pin on the floor. However, as James noted, the hypnotized subject is especially responsive to the operator's suggestions because of his induced freedom from competing or contradictory ideas. Spontaneous ideation is held in abeyance while his interest is dominated by the hypnotist; hence his robotlike compliance with all instructions that do not arouse antagonistic ideas. He complies readily to instructions involving overt action, such as thinking about hitting a golf ball or playing an accordion or opening an umbrella. This tendency, though more pronounced under hypnosis, is an ordinary experience common to all of us. It is shown in the strained posture of spectators watching a pole vault and in our muscular sets as we watch exciting scenes on stage or screen. Merely concentrating on the difference between right and left is likely to induce changes in muscular tension on right and left sides of the body. The ideas of right and left, up and down, have different motor consequences. According to the concept of ideomotor action, "*every representation of a movement awakens in some degree the actual movement which is its object; and awakens it in a maximum degree whenever it is not kept from so doing by an antagonistic representation present simultaneously to the mind*" (1890, 2:526; italics in original).

James argued against the popular notion that voluntary action involves a special kind of force or power. It is a "common prejudice," he noted, to attribute voluntary action to what people call willpower. This implies that some special inner force controls behavior by volitional fiats. James repudiated this prejudice and its consequent implication (1890, 2:526–27):

> The first point to start from in understanding voluntary action, and the possible occurrence of it with no fiat or express resolve, is the fact that consciousness is *in its very nature impulsive*. We do not have a sensation or a thought and then have to *add* something dynamic to it to get a movement. . . . The popular notion that mere consciousness as such is not essentially a forerunner of activity, that the latter must result from some superadded "will-force," is a very natural inference from those special cases in which we think of an act for an indefinite length of time without the action taking place. These cases, however, are not the norm; they are cases of inhibition by antagonistic thoughts. When the blocking is released we feel as if an inward spring were let loose, and this is the additional impulse or *fiat* upon which the act effectively succeeds. . . . But where there is no blocking, there is naturally no hiatus between the thought-process and the motor discharge. *Movement is the natural immediate effect of feeling, irrespective of what the quality of the feeling may be. It is so in reflex action, it is so in emotional expression, it is so in the voluntary life.* Ideo-motor action is thus no paradox, to be softened or explained away.

In thus calling attention to the impulsive aspect of feeling as related to "the voluntary life," James made the ideomotor theory a voluntaristic theory, noting that consciousness is by its very nature impulsive. This is altogether congruent with Wundt's *voluntarism* as well as with Spinoza's *conatus* and Schopenhauer's *will*. The voluntarism implicit in the ideomotor theory made for a dynamic psychology.

Voluntarism as a Dynamic Psychology

Voluntarism, especially as presented by Wundt, was manifestly a dynamic or motivational psychology, as shown by his analysis of motives into impelling feelings and moving reasons. In general, the former concern the *why* and the latter the *how* of action. The victim of poison ivy *feels* impelled to seek relief; hence his *reason* for scratching or applying lotion or consulting a dermatologist. Curiosity about the meaning of a word impels a student to consult the dictionary — desire for information as an impelling force results in the moving reason for seeking a dictionary. Similarly, dread of lung cancer may inhibit one's indulgence in cigarettes. Such everyday instances of motivated behavior reflect this distinction between the goad of a felt need and the means of satisfying the need. The need accounts for the *why* and the means account for the *how* of motivated behavior. Often, of course, the requisite means are unknown or unavailable so that there is a persistent search for a solution. This accounts for what rats learn in mazes as well for what men seek in laboratories, libraries, clinics, business conferences, and wherever their felt needs may take them.

The broader implications of this have become part of commonsense psychology as contrasted with technical psychology. In everyday discourse one comes across casual references to man's quest for identity, to Freudian wishes, to repressed desires, to wishful thinking, and to kindred motivational topics that are often considered especially relevant to man's psychiatric problems, particularly by those who sponsor a dynamic psychiatry. Because of their psychiatric orientation, some of these sponsors regard modern psychology's interest in motivation as a derivative of Freud's influence. From this viewpoint dynamic psychology is an outgrowth of dynamic psychiatry, and academic psychology is indebted to psychopathology for belated recognition of man as a creature of craving and impulse.[4]

Actually, a dynamic psychology was in evidence long before the rise of a dynamic psychiatry. In part it can be traced back to the basic conatus of Spinoza in the seventeenth century. Nineteenth-century leaders of academic psychology gave this conative theme explicit emphasis in varied terminology. It is reflected in Herbart's "dynamics of the soul," in Wundt's distinction between impelling forces and moving reasons, and in James's accounts of ideomotor action and impulsive consciousness. From James's accounts it was an easy transition to the kind of functionalism Thorndike recognized as a dynamic psychology.

Moreover, this kind of psychology received explicit recognition in Robert S. Woodworth's *Dynamic Psychology*,[5] published in 1918, some years before the phrase "dynamic psychiatry" appeared in the title of a publication. Woodworth did not see psychology's concern with the dynamics of mental life as derived from psychiatry's concern with psychopathology.

---

4. Among others, Boring apparently held this view, as indicated by this sentence from his *History* (1950, p. 707): "It was Freud who put the dynamic conception of psychology where psychologists could see it and take it." It is hard to understand how Boring came to overlook the non-Freudian origins of dynamic psychology. In his magnificent chapter on Wundt there is no mention of Wundt's voluntarism. His appreciative assessment of the psychology of James ignores the dynamic implications of James's account of instinct. In his list of Thorndike's writings there is no mention of the volume in which Thorndike equated functionalism with dynamic psychology. Finally, his review of psychology's philosophic past has nothing to say about Aristotle's appetitive soul or about the dynamism of Spinoza's basic conatus.

5. Freud must have known this title, for there was a copy of the book in his waiting room.

He saw it as implicit in the long history of psychology's efforts to understand the "workings of the mind" as revealed by introspection and by observation of behavior (1918, p. 43): "A dynamic psychology must utilize the observations of consciousness and behavior as indications of the 'workings of the mind'; and that, in spite of formal definitions to the contrary, is what psychologists have been attempting to accomplish since the beginning."

In tracing the influences that contributed to this dynamic orientation, Woodworth mentioned the impact of the doctrine of evolution on the thinking of psychologists. After publication of Darwin's *Origin of Species* in 1859 interest in biological evolution widened to include mental development both in the individual and in the race. Woodworth noted that "Darwin himself made the first systematic study of the mental development of a child" and that Darwin's cousin, Francis Galton (1822–1911), extended the scope of such study by investigating the role of heredity in mental endowment as well as by examining the nature of "individual differences in imagery and other mental traits." With the rise of voluntarism and then of functionalism, these studies engaged more and more psychologists. Evolution ceased to be exclusively biological as questions were raised regarding the emergence of consciousness and its influence on adaptation to the environment. Mind was studied as an agency in the struggle for survival. This interest in the evolution of mind and consciousness made for a dynamic psychology as Wundt and others considered the origin of instinct, emotion, and other motivating factors and their roles in human and animal behavior. A place was being found for mind in the biological scheme, and the stage was being set for grouping psychology with the life sciences. Study of the development of mind in the individual was extended to its development in the history of the species, bringing a transition from the ontogenetic to the phylogenetic viewpoint, or a shift from the study of the evolution of mind to a study of mind in evolution.

Mind in Evolution

I touched upon the evolution of mind in chapter 3 in connection with Titchener's teaching that mind and consciousness depend upon functioning neural structures. Because of such dependence Titchener regarded plants as mindless or nonsentient. But he did not seem to regard all reactions mediated by neural structures as indicative of mind, since he referred to reflexes as reactions to stimuli "received" both "mindlessly and mechanically" (1917, p. 32). Toward the end of his *Text-Book* he considered this issue in greater detail in discussing the origin of the earliest forms of organic action and the place of consciousness in regulating such action (1917, pp. 450–58). From an evolutionary perspective the issue involved this fundamental question: What was the character of the first actions of our biological ancestors? Titchener had this to say (p. 451):

There are two answers in current psychology and biology. The first is that consciousness is as old as animal life, and that the first movement of the first organisms were conscious movements. This is the answer which the author accepts. The other is that consciousness appeared later in life, and that the earliest movements were accordingly unconscious movements, of the nature of the physiological reflex.

In thus regarding reflexes and other automatic reactions as derivatives of conscious reactions in ancestral experience Titchener was not alone. Wundt had taken a similar stand in his defense of a voluntaristic psychology. In addition, as Titchener pointed out, the British psychologist James Ward (1843–1925) sponsored the same teaching, and so did the American zoologist E. D. Cope (1840–97).[6] Titchener listed four lines of evidence to support this teaching.

1. First he cited evidence from well-established facts concerning the role of consciousness in the mastery of physical skills such as swimming, typing, or cycling. At the start these voluntary undertakings are accompanied by awareness of a multiplicity of details as the learner eliminates incorrect moves and gains control over correct ones. With practice such awareness of particular maneuvers diminishes until it vanishes altogether as one masters the skill. This of course is the commonly recognized transition from voluntarism to automatism or from conscious intent to unconscious habit. Moreover, according to the functionalists, such automatically executed skills leave consciousness free to solve problems, confront difficulties, or develop new skills. In their view coping with novel situations was a chief function of consciousness.

On this Titchener the structuralist and Angell the functionalist were in agreement. Titchener had called attention to the difference between the "voluntary" or conscious initiation of actions and the later stage of their involuntary, nonconscious automatism. He regarded the latter stage as a quasi-reflex type of automatism and called its manifestations "secondary reflexes" to differentiate them from inherited or "ingrained" or "primary" reflexes. Since this shift from the voluntary to the "secondary" reflex is well established in the history of the individual, he believed "it is at least

6. Titchener supplied references to the writings of Wundt, Ward, and Cope in a footnote on page 452.

possible that the ingrained physiological reflexes may have a conscious ancestry in the history of the race."[7]

2. Titchener's second line of evidence also concerned reflexes. He noted that under given conditions both primary and secondary reflexes appeared to be subject to "cortical control and thus connected with conscious intent." He mentioned respiratory control by holding one's breath as well as the less well known ability to control automatic functions such as heart action, peristalsis, and sometimes even pupillary contraction.[8] Such control is akin to the cyclist's or swimmer's ability to reassert conscious control of their automatized skills. But this control over reflexes and acts of skill is hard to understand or explain "if we regard the reflexes as prior to consciousness."

3. For his third argument Titchener turned to the evolutionary implications of emotional expression as developed by Darwin. He stressed that

---

7. Titchener was not regarding reflexes as more "mechanical" than conscious or voluntary actions. In his view all actions, biologically considered, are "mechanical" in that eventually they will likely be explained "in psycho-chemical terms." Accordingly, "the antithesis of the reflex is not the conscious or voluntary action, but the complex coordinated action." An acceptable antithesis contrasted "movement with consciousness" and "movement without consciousness."

8. Titchener did not elaborate upon these instances of direct control of autonomic functions or supply any bibliographical references. Apparently he did not anticipate doubt about the reality of such control. In recent years Neal Miller and others have supplied experimental evidence of such control, and Miller brought the concept within the scope of learning theory. In his paper "Learning of Visceral and Glandular Responses" he posited that control of glandular responses is acquired by instrumental learning, and he objected to a prevalent belief "that instrumental learning is possible only for the cerebrospinal system and, conversely, that the autonomic system can be modified only by classical conditioning" (1969, p. 435). Miller's conclusion was based upon animal experiments, but its applicability to human beings is suggested by claims of autonomic control by yoga practitioners. In a summary of relevant experimental studies Kimble and Perlmutter report that "yogis can . . . control heart rate and pulse to some degree," but that claims of complete cardiac arrest have not yet been confirmed (1970, p. 374).

A most interesting example of autonomic control by a human being dates back to the 1930s and was reported by Lindsley and Sassman (1938). This involved a man who "since the age of 10 years has been aware of the ability to control the erection of hairs over the entire surface of his body. Experimental study has revealed the erection of hairs is accompanied by a number of other autonomic phenomena of which he was not aware. These consist of an increase in heart rate and depth of respiration, dilatation of the pupils, an increase in the electrical potentials of the skin over regions rich in sweat glands and characteristic changes in the electrical potentials over the premotor area of the brain" (p. 342). Furthermore, this man was able to prevent the reflex reaction of hairs known as "gooseflesh" — "normally induced by stepping out of a hot shower into a cold draft" (p. 348). When asked how he exercised such control the man replied that it was the same as controlling the flexion or extension of skeletal muscles. In recent years autonomic control has been acquired through biofeedback procedures, as described in Wickramasekera's report (1974) of the treatment of a cardiac patient.

Darwin's principle of serviceable associated habits was directly related to the issue under consideration. According to this principle some manifestations of emotional arousal, now devoid of utilitarian function, were originally associated with serviceable coping reactions in the organism's remote forebears.[9] Titchener quoted from Darwin's work on emotional expression with specific reference to this question: How has it come about that contemptuous disapproval is expressed by a sneering curl of the lip? Darwin proposed this answer. "Our semi-human progenitors uncovered their canine teeth when prepared for battle, as we still do when feeling ferocious, or when merely sneering at or defying someone, without any intention of making a real attack with our teeth." There is a similar suggestion of a biting attack in the forward thrust of head and torso in an enraged person. Wrinkling the nose in disgust might be another derivative of ancestral reactions to malodorous indications that food was no longer edible. Titchener regarded such signs of emotion as reflex reactions "which would be altogether unintelligible unless we could posit for them a remote conscious ancestry."

4. For his fourth line of evidence Titchener compared the secondary reflexes with the primary ones; that is, he compared acquired or conditioned reflexes with native or unconditioned ones. He was impressed that "as movements" they resemble[10] one another in being "definite, clean-cut, precise." Since the latter, secondary movement resulted from the "lapse

9. Darwin did not restrict this principle to ancestral experience. According to his original formulation it also applies to individual or personal experience (Darwin 1965, p. 28): "Certain complex actions are of direct or indirect service under certain states of the mind, in order to relieve or gratify certain sensations, desires, &c.; and whenever the same state of mind is induced, however feebly, there is a tendency through the force of habit and association for the same movements to be performed, though they may not be of the least use."

In applying the principle to the effects of ancestral experience Darwin first called attention to the force of habit and then noted the transition from attentive action to inattentive automatism (pp. 29–30): "The most complex and difficult movements can in time be performed without the least effort or consciousness. . . . That some physical change is produced in the nerve-cells . . . which are habitually used can hardly be doubted, for otherwise it is impossible to understand how the tendency to certain acquired movements is inherited. That they are inherited we see with horses in certain transmitted paces, such as cantering and ambling, which are not natural to them, — in the pointing of young setters — in the peculiar manner of flight of certain breeds of the pigeon, &c."

10. He was careful to say that they *resemble* one another, not that they are identical. Subsequent experimental studies justified this distinction. For example, Hamel (1919) found that the time for reaction to conditioned reflexes was different from the latent time of unconditioned reflexes. Then Liddell (1950) showed that a conditioned flexion reflex is not a duplicate of the unconditioned reflex in the precise nature of the movement. Even the conditioned salivary reaction, the paradigm of classical conditioning, may differ from the unconditioned reaction in rate and number of drops. The saliva may also differ in chemical composition; as the Iversens reported, "the chemical composition of saliva is different when it is naturally elicited than when it is conditioned to occur" (1975, p. 5).

of consciousness," he argued that a comparable lapse might have characterized the evolutionary emergence of the primary reflexes.

Titchener introduced the foregoing evidence to support his view regarding the evolution of mind, biologically considered. At what point in the evolutionary process, he asked, did the phenomena of consciousness first appear? Were such phenomena early or late in the genesis of organic development? Titchener had a definite answer: "the first movements of the first organisms were conscious movements." He traced the evolutionary beginnings of nonconscious primary reflexes to what might be called conscious protoreflexes, thus making "action consciousness" the matrix of mind. Moreover, he explained, in the individual this action consciousness gives rise to two lines of development. One line results in nonconscious automatism or fixity of behavior, and the other, paradoxically, enhances conscious processes and encourages plasticity of behavior (1917, p. 456):

> On the one hand, we are continually enlarging our sphere of action; conduct grows more complex; there is a tendency toward more and more complicated and specific coordination of movements; and the realization of this tendency is always accompanied by increasing complexity of consciousness, by the mental processes and attitudes known as choice, resolve, deliberation, comparison, judgment, doubt. On the other hand, there is a tendency toward the simplification of movement, and the realization of this tendency is accompanied by lapse of consciousness. Plasticity, that is, subsists alongside of fixity.

Titchener also noted that these two lines of development are reflected in the broad zoological division of animal forms into those with relatively stereotyped responses to stimulation and those whose responses are more flexible, plastic, and individualized. The former group includes ants, bees, and spiders and the latter the more complex vertebrates, including monkeys and men. Insects, spiders, and other invertebrates tend to be thought of as "pure automata, mindless reflex machines." However, in accordance with his "theory that consciousness is as old as life," Titchener speculated that the distant biological ancestors of these automatons may "have lost the flicker of mind that they at first possessed, and have hardened into unconscious machines." That they are governed by instinctive mechanisms in the struggle for survival is suggested by the fixed division of labor in colonies of ants and bees, by the symmetry of the spider's web, by the nest building of birds, and by any other pattern of behavior commonly regarded as unlearned or instinctive. All species—invertebrates as well as vertebrates—were credited with such patterns of behavior. Titchener's basic theory about the place of consciousness in evolutionary development was an outgrowth of Wundt's voluntarism, particularly Wundt's ideas about the origin of instinct. Just as Titchener had attributed the automatism of reflexes to "lapse of consciousness," Wundt had attributed the automatism of instinctive behavior to what came to be known as "lapsed intelligence."

Voluntarism as a Motivational Psychology

I have already pointed out that Wundt's voluntaristic psychology was basically concerned with wishes, desires, and related conative factors. It was thus a motivational psychology, reflecting the thinking of John Stuart Mill (1806–73). Wundt was familiar with Mill's writings,[11] and Mill had entertained the idea of an experimental psychology some years before Wundt introduced laboratory psychology. And long before Wundt sponsored a voluntaristic motivational psychology, Mill had already concluded that "volitions are determined by motives, and motives are expressible in terms of antecedent conditions including states of mind as well as states of the body" (Whitehead 1948, p. 79).

One way Wundt brought volitional considerations into the laboratory was in studying reaction time under a variety of experimental conditions. Consider the simple condition of reacting to a light flash by instantly depressing a telegraph key, where the reaction time is measured in thousandths of a second. To do this the subject has to understand and accept the experimenter's instructions, thus arousing an *intention* to depress the key the instant the light is flashed. H. C. Warren once suggested using the term intentional response time instead of reaction time (1934, p. 224), since the subject intends or is motivated to follow the instructions as he watches for the light and his reacting finger tenses. He is like the runner who prepares for a sprint by crouching when instructed to "get set." In both situations the time will vary from trial to trial, so many trials are needed to approximate the individual's best time, his average time, the deviation from the average, and other variables of special interest to the investigator.

One variable that interested Wundt was the influence of repetition during a long series of trials in a single session. In the early trials the subject was mindful or conscious of the intention to react with maximum speed; he was well aware of the purpose of the induced volitional set as he poised

11. Wundt was an admirer of Mill's *Logic,* the work in which Mill introduced his famous account of four methods of experimental science, and he wrote (Merz 1965, 3:375): "If the historian of science in the nineteenth century should wish to name the philosophical works which during and shortly after the middle of the century had the greatest influence, he will certainly have to place Mill's 'Logic' in the first rank." In his memorial tribute to Wundt, written shortly after Wundt's death in 1920, Titchener wrote that there was "no doubt of Wundt's indebtedness to Mill" (1921, p. 165).

himself for the light signal. But as the trials proceeded he gradually began to react more and more automatically until the reactions resembled reflexes, devoid both of experienced intention and of purpose. To Wundt this meant that what had begun as volitional had been transformed into an unconscious mechanical process. This was the interpretation Titchener adopted to account for the evolutionary origin of native or primary reflex mechanisms as distinguished from secondary reflexes.

Wundt attributed intentional factors to the phylogenetic origin of reflexes as well as instincts. As he saw it, both reflexes and instincts promote the welfare of the organism or the species. Though mechanically executed as inherited mechanisms, they appear to be biologically useful rather than aimless. The cough reflex, for example, acts *as if* to promote respiratory freedom, and the scratch reflex seems to reflect an intention to remove an irritant. More complex behavior commonly regarded as instinctive also seems to function *as if* instigated by a latent desire to safeguard the welfare of the organism or the species. Familiar instances of such instinctive patterns of behavior occur in broody hens, web-spinning spiders, and spawning salmon.

Wundt did not attribute any latent intentions to animals engaged in instinctive behavior; he did not regard them as driven by some dim foresight of useful results from reflexes and instincts. He thought of reflexes and instincts not as expressions of the unconscious mind, but as inherited endowments automatically activated by given stimuli. As *native* endowments they functioned independently of intention or purpose, as involuntary patterns of behavior. In this respect Wundt was a nativist.

Instincts as Lapsed Intelligence

With respect to his view of the phylogenetic origin of reflexes and instincts, however, Wundt is to be classified as an empiricist, since he thought of them as originating in the *experiences* of the biological forerunners of living species. He assumed that these experiences were crucial to survival and that no instinctive, stereotyped responses to them had yet come into existence. In these circumstances they and their descendants had to cope with such recurrent difficulties by deliberate effort. Thus they had to learn to escape from enemies, avoid painful substances, locate food and mates, safeguard the newborn, and find a suitable habitat in caves, trees, or marshes, in cold climates or warm ones. Wundt presumed that in the long run successful maneuvers would survive and others would be eliminated. He also presumed that the former indicated more intelligent patterns of behavior. Over countless generations these patterns gradually merged with the species' native equipment to form reflexes and instincts. In this way,

Wundt theorized, voluntary effort and problem-solving maneuvering were eventually transformed into automatic responses.

Wundt was not alone in this view of the origin of instincts. Lamarck (1744–1829) had sponsored a close approximation of it. It was also endorsed by the English philosophers Herbert Spencer (1820–1903) and George Henry Lewes (1817–78). Lewes suggested *lapsed intelligence theory* as a suitable designation for the view. Lamarck, as might be expected, took inheritance of acquired characters for granted, but, against expectations, Wundt followed this precedent. In theorizing about the origin of instincts Wundt wrote (1897, p. 280): "We may . . . explain the complex instincts as developed forms of originally simple impulses that have gradually differentiated more and more in the course of numberless generations through the gradual accumulation of habits that have been acquired by individuals and then transmitted."

Wundt did not elaborate upon this conclusion regarding the transmission of acquired habits, seeming content to take the mechanism of such transmission for granted as Lamarck had done. Prominent followers of Lamarck had done the same, including Darwin, as he indicated in his 1872 book on emotional expression (1965, p. 29): "That some physical change is produced in the nerve-cells or nerves which are habitually used can hardly be doubted, for otherwise it is impossible to understand how the tendency to certain acquired movements is inherited."

Ten years later Darwin had ceased to be a Lamarckian, as he demonstrated in his preface to the 1882 English translation of a book by August Weismann (1834–1914), whose experimental work was chiefly responsible for the replacement of Lamarckism by the germ plasm theory. By endorsing Weismann's theory Darwin showed that, instead of attributing evolutionary modification of structure and function to inherited habits, he now attributed it to random or chance variation of germ plasm's determiners of heredity.

Strangely enough, some fifteen years after Weismann's original experimental findings were published Wundt still based his lapsed intelligence theory on the inheritance of acquired characters. He continued to be a Lamarckian. Whether this was fatal to his theory as a plausible if speculative account of the origin of reflexes and instincts is questionable— Titchener may have rescued it.

Titchener on Lapsed Consciousness

With a few modifications, Titchener endorsed the general drift of Wundt's theory. In place of lapsed intelligence he referred to lapsed consciousness as marking the transition from voluntarism to automatism. This transition, in his view, accounted for the ontogenetic establishment of well-entrenched habitual skills as well as for phylogenetically derived "ingrained physiological reflexes." Unlike Wundt, in explaining his stand he made no appeal to inheritance of acquired reactions. He even called attention to this, not only urging caution about speculating on the evolutionary origins of psychological traits, but also going on record as unable to endorse the Lamarckian teaching (1917, p. 408):

> Speculations of this sort are permissible in psychology, but must be admitted only very cautiously into one's psychological thinking; their value depends partly upon their explanatory power, partly upon their agreement with what we know, or on other grounds can infer, of the nature of primitive mind; they are always speculations. It is clear that they involve the great question of biological heredity, into which it is here impossible to enter. The author can do no more than point out that they do not necessarily involve the direct transmission of mind, or of mental traits, from generation to generation, still less, the transmission of acquired characters.

Titchener was implying that the lapsed intelligence theory need not be discredited because it had depended on Lamarckism. It could be salvaged even though belief in the direct transmission of skills and traits could no longer be sustained. He did not say just how this was to be done, aside from his hasty reference to biological heredity. It may be that he thought of how animal breeders can change the inherited traits of horses and dogs by selective breeding and feared that considering genetic factors would take him too far afield, since the speed of race horses, the fat content of cow's milk, and the alertness of watchdogs are functions of genes, not of acquired habits of the parents.

Had Titchener lived a few years longer, he might have cited a famous laboratory study to support his conclusion—Tryon's investigation of the maze-learning ability of rats as genetically determined, first reported in 1929. By selective breeding Tryon was able to demonstrate a genetic influence on mastery of a maze. Successive generations of descendants of the more efficient or intelligent maze runners outperformed their ancestors. In effect Tryon developed strains of maze-bright rats. This did not mean inheritance of maze patterns acquired by previous generations. Each new generation of rats had to learn the maze, but later generations learned with fewer trials and fewer errors. What was inherited was a capacity or talent rather than knowledge of a particular maze pattern. Had Wundt and Titchener seen Tryon's brightest animals scamper through the maze speedily, mechanically, and without error, they might have thought this illustrated the automatism of lapsed intelligence or lapsed consciousness. They would have been viewing the performance as a derivative of prior conscious problem-solving maneuvering in either individual or ancestral experience. Such a view reflects a central teaching of functionalism — that conscious attention to the details of problems is replaced by the automatism of habit.

What Automatism Implies

The automatism of habit as a derivative of consciousness has dynamic implications. The word *automatism* connotes the nonconscious or mindless operation of clocks, slot machines, and electric fans. But even this restricted meaning involves the dynamics of coiled springs, moving plungers, and electrical energy. A breakdown in these mechanical contrivances stops their operation; but this is not true for the automatism of habit. Balked habits reinstate alertness to the conditions responsible for their frustration. The experienced driver can be absorbed in conversation with a passenger while the automatism of habit permits him to act as a quasi-mechanical chauffeur. He gives focal attention to the ideas being exchanged and only peripheral or subliminal attention to the engine and the road. This holds true as long as the situation is routine, but there is immediate and drastic reversal in the face of engine failure or hazardous road conditions, which precipitate maximum attention to the business of driving. If the engine fails, a veteran driver will stop the car at the side of the highway, as he will do if he hears a fire siren or sees an ambulance approaching. This is a commonplace maneuver for experienced drivers and becomes an inherent component of their entrenched driving habits, executed through *force* of habit.

The dynamism of habit is also reflected in the fact that habits are resistant to change. There are special clinics to deal with eating, smoking, and alcoholism, habits that, when not gratified, cause acute craving for the accustomed indulgence. Such craving demonstrates the imperiousness of habit. In these cases it can be attributed to disturbed tissue metabolism such as causes withdrawal symptoms in heroin addicts. But imperious needs are also experienced apart from biochemistry. Homesickness exemplifies this kind of longing — the stranger in new territory yearns for familiar faces, accustomed places, home cooking, and the idiom of his mother tongue. Nostalgia is a consequence of the disruption of a series of interrelated habits. To feel at home in his new country the immigrant must establish a whole array of new habits of language, gesture, dress, diet, recreation, business practice, coinage, politics, and sometimes even religious ritual. Needless to say, the dynamics of consciousness is involved in the struggle that brings such new habits into being.

Establishing new habits may be just as difficult as breaking old ones.

The dynamics of persistent motivation accounts for the automatism of the expert golfer's drives, the veteran tennis player's serves, the pianist's skill at the keyboard, and the adult's mastery of a foreign language. Without hours of concentrated practice such high-level automatism cannot be achieved. This is not limited to athletic, musical, and linguistic skills but is much vaster in scope, encompassing traits of personality and character such as courtesy, courage, friendliness, honesty, punctuality, tolerance, compassion, and sportsmanship. Fostering such presumably desirable traits involves the psychology of habit formation. A striking allusion to this phase of psychology is a notation William James made in his *Briefer Course* textbook, reported by Ralph Barton Perry (1935, 2:90): "At the head of the chapter on habit in his *Briefer Course* he wrote in his own hand: 'Sow an action, and you reap a habit; sow a habit and you reap a character; sow a character and you reap a destiny.' "

Unfortunately, this quotation was never included in any of James's published works and has remained buried in Perry's classic biography of James. But its essential meaning had already been elaborated upon in the *Principles* in the famous section on the "ethical implications of the law of habit" (1890, 1:120–27). This section, with its four maxims or principles of habit formation, may be construed as a contribution to the field of applied educational psychology. Although written many decades ago, these practical injunctions are by no means outmoded. The first[12] maxim says that "*to make our nervous system our ally instead of our enemy . . . we must make automatic and habitual, as early as possible, as many useful actions as we can.*"

This maxim epitomizes the drift of this discussion of the automatism of habit, with its latent dynamism as a derivative of volitional consciousness. It also reminds us of the definition of functionalism as "the science of the mind in action," since it urges the conscious initiation of "useful actions" in accordance with the law of habit. It was such initiation in problem situations that prompted Thorndike to call attention to functionalism as a dynamic psychology.

---

12. The other three maxims read as follows: "The second maxim is: *Never suffer an exception to occur till the new habit is securely rooted in your life. . . . Continuity of training is the great means of making the nervous system act infallibly right.* A third maxim: *Seize the very first possible opportunity to act on every resolution you make, and on every emotional prompting you may experience in the direction of the habits you aspire to gain.* As a final practical maxim: *Keep the faculty of effort alive in you by a little gratuitous exercise every day.*"

A current (1976) widely distributed book by W. W. Dyer entitled *Your Erroneous Zones* would have profited by attention to these maxims. Dyer might have avoided some dubious claims had he elaborated upon James's comment (1890, 1:127): "The physiological study of mental conditions is thus the most powerful ally of hortatory ethics."

Concluding Comments

The chief objective of this chapter has been to demonstrate that the founders of psychology as a science envisaged consciousness as dynamic and as part of the biological scheme. It was not an inert epiphenomenon; according to men like James, Wundt, and Brentano it had a "teleological function," served as a "selecting agency," revealed "moving reasons and impelling forces," and reflected the goal-directedness of intentionalism. Thus, contrary to an opinion sometimes expressed, psychology had a dynamic orientation before the rise of a dynamic psychiatry. The conscious motives of James and his contemporaries preceded the unconscious motives of Freud and his associates, but neither group influenced the other. The dynamics of James's functionalism owed nothing to the dynamics of Freud's psychoanalytic psychology, just as the latter developed independently. Nevertheless, in one respect both kinds of dynamism had a common origin in the dynamics of instinct, though they treated instinct very differently. James's long chapter on instinct in the *Principles* was more extensive and more detailed than what Freud included in his accounts of the subject. Their dynamic orientations were manifestly different, Freud's being far more restricted in range.

In Freud's view the organic matrix for the birth of instincts was supplied by gut and gonads; he attributed oral-anal drives to the former and libidinal drives to the latter in accord with the traditional division of instincts into those deemed to further self-preservation and those associated with preservation of the species. Taken together, the two sets of instincts were regarded as safeguarding or promoting life.

However, upon reflecting on World War I, Freud supplemented these life instincts by postulating a death instinct. The individual was thus equipped with two sets of inherent motivating forces: those belonging to eros, promoting growth and life, and those stemming from thanatos, the agency of destruction, decay, and death. These polar opposites were directed either toward or away from the self. Eros, when self-directed, accounted for self-love or narcissism or ego libido; when other-directed it accounted for object libido, or concern and affection for another individual. Analogously, thanatos moved against the self in self-disparagement, self-punishment, and self-destruction and moved against others in hatred, aggression, and murder. The death instinct accounted for both suicide and homicide. Freud's account of instinct thus broadly appears as an elaboration of the constructiveness of anabolism as contrasted with the destructiveness of catabolism, when reduced to essentials and examined from a biological perspective.

James's dynamic orientation, governed by a psychological perspective, promoted a different account of instinct. James introduces a guiding principle in the opening paragraph of his chapter on instincts by noting that instincts are "the functional correlatives of structure" and that in most instances "a native aptitude for its use" characterizes every organ. This is congruent in some respects with Freud's theorizing about gut and gonads, but not in other respects. James provided for a much broader range of inherent impulses to action than did Freud. Thus laryngeal structures provided for vocalization; striped muscle structures accounted for grasping, pulling, crawling, standing, shrinking, and pushing; sensory structures made it possible to see, hear, touch, smell, and taste, and to experience pain, pressure, tension, fatigue, hunger, and thirst; and, of course, pulmonary, gastric, and eliminative structures accounted for respiration, ingestion, and excretion.

The broad range of James's outlook is also reflected in his observation that, like reflexes, instinctive activation of bodily structures is elicited by specific excitants—as in coughing, sneezing, grimacing, sucking, swallowing, and smiling. It is also exemplified by "sighing, sobbing, gagging, vomiting, hiccuping, moving the limbs when tickled, touched, or blown upon, etc., etc." (James 1890, 2:403).

This quotation refers to "the first reflex movements" of infants. Whether some of these movements are to be called instincts rather than reflexes is a moot question. James recognized that there is no sharp line demarcating the two kinds of action: "The actions we call instinctive all conform to the general reflex type" (2:384). However, James also recognized that such instinctive actions are not rigidly fixed but may be modified by experience. An adult sneezes into a handkerchief and may strive to control his sobbing, coughing, vomiting, and eliminative urges in conformity to decency and etiquette. The actions have ceased to be purely instinctive. That James had already called attention to this in 1890 was either forgotten or overlooked by later writers who made their independent realization of it a chief reason for repudiating the concept of instinct.

The voluntarism of Wundt, the intentionalism of Brentano, and the instinct psychology of James all paved the way for twentieth-century functionalism. As early as 1905, "the science of mind in action" constituted recognition of functionalism as a dynamic psychology. Out of this recognition of the dynamism of consciousness, motivation emerged as a separate array of psychological problems that still persist.

References

Boring, E. G. 1950. *A history of experimental psychology.* New York: Appleton-Century-Crofts.

Darwin, C. 1965. *The expression of the emotions in men and animals.* Chicago: University of Chicago Press. First published 1872.

Dyer, W. W. 1976. *Your erroneous zones*. New York: Funk and Wagnalls.
Edman, I., ed. 1928. *The philosophy of Schopenhauer*. New York: Modern Library.
Hamel, I. A. 1919. A study and analysis of the conditioned reflex. *Psychological Monographs* 27:1–69.
Iversen, S. D., and Iversen, L. L. 1975. *Behavioral pharmacology*. New York and Oxford: Oxford University Press.
James, W. 1890. *Principles of psychology*. Vols. 1 and 2. New York: Henry Holt.
Kempf, E. J. 1918. The autonomic functions and the personality. *Nervous and Mental Disease Monograph,* no. 28.
Kimble, G. A., and Perlmutter, L. C. 1970. The problem of volition. *Psychological Review* 77: 361–84.
Liddell, H. 1950. Some specific factors that modify tolerance for environmental stress. In *Life stress and bodily disease,* 155–71. Proceedings for Research in Nervous and Mental Disease, vol. 29. Baltimore: Williams and Wilkins.
Lindsley, D. B., and Sassman, W. H. 1938. Autonomic activation and brain potentials associated with "voluntary" control of pilomotors. *Journal of Neurophysiology* 1:342–49.
Merz, J. T. 1965. *A history of European thought in the nineteenth century.* 4 vols. New York: Dover. First published 1904–12.
Miller, N. E. 1969. Learning of visceral and glandular responses. *Science* 163: 434–45.
Perry, R. B. 1935. *The thought and character of William James.* Vol. 2. Boston: Little, Brown.
Ratner, J., ed. 1927. *The philosophy of Spinoza: Selected from his chief works.* New York: Modern Library.
Thorndike, E. L. 1920. *The elements of psychology.* New York: A. G. Seiler. First published 1905.
Titchener, E. B. 1917. *A text-book of psychology.* New York: Macmillan.
———. 1921. Wilhelm Wundt. *American Journal of Psychology* 32:161–75.
Tryon, R. C. 1929. The genetics of learning ability in rats. *University of California Publications in Psychology* 4:71–89.
Warren, H. C. 1934. *Dictionary of psychology.* Boston: Houghton Mifflin.
Whitehead, A. N. 1948. *Science and the modern world.* New York: Mentor Books. First published 1925 by Macmillan.
Wickramasekera, I. 1974. Heart rate feedback and the management of cardiac neurosis. *Journal of Abnormal Psychology* 83:578–80.
Wolfson, H. A. 1934. *The philosophy of Spinoza.* Vol. 2. Cambridge: Harvard University Press.
Woodworth, R. S. 1918. *Dynamic psychology.* New York: Columbia University Press.
Wundt, W. 1897. *Outlines of psychology.* Translated with the cooperation of the author by C. H. Judd. Leipzig: Wilhelm Engelmann.

6 / Consciousness and Problems of Motivation

*I*n everyday use *motivation* is readily understood as accounting for the *why* of human and animal behavior. We take it for granted that behavior is instigated by needs, desires, cravings, intentions, purposes, urges, objectives, wants, and incentives, terms commonly regarded as having to do with motivation. When we wonder what induces such varied behaviors as hunting, writing poetry, cooking, sermonizing, gambling, golfing, whistling, voting, praying, watching a horror movie, joining a club, embezzling funds, rearing a family, or assuming responsibilities, we are inquiring about motivation, or the determiners of behavior. This kind of inquiry was connected with the impulsive and ideational aspects of Wundt's voluntarism, and it is common among psychoanalysts, who, following Freud, regard all human behavior as *motivated,* in accord with the determinism implicit in the concept of scientific law. Determinism attributes all change or all effects to antecedent causes—there can be no uncaused human behavior. But this is not the same as holding that there can be no unmotivated human behavior. Let us then examine the difference between causation and motivation.

On the Difference between Causation and Motivation

Both Freud and many contemporary psychoanalysts have interpreted the doctrine of determinism as meaning that *all* human behavior is motivated. This interpretation of what is sometimes called *psychic determinism* means that every human action or reaction is the product of a motive—there can be no unmotivated behavior. Freud ventured to attribute mistakes, blunders, mishaps, slips of the tongue, and failure to remember appointments to motivational influences, conscious or unconscious. Freudian slips thus reveal the ubiquity of motivational dynamics. This view makes motives the sole determinants or instigators of all behavior.

Freud said nothing about the question of unmotivated behavior. In examining what he termed the psychopathology of everyday life he was not concerned with possible instances of unmotivated behavior but deliberately looked for covert motives, especially in accidents, errors, or ineptitude commonly attributed to distraction or fatigue or other nonmotivational causes. His book on psychopathology in daily life is replete with instances of such covert motivation, but it lists no instances of unmotivated behavior. This may have prompted some interpreters to assume that Freud considered *all* behavior the outcome of motives or desires or wishes, though Freud never formulated a sentence reading "There can be no unmotivated behavior."

There is some justification for this interpretation in Freud's stress on the unconscious status of motives. Though he had little to say about conscious motives, he said a great deal about unconscious ones, perhaps failing to give due recognition to motivation as a *conscious* process, as it is now understood by psychologists. Dictionaries of psychology, in contrast to general dictionaries, stress this in defining *motive*. Warren defines the word as "a conscious experience" (1934, p. 171), and English and English define it as "that which one consciously assigns as the basis of his behavior" or as "the consciously sought goal which is considered to determine behavior" (1958, p. 331). They then add: "Originally, *motive* carried the meaning of a *conscious* factor, something of which one was aware," noting that the term later ceased to connote this factor and came to be applied to internal states calculated to alert, energize, and give direction to animal as well as human behavior. The latter qualification was introduced because animal experimenters had come to attribute motivational influences to animals in the form of instincts, needs, deprivations, or drives. Whether this broadened meaning is more clarifying than confusing is a separate question.[1]

One of Freud's central theses was that unconscious wishes determined

1. Such a broadened meaning was introduced by Allport (1961, p. 196): "By motive we mean any internal condition in the person that induces action or thought." Being restricted to persons, this definition does not apply to animal motivation, but it does exemplify the nonconscious phase of the enlarged meaning. Its adequacy, however, is questionable. Not every "internal condition in the person that induces action or thought" is a motive. The high fever of delirium induces agitated behavior and confused thinking; but the agitation and confusion are caused rather than motivated. Similarly, in epileptic automatism action is induced by an internal condition so that, as Penfield (1975, pp. 38–39) reported, one of his patients continued to drive his car during a seizure and only upon regaining consciousness discovered that he had failed to stop for red lights. Such automatic, perseverative, involuntary behavior is not to be classified as motivated. Like the speech of a stutterer, it is due to an "internal condition"; both are perseverative and involuntary, but hardly motivated.

dreams, speech, and action. Though the Freudian wish became a house-hold word, neither Freud nor others ever seem to have been concerned with wishing as a process. It was taken for granted that an unconscious wish, aside from being hidden, was the same as a conscious wish. Thus there was no need to define *wish;* it was conventionally interpreted as one's desire or longing or aspiration. This made it equivalent to goal-directed striving, one of the ordinary meanings of the word *motive;* hence the Freudian wish is manifestly motivational.

According to Freud, unconscious wishes always had some motivating effect on thought or behavior; psychoanalytic probing would reveal their dynamic effectiveness. Since they were never ineffective or inert, they became a prerequisite for ideational and behavioral changes. Freud overlooked or played down nonmotivational factors as instigators of such changes—factors such as illness, transportation difficulties, money problems, power failures, muggings, defective machinery, energy shortages, fatigue, misinformation, death in the family, contaminated food, loss of a job, sudden promotion, and kindred vicissitudes commonly regarded as due to luck, chance, fate, or acts of God. These are *causes* of change and in the vast majority of instances are altogether unrelated to motives or intentions. This difference between behavior as caused and behavior as motivated recalls the commonsense distinction between intentional and unintentional behavior. The young child makes this distinction when he says "I didn't mean it" or "I did it on purpose" or "It was an accident." When the child grows up and becomes a lawyer he makes the same distinction when he employs terms like involuntary manslaughter, malice aforethought, accidental death, premeditated murder, motiveless crimes, extenuating circumstances, and irresistible impulses.[2] This last phrase suggests that some impulses or motives can be resisted while others prove overwhelming. Motives vary in strength and consequently in their bearing on behavior.

The Strength and Duration of Motives

That motives vary in strength was not stressed in Freud's discussion of their influence on dreams, neuroses, and the psychopathology of everyday life. It may have seemed too obvious for special comment. Had he elaborated upon this fact, "Freudian wishes" might have been reinterpreted or qualified in terms of their significance and effectiveness. Those recognized as weak and transient would have called for different treatment than

2. How such impulses bear on the concept of insanity in criminal trials is a complex and difficult question. This is informatively discussed in Goldstein's *The Insanity Defense* (1967, chap. 5).

those regarded as moderate or as strong and persistent. Such observations are just as applicable to ordinary wishes and motives, which also range from feeble to strong and from evanescent to persistent. Awareness of such variance enhances our understanding of motivational dynamics.

Not all motives motivate, any more than all wishes result in wish fulfillment. They may be too feeble to induce action, like pious resolutions to give up smoking, start dieting, read the classics, exercise regularly, or spend more time with the children. Though intense as desires, they may prove futile in determining action. At sports events, partisan spectators, empathically identifying with a favorite team, vocalize strong motives, but they are powerless to physically influence the action of the game. Entertaining strong wishes for victory is not the same as playing the game. Kurt Lewin (1890–1947) would have called these wishes *quasi-needs,* akin to our "need" for the downfall of fictional villains and the triumph of heroes.

This distinction between a need or desire as an antecedent and some motivated act as a consequent obtains in criminal investigations. A crime is not solved with the arrest of individuals known to have motives for the crime. The murder of an oppressive dictator in a totalitarian regime may be welcomed by hundreds of his victims. Thus there are hundreds of motivated suspects for the police to consider. The problem is to find out whose motive resulted in an intended act—to close the gap between mere presence of a motive and execution of a crime. In so-called motiveless crimes guilt can be established upon proof of the act's execution; it is enough to show that the act took place without explaining *why*—which may be more difficult. Deciding on the *why* of behavior is the object of motivational research in general, and, far more than is commonly realized, the answers are elusive.[3]

The Elusive Why of Behavior

Inquiry into the motivation of behavior is not recent, nor is it limited to psychology. Its roots are old and widespread, extending into many other fields of study. The history of *philosophy,* for example, includes repeated efforts to account for the dynamics of behavior. I alluded to some when I discussed Aristotle, Descartes, Spinoza, and Schopenhauer. I also mentioned how *biology* has endeavored to determine the forces operative in evolution. Within biology, the field of *ethology* searches for the why of

3. Woodworth also considered the answers elusive (1918, p. 37): "Now science has come to regard the question 'Why?' with suspicion, and to substitute the question 'How?' since it has found that the answer to the question 'Why?' always calls for a further 'Why?' and that no stability or finality is reached in this direction, whereas the answer to the question 'How?' is always good as far as it is accurate, though, to be sure, it is seldom if ever complete."

such animal behaviors as hoarding, imprinting, territoriality, and dominance or submission, and *physiology* investigates the regnant drives of thirst, hunger, and sex with respect to their neural, endocrine, and related controls.

The why of behavior interests researchers in various social sciences. Students of *ethnology* are concerned with motives as they search for the anthropological origins of culture patterns in preliterate societies. Students of *sociology* are concerned with motivation as they ask about causes of divorce, crime, prostitution, suicide, and social pathology in general. The related subject of psychopathology has engaged students of *psychiatry* as they consider the reasons for manic excitement, catatonic posturing, compulsive hand washing, schizophrenic apathy, and other symptoms of neurosis, psychosis, or character disorder. Should they also be students of *psychoanalysis,* they would be especially alert for unconscious motives as determinants of behavior. Long before the rise of psychoanalysis, students of *history* strove to explain the rise and fall of empires and the drives to action of kings and commoners, knights and serfs, masters and slaves. The more recent specialty of *psychohistory* examines the lives of eminent men and women in light of psychodynamic influences. Such influences have long been considered by students of *economics* as contributing to the rise of labor unions, minimum wage legislation, conspicuous consumption, and other direct or indirect economic concerns.

Students of motivation fall into the natural sciences or the social sciences, reflecting a basic difference in outlook or orientation. The first group regards a motive as an internal force, while the second group sees more external influence—the difference between being impelled by thirst and being lured by the prospect of a promotion or, as Allport suggested (1961, p. 224), between being *pushed* by a motive and *pulled* by an intention. The intrinsic pushes for the most part are visceral and thus common to man and animals, but the extrinsic pulls of intention stemming from social tradition are unique to man. No animal is motivated to make a name for itself, join the right club, fight for justice, promote research, or strive for improvement. All such nonvisceral endeavors or intentions stem from our distinctively human identification with society's admonitions and prohibitions.

Intrinsic and extrinsic motives are not mutually exclusive, since society's admonitions and prohibitions influence both. Children are taught what and how and even when to eat. In toilet training their eliminative functions shift from uninhibited infantile impulsiveness to regulation by introjected imperious standards of self-control. Other spontaneous bodily functions are also brought under self-control as children assimilate society's codes of ethics and etiquette. They learn to reach for a handkerchief when about to sneeze or cough or drool, to avoid belching or spitting in public, and to inhibit masturbatory and other sexual impulses. The socialization of all these visceral impulses exemplifies the reciprocal interaction of intrinsic and extrinsic sources of motivation.

The Many Theories of Motivation

Motivation thus has not been studied only by psychologists, but has interested a wide range of other specialists in both biological and social sciences. Viewed in the abstract, however, motivation as an area of research belongs to the field of psychology along with subjects like memory, emotion, attention, and perception, though research psychologists are open to ideas from other disciplines. Psychology is a clearinghouse for what philosophers, biologists, physiologists, psychiatrists, and other specialists report about the why of behavior. These reports, added to the views developed within psychology itself, amount to a tremendous array of books and articles on motivation.

This vast body of writings contains an overwhelming amount of technical and often contradictory laboratory data on animal research as well as a bewildering number of theories of motivation. In his book on "modern theories of motivation" Madsen (1961) devotes considerable attention to nine theories and covers ten others more briefly.[4] Except for one psychiatrist and one ethologist, all nineteen theorists are psychologists. There are no psychoanalytic or sociological theories. Freud is omitted, presumably not "modern" enough. And Woodworth is not included, though he published a book on motivation in 1958, only three years before Madsen's book appeared. It is thus evident that there are more than nineteen "modern" theories of motivation and still more if we add the older theories. Precisely how many theories have been formulated through psychology's long past has never been determined.

Motivation appears to have given rise to more separate theories than any other psychological topic. One never reads about nineteen theories of memory or association or color vision or conditioning. Some topics have given rise to three or four theories and some, such as intelligence or learning, may have stimulated close to ten, but none even approximates the number of theories of motivation.

A fairly obvious reason for the proliferation of theories of motivation is the large number of biological and social sciences that have an interest in how motivation bears on issues germane to their specialties. Thus the physiologist's interest in the neurology and metabolism of thirst as a motive

4. The nine are discussed in this sequence: McDougall, Young, Allport, Lewin, Murray, Hull, Hebb, Tinbergen, and McClelland. The other ten include these familiar names: Skinner, Cattell, Frenkel-Brunswik, Masserman, and Maier.

in the life of an organism is different from the economist's interest in craving for alcoholic beverages as related to the liquor industry and excise taxes. Each specialist sees motivation from the viewpoint of his specialty, which gives rise to varied interpretations. Moreover, directly or indirectly such interpretations influence psychologists' efforts to come to terms with motivation as a distinct psychological topic.

Individual psychologists may become interested in particular phases of motivation. Some are concerned with the why of suicide, others with the why of obesity, still others with the why of crime, of achievement, of isolation, of gregariousness, of susceptibility to hypnosis, of food preferences and aversions, of religiosity, or of other delimited phases of motivation. For many years they have been issuing an impressive number of specialized reports on a wide variety of aspects of motivation. Early in the 1950s this burgeoning of psychological interest in motivation was recognized by the establishment of an annual symposium on motivation at the University of Nebraska. Each year's symposium was published in a separate volume, the twenty-ninth appearing in 1982. Since the volumes contain an average of six papers, the total number of papers accumulated through the years exceeds one hundred and seventy.[5] Each paper is much like a monograph, since participants are given more space than is customary in journals. The result is an entire shelf of bound volumes devoted to the topic of motivation. It is an impressive series.

No series of similar duration has been devoted to any other psychological topic, emphasizing that motivation has given rise to more theories than any other area of psychology. Despite all the years of study, clinical experience, and experimentation devoted to the subject, the proliferation of theories indicates that science has failed to reach agreement on motivation as a concept. David McClelland, in his *Encyclopaedia Britannica* article on motivation, arrived at the following conclusion (1970, p. 920): "In general the wide variety in points of view as to the ultimate nature of human motivation reflects the fact that scientific knowledge about the subject is still extremely limited."

This conclusion does not mean there has been no enhanced understanding of motivation over these many years of reflection and research by generations of investigators. Provocative insights and relevant data have come to light, their very abundance revealing the complexity of the subject,

5. A clarifying introduction to the diverse aspects of motivation the series covers is supplied by the volume of thirty-six selected readings edited by Bindra and Stewart and published in 1971. The papers were presented under the following six captions: (1) Motivation as Instinct; (2) Motivation as Drive; (3) Motivation as a Correlate of Reinforcement; (4) Motivation as Incentive Stimulation; (5) Unified Interpretation of Motivation and Reinforcement; (6) Neural Mechanisms of Motivation and Reinforcement. The oldest paper dates back to 1872, and 1970 is the date of the most recent.

which readily lends itself to being studied from "the wide variety in points of view" mentioned by McClelland. These distinctive viewpoints tend to become identified with distinctive theories of motivation, such as those promoted by Woodworth, McDougall, Adler, Jung, Lewin, Horney, Fromm, Allport, Maslow, Thorpe, and others. There are as many separate theories of motivation as there are distinctive theories of personality, and I shall not venture to elaborate upon them. However, because of its bearing on the main objectives of this chapter, let us consider the venerable philosophical theory of hedonism.

The Hedonistic Theory

The hedonistic theory concerns desire for pleasure and dread of pain and dates back to psychology's philosophic past. It has roots in Greek philosophy, Epicurus (341–270 B.C.) being one of its first sponsors. He taught that the pursuit of happiness did not entail immediate, impulsive gratification of desire but required due evaluation of possible consequences of such indulgence. Avoiding pain or distress was as important as pursuing pleasure. This entailed planning and control over desire so as to realize what Epicurus called *ataraxia,* the freedom from disturbance essential for inner peace and a tranquil life. In its Greek origin hedonism was thus very different from unbridled, sybaritic self-indulgence.

With its dual emphasis on pursuit of pleasure and prevention of pain, hedonism has become a commonsense theory of motivation. It reflects the widespread use of reward and punishment in rearing children, training animals, and administering prisons and military installations. It accounts for the prizes, medals, bonuses, honorary degrees, and standing ovations on the one hand, and forfeits, spankings, solitary confinement, scoldings, dishonorable discharges, excommunication, monetary fines, and failing grades on the other. In general we take it for granted that law violators must be punished—by implication the reward for obedience is the absence of punishment.

This commonsense application of hedonism accounts for some familiar psychological views of the learning process. Thorndike stressed what he called the law of effect as a principle of learning.[6] He used the word *effect* in accordance with his prior introduction of the phrase "hedonic effect," intending to call attention to the satisfying or annoying consequences of action. The law held that for both man and beast actions leading to a satisfying state of affairs will be strengthened and retained while those

6. For an informative account of Thorndike's views of learning as influenced by his understanding of the law of effect, see Hilgard's *Theories of Learning* (1956, pp. 15–47). How others understood the law is considered in the critical reviews he lists on page 46.

resulting in annoyance will be weakened or eliminated. As a principle of learning it is supposed to show how children learn to cipher and spell and how animals learn maze patterns and new tricks. Thorndike's notion of satisfaction as contrasted with annoyance is not alien to contemporary notions of positive and negative reinforcement. Both sets of terms echo hedonism's reward/punishment dichotomy.

As George Kelly noted (1960, p. 50), the reward/punishment dichotomy involves two types of motivational theories, the "push theories" and the "pull theories." The push theories concern drives and goads to action, while the pull theories concern the purposes and goals of action. Kelly added, "these are the pitchfork theories on the one hand and the carrot theories on the other," the pitchfork suggesting the annoyance of negative reinforcement and the carrot the satisfaction of positive reinforcement.

These pitchfork and carrot theories with their connotations of pain and pleasure are thus hedonistic theories, implicit in the array of punishments and rewards used by parents, teachers, penologists, and drill sergeants. The array of goads and lures is presumed to prevent the wrong and promote the right way of doing things.

These educational reinforcements are introduced in two very different sets of circumstances. The first set has to do with acts, skills, or habits already acquired that need to be reinforced. Thus children are praised for helping with the dishes and reprimanded for teasing their brothers. Truck drivers may be fined for speeding or given a bonus for years of safe driving. Here no new skill is to be mastered and no new information acquired. An existing mode of behavior is to be encouraged or inhibited.

In the other set of circumstances the reinforcements are intended to initiate new skills and abilities. In the academic world, for example, the dread of failing grades and the desire for high ones are expected to promote knowledge of chemistry, calculus, biology, and the rest of the curriculum. The dread and desire may induce persistent effort, but effort per se will not provide the intelligence, talent, and interest needed for mastery of academic subjects — otherwise all school failure could be eliminated by sharp enough pitchforks and big enough carrots and, in theory, all students should receive equally high grades.

Thus hedonism, as expressed in the law of effect, may explain why a given act is retained or eliminated, but it fails to explain why or how it came to be introduced. Moreover, with respect to the unpleasant effects of punishment the law of effect is not altogether dependable. If it were, then released convicts should never again commit crimes — yet the incidence of recidivism shows that this is not the case. Alcoholics continue to drink to excess despite the punishment of hangovers, with their nausea, headaches, and self-disparagement. Here the punishment is administered after the act, not during it, as when children's punishment is delayed until father gets home from the office. By contrast, the child who touches a hot stove does not have to be scolded. Being burned once will ensure that he avoids fire or hot objects. This exemplifies *traumatic avoidance learning,*[7] which involves very severe punishment. As Solomon and Wynne noted in their experiment with dogs subjected to electric shock, traumatic punishment results in widespread autonomic upheaval; the animal's "pupils will dilate, portions of his hair will stand on end, small muscle groups all over his body will tremble, and his breathing will consist of short, irregular gasps" (1953, p. 1).

It is exceedingly difficult to undo the disruptive effects of traumatic avoidance learning. Conditioned emotional reactions resist extinction, so that any remainder of the original trauma may reinstate the autonomic upheaval. Such upheaval is also common in human victims of punitive assaults, as in the battered child syndrome. The disruptive effects of cruelty may prove refractory to treatment; this is true of any terrifying experience, especially in a young child.[8]

7. This kind of learning was the subject of special study during the 1950s by Richard Solomon and his colleagues (see Solomon and Wynne 1953). An account of some later studies and a survey of the problem as a whole are supplied by Brown and Herrnstein (1975, pp. 103–8). Their discussion of the relation between efficiency of learning and intensity of punishment on tasks of varying difficulty elaborates upon the complexity of avoidance learning. As they point out, the first experimental report on this was by Yerkes and Dodson (1908), whose conclusions are now known as the Yerkes-Dodson law. Although the law was based on animal experiments, it seems to apply to some problems confronting the human learner. Consider a learner taking a driver's test who is told about being penalized for every mistake as he drives a fixed route with the examiner taking notes. His final score will be a function of the route's difficulty and the magnitude of each penalty. A route through heavy traffic will occasion more tension than one along uncongested roads, and a demerit of twenty points per error will make for more tension than a demerit of two points. According to the Yerkes-Dodson law, optimal performance will call for a kind of golden mean between easy and difficult routes and between low and high penalty scores. For efficient performance an undertaking should be challenging without being overwhelming, and the prospect of failure should not precipitate paralyzing panic.

8. A dramatic account of such a terrifying experience is described in *The Locomotive God,* written in the 1920s by William Ellery Leonard, a poet and a professor of English at the University of Wisconsin. He was subject to paralyzing fright whenever he ventured too far from home—a rare form of *agoraphobia.* His psychotherapist traced the phobia to an experience in his early childhood when he disobeyed his mother by wandering away from her side as they waited for a train. To the child the locomotive coming down the track was an overpowering God of vengeance coming to punish his disobedience, and he fled back to his mother for protection. Even after he acquired insight into the origin of his phobia, it not only remained but increased in severity.

Misleading Interpretations of Hedonism

As Spinoza observed centuries ago, interpretations of hedonism that make pursuit of pleasure and avoidance of pain the chief objectives of human endeavor may turn out to be misleading or even hazardous. He recognized the relativity of good and evil and gave it this succinct formulation (Ratner 1927, pp. 254–55):

> For one and the same thing may at the same time be both good and evil or indifferent. Music, for example, is good to a melancholy person, bad to one mourning, while to a deaf man it is neither good nor bad.
>
> By *good,* therefore, I understand . . . everything we are certain is a means by which we may approach nearer and nearer to the model of human nature we set before us. By *evil,* on the contrary, I understand everything which we are certain hinders us from reaching that model.

Spinoza was thus sponsoring a goal-oriented theory of motivation, viewing pleasure as a by-product, not as the objective of motivated effort. In opposition to hedonism this was a conative theory, and Spinoza wrote (Ratner 1927, p. 216): "We neither strive for, wish, seek, nor desire anything because we think it to be good, but on the contrary we adjudge a thing to be good because we strive for, wish, seek, or desire it." Thus we do not hunger for something because it gives us pleasure; it gives us pleasure because we hunger for it—the seasick passenger is never tempted by food. This view of motivation, in which pleasure is contingent upon antecedent desire, is at variance with the hedonism implied in Freud's attributing such importance to the pleasure principle as a chief characteristic of the id.

The pleasure principle construed striving for pleasure as an inherent attribute of the id, inborn rather than a product of experience. Id impulses were endowed with a priori anticipation of their own gratification. Although Freud never explicitly expressed a priori anticipation, it seems implicit in the untutored regnancy he ascribed to the pleasure principle. Nor did he explain his supposition of innate knowledge of pleasure, at least in the one paper that gives a critical analysis of the pleasure principle (1950). This was a paper on masochism, which at first glance seems impossible to reconcile with the pleasure principle. The masochist talks and acts as though being beaten and humiliated is pleasurable. Freud suggested that feelings of guilt provoke a "need for punishment" (p. 263), and he also linked masochism to the death instinct, the Nirvana principle, and the Oedipus complex. In making desire antecedent to the pleasure of punishment, he was following Spinoza.

Thus there is no pursuit of pleasure in the abstract; it is always in response to some concrete need or desire. The hungry man desires particular items on the menu, not just any kind of food. The music lover buys certain kinds of records, not just any record. Those who enjoy reading do not reach for any novel indiscriminately, but thoughtfully consider a restricted list of possible choices. Such specificity of choice governs all options in the pursuit of pleasure—games to be played, clubs to join, friendships to cultivate, charities to support, garments to purchase, and, of course, the person to marry.

A multiplicity of desires, needs, and interests are involved in the dynamics of motivation. As individual motives, each calls for its own gratification, with pleasure as its distinctive by-product. Hedonism notwithstanding, there is no pursuit of pleasure in the abstract, but just a quest for goal objects congruent with a specific motive, such as a candidate's desire for votes, a detective's search for a murderer, or a preacher's quest for converts. A defender of hedonism might challenge this generalization, however, saying "We now have evidence that there can be pursuit of pleasure in the abstract, because the brain has definite pleasure centers." This is a provocative statement and merits examination.

The Brain's Pleasure Centers

This evidence is based on the experimental work of James Olds (1922–76) and others in which electrodes were implanted in the brain of an animal, usually a rat, with subsequent electrical intracranial stimulation. The first report of this experimentation by Olds and Milner appeared in 1954 and many later reports have been published by Olds and by other investigators.[9] In a 1956 article on "pleasure centers in the brain," Olds told about some of his findings. He had placed his experimental animal in a Skinner box arranged to yield one or two volts of electricity for no more than a second. When the animal pressed a bar with its forepaws a circuit was closed and current was transmitted to the septal area of the hypothalamus which Olds regarded as the locus of the brain's "pleasure centers" owing to the animal's insatiable, repetitive electrical self-stimulation. Hour after hour without interruption the animal kept pressing the bar at the startling rate of five thousand times an hour. A rate of eight thousand per hour is mentioned by McLeary and Moore, and the rats kept this up "for twenty-four hours or more until they finally drop from exhaustion" (1965, p. 104).[10]

9. The articles by Olds and other students of intracranial stimulation are numerous and scattered. For the more important ones consult Hokanson (1969), *The Physiological Bases of Motivation,* and Wong (1976), *Motivation.*

10. McCleary and Moore (1965, p. 103) contains explanatory diagrams. Keesey and Powley (1975), "Hypothalamic Regulation of Body Weight," contains a photomicrograph of a section of a rat brain with clear locations of lateral and ventromedial areas.

That the electrical impulses were responsible for such orgiastic self-stimulation was readily demonstrated by shutting off the current, after which the bar pressing was soon extinguished. What could not be demonstrated was the exact nature of the rat's sensations during its electrical self-indulgence. By referring to "pleasure centers" Olds was identifying these areas with pleasurable feelings,[11] perhaps like those aroused by cooling drinks on a parched throat or soothing warmth on cold skin, but he did not describe the kind of pleasure he attributed to the animal. It seemed to be the equivalent of pleasure in the abstract, or what in human terms might be described as a good feeling or exciting fun. But this remains altogether speculative, since animals cannot describe whatever feelings, sensations, or sensory impressions we attribute to them. It will cease to be speculative when it becomes possible to have a mentally healthy human observer report on his experiences while undergoing electrical stimulation of his septal area.

For obvious reasons no healthy human brain has ever been subjected to hypothalamic electrode implantation, though some years ago this was tried on some seriously disturbed psychiatric patients, by Bishop and two associates at the Tulane University School of Medicine. This was undertaken as a last resort on schizophrenic patients who had failed to respond to any therapeutic effort. Electrodes were placed in the septal area and some adjacent areas. The general nature of the study is clearly summarized in this sentence (Bishop, Elder, and Heath 1963, p. 394):

> With schizophrenic patients, focal electrical stimulation to selected subcortical sites has been shown to produce at least temporary therapeutic benefits and in the Tulane studies, stimulation of activating and "pleasure-inducing" regions has particularly benefited retarded, anhedonic, chronic schizophrenic patients.

The reference to pleasure-inducing regions means that the septal area was not the sole locus of hedonic stimulation. Other loci of such "rewarding" stimulation were the midhypothalamus, the amygdala, the posterior hypothalamus, and two other sites. Except for the septal area, the areas tested proved "rewarding" at low intensities of stimulation but "aversive" at higher intensities. The terms "rewarding" and "aversive" were based not upon the subjects' remarks, but upon their lever-pressing behavior.

---

11. Hedonism is concerned with affective experiences, or feelings of pleasantness and unpleasantness. Pleasure is a feeling of pleasantness and dread a feeling of unpleasantness. Intense feelings merge into emotions; thus feelings may be regarded as incipient emotions and emotions as intensified feelings. The psychology of feeling is a complex and difficult subject. An informative introduction to its complexities was published in the 1930s by Beebe-Center, *The Psychology of Pleasantness and Unpleasantness* (1932), and the same author contributed an article on feeling to the 1970 edition of *Encyclopaedia Britannica*.

An unexpected finding was that this "rewarding" behavior continued when the current was turned off. In the animal studies, bar-pressing stopped when the current ceased. But one patient, even though the current had been stopped, continued to press the lever at least two thousand times until urged to stop. This was also true for stimulation of the septal area, and for that site the researchers reached the following conclusion (p. 396):

> These data appear to provide sound evidence of the reinforcing or rewarding properties of electrical stimulation at this site. Again, however, when the current was turned off entirely, this subject vacillated back and forth a few times and then continued to press the lever without reinforcement for more than half an hour until stopped.

Because of such perseveration of lever pressing in the absence of current, it was impossible to determine the reward value of the electrical stimulation. It was also difficult to be confident that septal stimulation alone was rewarding, since the possible "spread of the field of excitation to other structures" raised questions about whether the stimulation was isolated. The septal area is close to other hypothalamic areas such as the lateral area, concerned with eating and drinking, and the anterior area, related to sexual behavior under parasympathetic influence. If there was neural irradiation from the septal area to one or more other areas, then the hypothesized pleasure would not be abstract but indigenous to stimulation of the irradiated area.

Another possibility is that afferent impulses from these other subthalamic areas converge in the septal area, making it a clearinghouse for all pleasurable feelings and thus the brain's pleasure center. However, this is altogether conjectural and not based upon established neural connections. The septal area belongs to the limbic system and, as McCleary and Moore noted, even though that system has widespread connections throughout the brain, "not all of its anatomic connections are as yet understood" (1965, p. 110). Fortunately, despite this uncertainty regarding the neurology of pleasure and related hedonic processes, some phases of their psychology are not quite so conjectural—particularly factors governing the selection and rejection of food.

Food Preferences and Aversions

Both psychological and physiological issues are considered in extensive discussions about nutrition, appetite, organic foods, reducing diets, and kindred themes. Sometimes people ask whether cravings for specific foods indicate a metabolic need for certain chemicals—for example, whether craving salt indicates a biochemical need for sodium chloride. Evidence for such a need was reported by Wilkins and Richter (1940), who wrote about a boy three and a half years old who had eaten great quantities of salt for many months. The boy rejected cake, candy, puddings, and other sweets. The parents wrote about first realizing the child's craving for salt (p. 867): "When he was a year old he started licking all the salt off the crackers and always asked for more. He didn't say any words at this time, but he had a certain sound for everything and a way of letting us know what he wanted." He did not swallow the crackers, and later he refused any food without salt, even at breakfast.

He was admitted to a hospital for study. Since the child did not seem very sick, no special diet was prescribed, but his appetite was poor and he ate very little. Forced feeding tended to induce vomiting. Lack of the extra salt proved fatal, for the boy died rather suddenly one week after admission. In the laconic words of the case history, by increased salt intake the boy had "kept himself alive for at least two and a half years" (p. 868).

Upon postmortem both adrenal glands were found to be enlarged, with a reduced number of healthy cortical cells. This finding of adrenal pathology, Wilkins and Richter note, is congruent with results of experiments in which "rats die within ten to fifteen days after adrenalectomy" in consequence of loss of salt. When salt was supplied, adrenalectomized rats warded off symptoms by ingesting large amounts, and if adrenals were implanted the craving disappeared. The experimental rats were more sensitive to the presence of salt than normal rats, being able to discriminate between distilled water and a salt solution of 1 part to 33,000 whereas normal rats require a solution of 1 to 2,000. There is thus an inherent change in sensitivity to the taste of salt after adrenalectomy, apparently independent of learning. As Wong noted (1976, p. 99), "Sodium preference of animals following sodium depletion occurs without any specific learning. Sodium-deficient animals appear to be innately attracted to the taste of sodium."

The possibility that preference for given foods is metabolically determined was suggested in the late 1920s by Clara M. Davis in a study of newly weaned infants. Infants were given free access to a representative assortment of foods on a tray. With no interference or guidance by parents or others, they were permitted to choose for themselves irrespective of the amount eaten. Because of such unrestricted free choice individual meals were very poorly unbalanced in terms of conventions of optimal nutrition. But in overall consumption from one month to the next the amounts of proteins, fats, and carbohydrates selected were found to accord with requirements for healthy growth. Dr. Davis reported that one child with a vitamin A deficiency compensated by choosing large amounts of cod-liver oil.[12] She also reported appropriate shifts in choices as the weather

12. I am indebted to Professor Eliot Stellar for this reference.

changed. On hot, humid days the infants reduced their caloric intake and took more fluids. When the weather turned cold they chose more heat-producing foods. The Davis study thus appeared to establish an *innate* relationship between metabolic needs and food preferences, suggesting that biological factors rather than experience are responsible for some food choices.

Concerning Innate Factors

We know that innate factors account for the food choices of herbivorous and carnivorous animals. Cud-chewers' stomachs are structurally different from the stomachs of carnivores, being divided into four compartments. Presumably this anatomical difference predisposes goats, bison, cattle, and other ruminants to eat plants rather than meat. A cow does not have to *learn* to avoid a bone any more than a dog has to be coaxed into gnawing one, though a ruminant might gnaw at a bone in a case of abnormal or perverted appetite. Many years ago H. H. Green, a South African veterinarian, reported such bone eating by cattle among his experiences with different kinds of abnormal eating by animals (Green 1925).

Green explained that the craving, called *osteophagia* from the Greek for "bone eating," was caused by a phosphorous deficiency in the diet. These phosphorous-deficient animals appeared to be attracted to bones as a source of phosphorous. In his words, a herd of such animals "may provide a veritable concert" as they crunch away on the bones of some discovered skeleton. In the later stages of the deficiency the craving becomes extreme (p. 347): "A mild craver is fastidious in its selection of clean weathered bones, but an extreme craver has even been observed crunching a living tortoise with the blood dripping from its jaws; or eating pieces of hide with adherent putrefying flesh."

The craving for bones is not learned, since "young cattle brought up in an area carefully cleaned of all bone debris have yet been found to manifest osteophagia the first time bones were displayed before them," suggesting an inherent predisposition for phosphorous-deficient animals to seek phosphorous compounds. However, Green reported that osteophagic cattle refused a precipitate of calcium phosphate presented in troughs; the craving was limited to bones and did not encompass their chemical equivalent.

Richter (1950) reported a rejection of strange foods by wild rats as contrasted with domestic rats. The rats had access to the entire gamut of essential foodstuffs, with protein supplied in one container, carbohydrate in another, fat in a third, and a vitamin solution in a fourth:

The domestic rats freely sampled all of the solids and fluids and on their selections grew and thrived while the wild rats did not sample any of the foods, except olive oil, and as a result lost weight and died. It appears that they literally would rather die than touch any of the new unknown substances. (p. 201)

The wild rats were *neophobic,* or wary of the unfamiliar, while the domestic rats were *neophilic,* or drawn to the novel. By their readiness to sample the new foods the latter animals met their nutritional needs just as the babies did in the Davis investigation. The wild rats' aversion to these same foods was not due to unpleasant taste experiences, since they refused to sample them: "they are highly suspicious of all new foods and differ in many other ways from domestic Norway rats with which most laboratory workers are familiar." One conspicuous characteristic associated with their wildness is that their adrenal glands were three or four times larger than those of the domestic rats. This was reflected in their wariness when confronted with strange food and in their increased suspicion after eating poisoned food. Some of the rats, after repeated exposure to poisoned food, rejected both poisoned and unpoisoned food and thus died of starvation: "Despite the great hunger that these animals must have had they still refused to touch the unpoisoned food" (pp. 196–97).

Richter interpreted this avoidance of the unpoisoned food as due to psychotic disturbance induced by repeated experience with poisoned diets over many days. The rats exhibited a prolonged postural rigidity similar to catalepsy, but it seemed to be a paralyzing terror rather than a toxic effect of the poison—perhaps the equivalent of human dread of acute nausea or illness. It was thus a product of traumatic avoidance learning like that in the dogs terrified by electric shocks. The dogs persisted in frantic escape attempts in the absence of shocks, and Richter's rats rejected food despite absence of poison. Desire for food apparently had ceased, either through loss of appetite or through disappearance of hunger.

Hunger versus Appetite

As everyday words hunger and appetite both signify desire for food. As desires, they thus are directly relevant to the psychophysiology of motivation. We can see the difference in meaning between them in that we speak of loss of appetite but never loss of hunger. In medicine loss of appetite is indicated by the word *anorexia,* but there is no comparable technical word for loss of hunger.[13]

13. The medical term *aphagia,* from the Greek *phagein,* "to eat," might be considered in this connection, since it suggests loss of ability to eat, but medical writings define it more narrowly as loss of ability to swallow owing to stricture or some other disturbance of the

We sometimes wish a diner *bon appétit,* but we never speak of *good hunger,* though we may say we are "good and hungry" and then order a heavy meal. If we order a light meal, we might say we are "not that hungry" or that we "don't have a keen appetite." In everyday speech *hunger* and *appetite* thus refer to differing motivational states, but the precise nature of the difference may not be obvious.

It seems clear that one does not have to learn to be hungry. Some hours after eating one feels an easily recognized gnawing in the abdomen. Physiologists have demonstrated that this sensation is associated with characteristic contractions of the stomach, and many years ago a Chicago physiologist, A. J. Carlson, demonstrated hunger contractions[14] in the newborn infant (1916, pp. 40–41). This makes hunger an unlearned or innate phenomenon.

What we describe as appetite is not referable to a particular body region. Ordinarily it is characterized by a desire for specific foods or by anticipation of a meal, reflecting earlier eating experiences. Thus appetite differs from hunger in being acquired or learned. Appetite also differs from hunger in that a definite organic sensory complex identifies the state of being hungry, whereas appetite is devoid of such a complex.

Appetite connotes taste, aroma, pungency, and flavor as characteristics of our food experiences, which we gradually learn as we try out different foods. The way food is served or who offers it may influence appetite; aesthetic factors and the social setting have a bearing on our likes and dislikes for certain foods or restaurants. Woodworth called attention to such factors (1958, p. 119): "A hungry man entering a restaurant is assailed by a disagreeable odor which quickly reduces his need or at least his drive (appetite) but notably fails to strengthen the instrumental act of entering that restaurant when again in need of food. A similar case is sex desire reduced by something repulsive in the person desired."

The palatability of food is thus reduced by a disagreeable or reuplsive concomitant, just as it can be enhanced by flowers, glistening tumblers, and fine linen. However, attractive concomitants will not improve the taste

---

esophagus. This medical usage limits aphagia to the gullet as the swallowing organ and does not extend it to the stomach as the organ of hunger. Nevertheless, its literal meaning of loss of ability to eat does pertain to the stomach, and the term has been so used in physiological psychology. For example, Hokanson used its literal meaning as follows (p. 42): "Destruction of the lateral hypothalamus results in a condition known as *aphagia,* the inability of the organism to eat or drink, resulting in eventual death."

14. Such contractions are different from those associated with digestion. Digestive contractions involve more activity of the lower part of the stomach, near the pyloric end, whereas hunger contractions start at the upper or cardiac end. Just what initiates the hunger contractions is a separate question having to do with changes in blood chemistry. A brief account of this phase of the problem is supplied by Kimble's discussion of factors involved in the neural and biochemical regulation of ingestion (1977, pp. 148–51).

of repulsive food. Rancid butter will still be rancid no matter how attractive the table setting. The effect of food in the mouth is the crucial determinant of its appeal, making appetite an oral rather than a gastric phenomenon.

Carlson (1916) held that to some degree appetite is influenced by sensations aroused as food comes into contact with the stomach's lining. In their experimental investigation of the psychology of appetite, Boring and Luce (1917) used a gastric balloon and two rubber tubes to enable trained observers to report their sensory impressions as food reached the stomach during hunger contractions. They were unable to confirm Carlson's view —the only reports of sensory impressions were those deemed characteristic of feeling hungry, which one observer described as a "complex of kinesthetic pressure and pain" and about which another observer said (1917, p. 445): "Hunger is just a pressure, constant, which varies in intensity and is very profuse. And there is a pain which is the same as the pain in extreme pressure."

Boring and Luce thus concluded that consciousness of hunger as a gastric phenomenon was not related to consciousness of appetite as an oral experience. To determine the nature of such oral experience they introduced a different method, but before describing this part of their investigation let me return to the rejected Carlson view.

In a recent investigation, Carlson's contention appears to have been confirmed. Deutsch and Wang (1977) placed stomach tubes in "15 native male rats" providing direct access to the stomach through the gastric fistula. Of these fifteen animals, ten were used as test animals and the other five were used to predigest milk, which was then removed from their stomachs and used as test material.

The experimental animals were offered a choice between an almond-flavored drink and a banana-flavored one. For half the sample, if a rat chose the banana drink, the predigested milk was injected into its stomach. If it chose the other flavor, a physiological salt solution was injected. Thus one choice resulted in nourishing calories and the other in zero calories. For the other five rats the milk was paired with the almond flavor and the salt water with the banana flavor. Each day for five days the experiment was conducted in five ten-minute periods.

During the daily ten-minute sessions the rats sampled both solutions, but there was a steady and statistically significant increase from day to day in the choice of the flavor that resulted in milk and a concomitant reduction in the choice that brought the salt solution. This change in preference was interpreted to mean gastric sensitivity to the difference between nourishing and nonnourishing material: "The preference of rats for the nutrient-paired flavors indicates that the stomach alone can rapidly detect the arrival of nutritive substances" (1977, p. 89).

Although Deutsch and Wang attribute the discrimination between nutritive and nonnutritive substances to "sensors" in the stomach, they were not equating the "sensors" with the taste buds of the tongue. They said nothing about the structure or precise location of the "sensors," nor did they assign them to different parts of the stomach as taste buds are distributed over the tongue. They postulated these structures, just as "the presence of nutrient sensors in the duodenum . . . has been postulated" (p. 90). There was no way to determine what the animals were experiencing upon stimulation of the postulated sensors. Though they obviously differentiated between milk and salt water, this was not the equivalent of the delicate discriminations made by professional wine tasters and gourmet cooks. The tasters and the cooks have cultivated appetites, but unless we assume that the rats *tasted* the milk injected into their stomachs, it would be misleading to apply the concept of appetite to gastric stimulation. The rats' sensitivity to the predigested milk appears to be a consciousness of gastric fullness, which is different from one's consciousness of the palatability of food.

Boring and Luce implied that palatability is an oral experience and hunger a gastric experience. In recognizing consciousness of hunger, they were assuming the existence of gastric sensors just as they assumed the existence of gustatory sensors in recognizing consciousness of appetite.

In studying the psychological basis of appetite, Boring and Luce were not concerned with gustatory sensors or taste buds as anatomical structures. They took their existence for granted and instructed the experimental subjects to give critical attention to all mental processes connected with eating. In particular, they were to be alert for phenomenological differences between hunger and appetite. Although there was considerable variation in the mental processes they described as concomitants of appetite, they were unanimous about the difference between being conscious of hunger and being conscious of appetite. In contrast with the description of gnawing hunger as a fusion of pain and kinesthetic pressure, appetite was summed up as follows (1917, p. 452): "Appetite can be adequately described only as a food-seeking attitude or meaning, a reaching-out-after food."

The "reaching-out-after" characteristic of appetite makes it more intentional or conative than hunger. Hunger is a longing for nourishment, while appetite is a desire for specific taste experiences. Anticipation of specific tastes involves all the sense modalities related to food enjoyment. Thus one's anticipation of hot apple pie may be a medley of olfactory, gustatory, visual, and even thermal recollections. Unlike hunger, appetite is a function of experience or learning, the outcome of many discriminating choices of food; hence we speak of a *cultivated* appetite but not of a cultivated hunger. This reflects a physiological difference — appetite is more a cortical function and hunger is more a hypothalamic function.

The Physiology of Motivation

Physiological aspects of motivation are evoked when people refer to the stomach as empty, the throat as dry, and the bladder as full when they talk about impulses or desires to eat, drink, and urinate. In their technical writings physiologists refer to the same three motives in terms of gastric contractions, pharyngeal dryness, and intravesicular tension. These differences in descriptive vocabulary reflect underlying differences between popular and scientific physiology, between the layman and the specialist. The layman is content with simple, unexamined allusions to body functions. For him it suffices to know that the stomach digests food and the heart pumps blood. He has no interest in the chemistry of digestion and in the intricate details of cardiac valves, tachycardia, the sinoatrial node, or other technical details of how the heart pumps blood. His consciousness of digestion and circulation is very different from the physiologist's understanding of these processes.

The layman's outlook on motivation is thus very different from that of the physiologist. As he sees it, consciousness of a dry throat or a feeling of hunger motivates drinking and eating, and he attributes sexual motives to urges localized in the genitals. He does not ask about the neurology and biochemistry of drinking, eating, and mating, since to him these motives arise from abstention from water, food, or sexual release. This commonsense view of motivation can be contrasted with a more technically sophisticated or scientific view.

Is this commonsense view to be discarded as misleading or contrary to fact or no longer fruitful from the viewpoint of psychological theory? Stellar (1954) discussed this in a provocative paper on psychology's interest in the physiology of motivation, in which he described the vocabulary of the empty stomach and the dry throat as involving "local theories of hunger and thirst." These theories, he noted, were based upon an "outmoded model" that had been replaced. The new model was more central, since it attributed the crux of motivation to "a *central motive state (c.m.s.)* built up in the organism by the combined influences of the sensory, humoral, and neural factors. Presumably, the amount of motivated behavior is determined by the level of the *c.m.s.*" Moreover, he emphasized that the amount in question "*is a direct function of the amount of activity in certain excitatory centers of the hypothalamus*" (p. 6; his italics).

Stellar's paper elaborated on the nature and scope of these excitatory hypothalamic centers to explain the new model of motivation. He did not explain why the old model was outmoded except in noting the advantages of the new model from the viewpoint of "new" physiological facts. The facts he cited pertained to the excitatory brain centers, but there were others he might have mentioned to supply a factual basis for rejecting the old model, with its emphasis on hunger and thirst as induced by stomach contractions and by pharyngeal dryness.

Later experiments brought into question traditional teachings regarding the nature of hunger and thirst. It was discovered that removing an animal's stomach and suturing the gullet to the duodenum was not followed by decreased food consumption. The same operation on people had the same outcome, along with this important additional finding; subjects reported *feelings of hunger*. Comparable findings resulted with thirst: animals deprived of salivary activity and thus doomed to chronically dry throats did not drink to excess, nor is there an abnormal intake of fluids in humans born without salivary glands.

Such findings made researchers recognize the need to revise older teachings regarding hunger and thirst, since they concluded that gastric contractions and pharyngeal dryness were incidental concomitants, not essential causes, of our desire for food and water. They thus shifted from peripheral to central theories of such causation, considering the contractions and dryness consequences of the excitation of given centers of the hypothalamus.

Hypothalamic centers have been investigated since the 1930s, and a vast research literature has accumulated.[15] I have already mentioned a few of these areas in connection with the "pleasure centers" studied by Olds and others. To give detailed attention to them all one would need to draw on the fields of neurology, physiology, and endocrinology. Here it is enough to note a few salient hypothalamic findings that outline the nature and scope of the influences exerted by the central motive state.

Some Hypothalamic Findings

The hypothalamus regulates vital biological functions indispensable for individual and species survival. Some of these functions are associated with the metabolism of digestion, water retention, sexual arousal, vigilance, ovulation, sleep, and whatever else used to be attributed to the instincts of self-preservation and race preservation. Instead of appealing to such vague and unanalyzed concepts as these instincts, we can now analyze metabolic functions in terms of specific hypothalamic areas—clusters of specialized cells or nuclei that control particular functions.

The nature of specific functions may be inferred from the consequences of disease or lesions in an area, stimulation of an area by implanted elec-

15. Introductions to the relevant literature are found in some current books on motivation. Hokanson (1969), for example, lists close to 400 references, and Wong (1976) lists almost 350. For references to views of motivation dating back to the 1950s see Irwin (1950).

trodes, or drugs or chemicals applied to the area. Additional information can sometimes be obtained by tracing nerve tracts linking a given area with some remote target. For example, such tracts link the hypothalamus with the parasympathetic and sympathetic branches of the autonomic nervous system. This permits a more precise localization of function, since the parasympathetic branch is connected with an anterior hypothalamic area while the sympathetic branch engages a posterior area.

The two divisions of the autonomic nervous system have antithetical effects on organs and tissues. In general, the sympathetic division energizes and alerts the organism while parasympathetic division promotes relaxed and less vigilant states. The sympathetic division releases adrenaline, activates the heart and muscles, inhibits gastrointestinal functions, and arouses strong emotion and concomitant vigilance. The parasympathetic division reduces heart action, promotes digestion, inhibits strong emotion, and initiates sexual behavior and other activities compatible with the relaxed assurance of freedom from attack or danger conducive to sleep. Motives involving excited vigilance thus appear to have their hypothalamic roots in the posterior area, while those involving calm self-assurance are more likely to be rooted in the anterior area.

Two areas are of special interest because of their influence on eating—the lateral and ventromedial areas. Two sets of impulses must also be considered: those that initiate eating and those that inhibit it. The common belief that eating continues until the needs of depleted tissues have been met is altogether erroneous. Irwin referred to this when he wrote, "The fact that animals and humans stop eating and drinking long before the water and food can have had opportunity to supply bodily needs by being assimilated into the tissues is as obvious as it is often disregarded" (1950, pp. 215–16). We are conscious that we have eaten enough and are no longer hungry three hours or more before the food has been assimilated; we stop eating before gastric digestion has been completed. Why?

Apparently we stop because of changes initiated by the ventromedial nucleus—changes involving afferent impulses *from* and efferent impulses *to* the stomach. Efferent impulses have been demonstrated by direct stimulation of this nucleus, which causes immediate cessation of eating, and surgical destruction of this hypothalamic area prolongs eating.

If the ventromedial nucleus is a *stop* center, then the lateral hypothalamic nucleus becomes the *go* center, for it is directly implicated in the initiation of eating behavior. As already noted (see note 13), when this nucleus is destroyed the animal ceases to eat, a condition known as *aphagia*. However, when this *go* center is intact and the *stop* center is destroyed, a condition known as *hyperphagia* ensues, characterized by voracious eating and obesity. Obesity in humans is sometimes caused by a tumor encroaching upon the cells of the ventromedial nucleus, resulting in loss of control over impulses from the undamaged lateral hypothalamus[16] and thus in compulsive eating. However, though compulsive eating is not unusual, it is rarely due to hypothalamic tissue damage; such excessive eating and the consequent obesity can be caused by many other factors. As is brought out in Rodin's current (1981) review of the status of obesity as a psychophysiological problem, these many factors include enlarged fat cells, abnormally high levels of insulin, reduced metabolic rates, and a variety of nonmetabolic factors. As Rodin points out, "onset and degree of overweight are determined by a combination of genetic, metabolic, psychological, and environmental events." She also points out that "obesity is not a single syndrome, has no single cause, and therefore does not have a single cure."

Along with recognition of the complexity of factors responsible for obesity has come recognition of the obese patient as a compulsive eater. Salzman, for example, noted this in his article "Obesity: Understanding the Compulsion" (1975, p. 89):

> Both psychological and physiological issues, including genetics, biochemistry, energy output, and caloric intake must be considered in the effort to fully comprehend this disorder. The tendency to emphasize the physiological factors, however, derives not only from the failure of physician and patient to acknowledge the psychological issues, but also from the nature of the obese person's character structure which encourages denial and assumes an omnipotent capacity to be exempt from the consequences of cause and effect.

Salzman manifestly regards the compulsive eater as a driven personality. He describes obese patients as feeling empty and being impelled by urges they can neither comprehend nor control. Often, he reports, they eat sparsely at mealtime but eat voraciously in secret. They then delude themselves that they eat little because they abstain at mealtime. Thus the compulsion is characterized by disordered or warped thinking. We might ask whether motivation has the same effect on thinking—whether compulsive eating is the same as motivated eating—which brings up the important difference between compulsion and motivation.

The Difference between Compulsion and Motivation

The difference between *compulsion* and *motivation* is related to an issue introduced at the beginning of this chapter, the difference between *causation* and *motivation*. I stated that, while all behavior is caused, not all

16. The literature on this subject is vast, and the problems involved are both complex and controversial. For an excellent introduction to the range and diversity of these problems see the articles collected by Brent Q. Hafen in *Overweight and Obesity* (1975).

behavior is motivated and cited the distinction between intentional and unintentional behavior as illustrated by the legal distinction between pre-meditated murder and involuntary manslaughter. I also alluded to irresistible impulse as a defense in criminal trials.

A phrase like irresistible impulse implies a distinction between impulses amenable to control[17] and those too intense or overwhelming to be resisted. Acute pain may force an outcry and a grimace of agony, but, being irresistible, the outcry and the grimace would be unmotivated. In fact, often one is motivated to be brave and avoid an outcry, but such resolve is of no avail when the dentist's drill strikes a nerve. People who must speak in public sometimes report that they have strong desire or motivation to remain calm and controlled but are overwhelmed by stage fright, which may result in panic and inability to deliver the intended address. The impulse to flee the platform militates against the desire to speak, with consequent loss of control of the muscles of articulation. The speaker is *motivated* to speak, but the uprush of fear *impels* the panic. In a similar way we might say that a mourner's convulsive sobbing is *impelled* rather than motivated by grief. Motivation involves intentions or purposes to be accomplished; there is no such involvement in the mourner's sobbing, which is an involuntary, unintentional outburst that may be at variance with his original resolve to keep his emotions under control. Failure to curb his feelings results in the *impulsive* sobbing.

I emphasize the word *impulsive* to differentiate it from *compulsive*. The public speaker was not compelled to experience stage fright, nor was the mourner compelled to give way to convulsive sobbing. Psychopathologists refer to obsessive-compulsive neuroses, not impulsive neuroses, because they regard compulsive behavior as inappropriate or irrational. In the familiar hand-washing compulsion the superfluous, repetitive washing ritual is the focus of irrepressible morbid preoccupation. The ritual makes efficient work impossible and is a source of distress to the victims, who themselves tend to consider it "crazy" behavior. They recognize it as annoying and unjustified but are unable to inhibit it. Since it is alien to their desires, they may deem it both forced and unmotivated, in accord with the psychiatric verdict of compulsive behavior.[18]

17. In explaining how the courts interpret the phrase Goldstein notes that "there is no monolith called the 'irresistible impulse' test. Most of the cases do not even use the phrase. It is much more accurate to describe the rules as concerned with lack of control and to use the shorthand designation 'control' test" (1967, p. 69).

18. In comparable fashion habitual alcoholics come to recognize their drinking as a psychiatric compulsion. Even when strongly motivated to remain sober, they are unable to curb the craving for alcohol. Their addiction has often been regarded as a sickness attributable to some metabolic disturbance. Support for this view has been contributed by Myers and Melchior (1977), who took a direct experimental approach, introducing specific amine metabolites into the brain ventricles of rats. Rats ordinarily will not drink ethyl alcohol,

A Note on Impulsive Behavior

Earlier I cited as examples of impulsive behavior reaction to the dentist's drill, stage fright, and uncontrollable sobbing. Such behavior is forced, unmotivated, and unwelcome, especially when the loss of control conflicts with an intention to be brave and not yield during an ordeal. Unlike compulsive behavior, it is neither inappropriate nor irrational. Other familiar instances of such unwelcome, impulsive outbursts are uncontrollable giggling in church and persistent coughing during a concert. Such outbursts are forced, instinctive, involuntary, and *unmotivated*. Like sneezing and hiccupping, they are reflex automatisms and illustrate one kind of impulsive behavior. But there is also a very different kind to be considered.

One kind of impulsive behavior is both welcomed and highly motivated, a product of mature character development and personal commitment to a given value system. Far from constituting reflex automatism, it reflects an intimate identification with the ethicosocial implications of concepts of right and wrong and is essential to integrity of character. Acquiring certain personal values gives rise to this kind of motivated impulsive behavior, and once they are genuinely assimilated a person cannot bear false witness, embezzle funds, or forge a check. It would be impossible for such a person to be an arsonist or a robber or a kidnapper; in this sense his behavior is *forced,* since he is no longer free to act in ways at variance with his principles of conduct. This negative coercion is supported by the positive coercion of allegiance to these authoritative principles, which entails immediate and virtually *forced* recognition of the proper action to take when these principles are involved.

Such principles of conduct are implicit in a person's sense of duty or pride of workmanship or loyalty to a professional code or devotion to artistic ideals or faith in the honor system or business ethics; they prompt adherence to ideals of conscientious behavior. They explain why some writers find it impossible to write shoddy but lucrative articles and why some carpenters, masons, and other artisans cannot bring themselves to do slipshod work, being governed by self-imposed standards of excellence. The same applies to architects, homemakers, bankers, farmers, teachers, and all whose standards of competence are expressed in their work.

Such people are impelled to act in accordance with such introjected standards. They cannot bring themselves to violate them, free-will doctrine notwithstanding. Since it expresses a personally cherished value

---

but in a few days the experimental animals, given access to both water and alcohol, "drank alcohol solutions in increasingly excessive amounts" and displayed muscular and other disturbances characteristic of intoxication. A change in brain metabolism had transformed healthy rats into compulsive drinkers.

system, their behavior is impulsive rather than compulsive. Being ego syntonic, it exemplifies conflict-free, goal-directed motivation as differentiated from ego-alien compulsion. It also exemplifies the psychiatric idea of an integrated personality and thus demonstrates the centrality of motivation to mental health and personality organization. Thus it seems safe to say that there are as many theories of motivation as there are distinctive theories of personality.

Concluding Comments: Three Recurrent Themes

The diversity of topics pertaining to motivation is a reminder of the complexity of the subject. I have had to ignore or merely touch on many important areas. I have adopted a commonsense view of motivation, approaching it as a conscious experience of goal-directed striving accompanied by awareness of intention and initiation of a conative set. This conative set suggests emotional arousal incident to effort directed toward an objective; thus emotion constitutes the *affective* phase of conation and motivation is its *effective* phase. From the perspective of systematic psychology, activated conation can be contrasted with the serenity of undisturbed homeostasis, and motivation falls within a biological or a physiological perspective.

We saw that the range of motivational problems cuts across many specialized fields of investigation, from biology to virtually all the social sciences. Motivation looms large in the thinking of neurophysiologists, animal psychologists, economists, psychiatrists, and psychoanalysts, and the conclusions of workers in these different fields do not always agree. Though the core of fact thus is often obscured in a tangle of speculation and contradictory supposition, a retrospective broad survey of these crosscurrents reveals a few basic themes.

Implicit in many theories of motivation is the *approach-avoidance* theme, a venerable theme that dates back to Aristotle's idea of the "appetitive" faculty's "pursuit and avoidance" of objects. Aristotle wrote that "appetite can originate movement" and that "wish is a form of appetite," observations that mark the beginnings of both a psychological and a psychoanalytic theory of motivation. Even before the age of psychology this approach-avoidance theme had received philosophic attention, as Roy Lawrence made clear in his *Motive and Intention*, quoting a 1751 publication of the Scottish philosopher Henry Home Kames (Lawrence 1972, p. 32):

> No man can be conceived to act without some principle leading him to action. All our principles of action resolve into *desires* and *aversions;* for nothing can prompt us to move or exert ourselves in

any shape, but what presents some object to be either pursued or avoided. A motive is an object so operating upon the mind, as to produce either desire or aversion.

This eighteenth-century view of motives as instigating desires and aversions has not vanished from the scene. The layman uses punishment and reward to inhibit wrong behavior and promote right behavior, and the psychologist uses negative reinforcement to elicit aversive behavior and positive reinforcement to elicit approach behavior. These two kinds of reinforcement remind us of the law of effect, with its emphasis on results as satisfying or annoying. Since this law originally was known as the law of hedonic effect, the approach-avoidance theme can be viewed as congruent with hedonistic theories of motivation.

Another recurrent theme pertains to the source of given motives. It may be called the *endogenous-exogenous* theme, since it differentiates intraorganic from extraorganic motives.[19] The former are physiological motives such as hunger and thirst, while the latter are social motives such as prestige and achievement. Thus this theme highlights the distinction between being driven by an inner urge and being lured by some external incentive. Woodworth contrasted "a need primacy theory of motivation" with "a behavior primacy theory of motivation" (1958, pp. 109–33). Sponsors of need primacy perceive motivation as springing from organic needs for relief of inner tensions—fatigue demands sleep, thirst requires water, and anxiety calls for reassurance. Motivation is thus a process of need reduction.

But is need reduction characteristic of every motivated act? Examining the behavior primacy theory sheds light on this question, for the theory recognizes that neither man nor beast is just a passive recipient of external stimuli. Instead, in Woodworth's phrase, there is an exchange, or a "dealing with the environment." The healthy organism is *actively* involved with its surroundings. Children climb trees, dig in the sand, throw snowballs, frolic with their dogs, and engage in countless energetic dealings with the outdoors. Instead of need reduction, they are displaying need *enhancement* as they discover absorbing interests and seek thrills or excitement. Children often ignore mother's call to dinner during an exciting game— need primacy as an internal process, or goad, is yielding to behavior primacy as an external process, or lure. The endogenous-exogenous theme thus reflects the *spatial* locus of motives as organic needs and cravings or as external concerns and interests.

A correlative of this spatial theme is a *temporal* theme, concerned with the three dimensions of time. Some present motives as derivatives of past

19. Guilford recognized a similar differentiation in his Nebraska lecture on motivation when he attributed "input of information" both to "internal somatic sources" and to "external environmental sources" (1965, p. 328).

experience, others discount the past in favor of the present, and still others stress the future in terms of hopes to be fulfilled, hazards to be guarded against, and plans to be executed. For example, a Freudian may attribute fear of a domineering employer to an unresolved oedipal conflict dating back to childhood. An Adlerian might attribute the same fear to current feelings of masculine inferiority as the worker finds himself meekly submissive. The aroused sense of inferiority is regarded as an event of the present, not a relic of the past or a prospective apprehension. To a Jungian such apprehension might suggest anxiety about future chances of promotion.

The temporal theme is especially prominent in Allport's account of motivation, with its emphasis on human behavior as *proactive,* not just reactive. We are future oriented as we schedule next month's appointments, plan a summer vacation, purchase life insurance, and deal with innumerable objectives and contingencies, acting in terms of progression rather than regression (Allport 1961, p. 206): "We hear much of *reaction* but seldom if ever of *proaction.* We hear of regression, but not of *progression.* We conclude that while human beings are busy living their lives into the future, much psychological theory is busy tracing these lives backward into the past."

The noun *proaction* has not yet gained currency; it is not listed even in dictionaries of psychology. However, the adjective *proactive* is defined by English and English as "a process that affects a subsequent related process," in contrast with "retroactive" processes (1958, p. 408). Accordingly, the temporal theme can be designated retroactive-proactive to parallel the approach-avoidance and endogenous-exogenous themes.

Directly or indirectly, the problems and theories of motivation reflect one or more of these three themes. Some motives prompt action toward or away from goal objects, others are pitchfork prods or carrot pulls, and still others involve the past-future antithesis. The vast array of facts and conjectures amassed by students of motivation can all be encompassed within this scheme.

References

Allport, G. 1961. *Pattern and growth in personality.* New York: Holt, Rinehart and Winston.

Beebe-Center, J. G. 1932. *The psychology of pleasantness and unpleasantness.* New York: Van Nostrand.

————. 1970. The psychology of feeling. In *Encyclopaedia Britannica,* 9:148–53.

Bindra, D., and Stewart, J. 1971. *Motivation: Selected readings.* 2d ed. Harmondsworth, England: Penguin Books.

Bishop, M. P.; Elder, S. T.; and Heath, R. G. 1963. Intracranial self-stimulation in man. *Science* 140:394–96.

Boring, E. G., and Luce, A. 1917. The psychological basis of appetite. *American Journal of Psychology* 28:443–53.

Brown, R., and Herrnstein, R. J. 1975. *Psychology*. Boston: Little, Brown.

Carlson, A. J. 1916. *The control of hunger in health and disease*. Chicago: University of Chicago Press.

Davis, C. M. 1928. Self selection of diet by newly weaned infants. *American Journal of Diseases of Children* 36:651–79.

Deutsch, J. A., and Wang, M. L. 1977. The stomach as a site for rapid nutrient reinforcement sensors. *Science* 195:89–90.

English, H. B., and English, A. C. 1958. *A comprehensive dictionary of psychological and psychoanalytical terms*. New York: Longmans, Green.

Freud, S. 1950. The economic problem in masochism. In *Collected Papers*, vol. 2, trans. Joan Riviere, 255–68. London: Hogarth Press.

Garrison, F. H. 1960. *An introduction to the history of medicine*. 4th ed. Philadelphia: W. B. Saunders.

Goldstein, A. S. 1967. *The insanity defense*. New Haven: Yale University Press.

Green, H. H. 1925. Perverted appetites. *Physiological Review* 5:336–48.

Guilford, J. P. 1965. Motivation in an informational psychology. In *Nebraska symposium on motivation*, ed. D. Levine, 313–32. Lincoln: University of Nebraska Press.

Hafen, B. Q., ed. 1975. *Overweight and obesity: Causes, fallacies, treatment*. Provo, Utah: Brigham Young University Press.

Hilgard, E. R. 1956. *Theories of learning*. 2d ed. New York: Appleton-Century-Crofts.

Hokanson, J. E. 1969. *The physiological bases of motivation*. New York: John Wiley.

Irwin, F. W. 1950. Motivation. In *Theoretical foundations of psychology*, ed. Harry Helson, 200–253. New York: Van Nostrand.

Keesey, R. E., and Powley, T. L. 1975. Hypothalamic regulation of body weight. *American Scientist* 63:558–65.

Kelly, G. A. 1960. Man's construction of his alternatives. In *Assessment of human motives*, ed. G. Lindsey, 33–64. New York: Grove Press.

Kimble, D. P. 1977. *Psychology as a biological science*. 2d ed. Santa Monica, Calif.: Goodyear.

Lawrence, R. 1972. *Motive and intention: An essay in the appreciation of action*. Evanston, Ill.: Northwestern University Press.

Leonard, W. E. 1927. *The locomotive God*. New York: Century.

McCleary, R. A., and Moore, R. Y. 1965. *Subcortical mechanisms of behavior: The psychological functions of primitive parts of the brain*. New York: Basic Books.

McClelland, D. 1970. Motivation. In *Encyclopaedia Britannica*, 15:919–24.

Madsen, K. B. 1961. *Theories of motivation: A comparative study of modern theories of motivation*. 2d ed. Copenhagen: Munksgaard.

Myers, R. D., and Melchior, C. L. 1977. Alcohol and drinking: Abnormal intake caused by tetrahydropapaveroline in brain. *Science* 196:554–55.

Olds, J. 1956. Pleasure centers in the brain. *Scientific American* 193:105–16.

Olds, J., and Milner, P. 1954. Positive reinforcement produced by electrical stimulation of septal area and other regions of rat brain. *Journal of Comparative and Physiological Psychology* 47:419–27.

Penfield, W. 1975. *The mystery of the mind: A critical study of consciousness and the human brain.* Princeton: Princeton University Press.

Ratner, J., ed. 1927. *The philosophy of Spinoza: Selected from his chief works.* New York: Modern Library.

Richter, C. P. 1950. Psychotic behavior produced in wild Norway and Alexandrian rats apparently by the fear of food poisoning. In *Feelings and emotions,* ed. M. L. Reynert, 189–202. New York: McGraw-Hill.

Rodin, J. 1981. Current status of the internal-external hypothesis for obesity: What went wrong? *American Psychologist* 36:361–72.

Rozin, P., and Kalat, J. W. 1971. Specific hungers and poison avoidance as adaptive specializations of learning. *Psychological Review* 78:459–86.

Salzman, L. 1975. Obesity: Understanding the compulsion. In *Overweight and obesity,* ed. B. Q. Hafen, 89–93. Provo, Utah: Brigham Young University Press.

Solomon, R. L., and Wynne, L. C. 1953. Traumatic avoidance learning: Acquisition in normal dogs. *Psychological Monographs* 67:1–19.

Stellar, E. 1954. The physiology of motivation. *Psychological Review* 61:5–22.

Warren, H. C. 1934. *Dictionary of psychology.* Boston: Houghton Mifflin.

Wilkins, L., and Richter, C. P. 1940. A great craving for salt by a child with corticoadrenal insufficiency. *Journal of the American Medical Association* 114:866–68.

Wong, R. 1976. *Motivation: A biobehavioral analysis of consummatory activities.* New York: Macmillan.

Woodworth, R. S. 1918. *Dynamic psychology.* New York: Columbia University Press.

———. 1958. *Dynamics of behavior.* New York: Henry Holt.

Yerkes, R. M., and Dodson, J. D. 1908. The relation of strength of stimulus to rapidity of habit-formation. *Journal of Comparative Neurology and Psychology* 18:459–82.

7 / Consciousness and Lateral Dominance

*T*he title of this chapter could have read "lateral dominance and consciousness," and some might prefer to see the greater emphasis on lateral dominance. Taken in the abstract, the concept owes more to students of brain anatomy and brain physiology than to students of psychology. It is an outgrowth of a finding reported in the early 1860s by a French brain surgeon, Paul Broca (1824–80), that motor aphasia, or loss of control of speech muscles, almost always involves damage to the left brain hemisphere. According to Broca, the lesion occurred in the posterior portion of the lowest convolution of the frontal lobe, a location now known as Broca's area. Damage to the corresponding area of the right hemisphere affects language control only in some left-handed patients. For the vast majority the left hemisphere is dominant with respect to language mastery; hence the concept of lateral dominance.

Lateral dominance is a neurological rather than a psychological discovery; before Broca's work speech was not recognized as a function of the left brain cortex. Moreover, there is no direct conscious experience of particular functions that students of brain physiology attribute to given sides of the brain. Thus there can be no introspective confirmation of lateral dominance. We are never conscious of it in the way we note pains, sights, noises, thoughts, and other conscious events.

Even though we are not aware of lateral dominance, we commonly are aware of its bodily consequences. Early in life children learn whether they are left- or right-handed and whether they kick a ball better with one foot or the other. When first confronted with a microscope they may find out whether they are right-eyed or left-eyed. They take it for granted that it is easier to do things with one side of the body. We implicitly recognize the body's bilateral symmetry, but unless we are exposed to special reading or instruction, we do not recognize the brain's bilateral symmetry.

The Brain's Bilateral Symmetry

The human brain is divided into two equal hemispheres, one on each side of the prominent longitudinal fissure. Without evidence to the contrary, one might attribute right-handedness to the right hemisphere and left-handedness to the left hemisphere. But such contrary evidence has been supplied by brain injury. Rupture of blood vessels in the right hemisphere causes paralysis of the left half of the body, and a stroke in the left hemisphere causes right hemiplegia, because the nerves that innervate a given side of the body originate in the opposite brain hemisphere. Because of such crossing over or decussation of nerves, the right hemisphere controls the left half of the body and vice versa. This applies both to motor nerves and to sensory nerves, so that afferent impulses stemming from receptors on one side are transmitted to the contralateral hemisphere and efferent impulses originating in one hemisphere terminate in the contralateral musculature. Thus a principle of reversed laterality in neural organization characterizes the body's bilateral symmetry.

It is readily understandable that reversed laterality applies to all *pairs* of bodily structures such as arms and legs, but a question might be raised about an *unpaired* structure like the tongue. In reality the tongue conforms to the pairing of bilateral symmetry, for it consists of two halves separated along the midline by a fibrous septum, each with its own set of five nerves—three sensory nerves and two motor nerves. Like the nerves of the arms and legs, these nerves of the tongue also cross over; but there is a difference. Neither side of the tongue is dominant; instead, both halves are equipollent, permitting smooth, balanced unitary action in chewing, swallowing, and talking.

This unitary action is not true of victims of motor aphasia. They can chew and swallow, but their talking is impaired. The tongue, jaws, and lips function normally at mealtime and are thus under control as eating muscles. But though the structures are undamaged, their function in speech is impaired by damage to brain tissues. The aphasic knows what he wants to say, yet the words elude him.[1] He recognizes the words when they are suggested to him, but he may still have trouble uttering them. He cannot effect the transition from intention to execution. The loss of control is intracerebral rather than peripheral, and in the vast majority of cases it is associated with a lesion in the left hemisphere involving Broca's area. This demonstrates that hemisphere's dominance with respect to vocal speech.

---

1. This distinction between ideation and verbalization has long been recognized and is reflected in some biblical passages. In Psalm 19:14 one reads about "the words of my mouth and the meditation of my heart." In the Bible the heart, not the brain, was regarded as the seat of the intellect.

To regard one hemisphere as dominant in any respect is hard to reconcile with the concept of bilateral symmetry, which implies equality of measurement and thus equality of structure. This suggests that the two hemispheres are duplicates, and identity of structure implies identity of function. In turn, identity of structure and function implies that there is no difference between the hemispheres. But the fact of lateral dominance indicates that there are differences and that the brain exhibits bilateral asymmetries.

On the Brain's Bilateral Asymmetries

To regard the two halves of the brain as both symmetrical and asymmetrical may be a paradox rather than a contradiction, a result of differing viewpoints resulting from superficial or casual inspection as opposed to careful or measured examination. Thus as people pass us on the street their bodies appear symmetrically proportioned and yet, as any orthopedist can testify, were any of these bodies subjected to anthropometric scrutiny asymmetries would emerge. One arm might be slightly longer than the other, the left shoulder lower than the right, the muscles of one arm larger than those of the opposite arm, and so forth.

In similar fashion, as some neurologists are now ready to testify, appropriate methods of examination reveal such structural discrepancies in the cerebral hemispheres. As reported by Galaburda et al. (1978), "the human brain contains regions that are typically different in size on the two sides" (p. 852). In particular they report that a portion of the temporal lobe close to the lateral fissure[2] has definite asymmetries. One study found that in the left hemisphere the gyrus in question averaged one-third larger, based on examination of one hundred adult brains. In some individuals the left gyrus measured five times larger than the right. Such asymmetries have also been found early in fetal life and in the newborn.

There appears to be a definite relation between handedness and bilateral asymmetry. Both the frontal and the occipital lobes were found to be wider in right-handed than in left-handed subjects in almost every instance among 174 right-handed and 49 left-handed persons, as measured by an X-ray technique known as tomography. In the right-handed subjects the right frontal lobe was the wider nine times as often, and the left occipital lobe was the wider four times as often. No such striking differences characterized left-handed subjects (pp. 853–54). Furthermore, these asymmetric differences correlated with handedness were not limited to the cerebral

2. Brain anatomists refer to this part of the temporal lobe both as the anterior transverse gyrus and as Heschl's gyrus.

lobes; air studies of the brain ventricles showed that the left occipital branch of the lateral ventricle was longer than the corresponding branch of right ventricle in most of the right-handed persons studied.

Galaburda et al. did not interpret such differences as meaning that right-handedness was caused by dominance of the left cerebral hemisphere and vice versa. They merely noted that handedness was correlated with these differences. They introduced no explanation for why the computerized tomograms showed wider right frontal and left occipital lobes for the right-handed subjects. In terms of these measurements one might be tempted to ascribe right-handedness to right frontal lobe dominance and left occipital lobe dominance, but the concept of *cerebral* dominance, as ordinarily understood, has not provided for *lobular* dominance. It is thus advisable to suspend judgment on the significance of these measurements. Moreover, there are some perplexing exceptions to the reported findings. Not every right-handed subject showed such lobular differences. In a few the right/left measurements were equal, and in a few others the left frontal and the right occipital were wider. A comparable reversal was found in a few left-handed subjects. All we can say with confidence is that in the vast majority of cases the superior control of the muscles of the right side in the right-handed suggests left cerebral dominance and vice versa for the left-handed.

Presumably the ambidextrous lack this dominance, though there may be no genuinely ambidextrous individuals. The switch-hitter may not be able to sign his name with equal ease and quasi-automatism using either hand. Such relativity in dominance is also applicable to the concept of handedness in general. Luria (1973) cited investigations from the 1960s reporting that absolute left cerebral dominance applies to no more than one-quarter of the population—people who are not only right-handed, but also right-footed, right-eyed, and right-eared and thus what Luria describes as "completely right-handed." Another one-third of the population exhibits marked dominance, some show slight dominance of the left hemisphere, and "in one-tenth of all cases the dominance of the left hemisphere is totally absent" (pp. 78–79)—those who are wholly or markedly left-handed. In individuals whose ambidexterity applies to all aspects of handedness, neither hemisphere would be regarded as dominant. Ambidextrous tennis players, at least in theory, should be able to serve equally well with either hand; soccer players should control the ball equally well with either foot. But establishing such equal proficiency would call for special study.

The whole question of handedness involves special study, not only with respect to its nature and scope but also with respect to lateral dominance. The question cannot be disposed of by having hundreds of college sophomores classify themselves as right-handed, left-handed, or ambidextrous,[3] nor could they relate their answers to lateral dominance. Nobody is ever conscious of such dominance in his own brain, or of any mental process as it occurs; one can never have introspective access to brain events. Thus one must determine criteria for handedness, as well as measures or estimates of relevance, frequency, and modifiability.

Criteria for Handedness

How does one decide whether a young child is right-handed or left-handed? This question confronted Helen Koch in her classic critical study *Twins and Twin Relations*. Her ninety pairs of twins, aged between five and six, included both identical and fraternal twins. To determine each child's handedness she collected five kinds of data: (1) the mothers reported their observations; (2) the twins' teachers gave estimates; (3) two adult examiners gave their "general impression" of each twin's hand preference after observing for a day; (4) each child was asked to draw a picture, and the hand used was noted; (5) while being interviewed each child had access to a box of toys and the interviewer noted the hand used in reaching for a distant toy, in holding a toy, and in handling a difficult toy.

These five modes of observation did not measure "strength" of hand preference; they gave only general estimates. For left-handed children there was general agreement in the five lines of evidence, but there were some doubtful cases. In Koch's words, "there are all degrees of preference" (p. 73) — some children used either hand for some maneuvers and the right hand (or the left) for most others. There are also degrees of preference in the sense that in some people dextrality or sinistrality refers to the hands but not the eyes or ears.

Koch noted that investigators disagree about the frequency of left-handedness, in part because they use different criteria. One investigator studying identical versus fraternal twins, using cutting with scissors and throwing a ball as indicators, found twice as many left-handed children among the identical twins as among the fraternal twins. Another investigator, using hammering, shuffling cards, and cutting as indicators, reported no significant differences between the two kinds of twins. But according to most reports there is a somewhat higher incidence of left-handedness among twins than among singletons.

3. Hicks and Kinsbourne expressed a contrary opinion in their study of the handedness of college students compared with that of their parents and stepparents. The authors regarded the results as "contrary to a learning theory of handedness" and as "consistent with a genetic theory." Whether this settles the issue is open to question.

Why a Left Preference in Twins?

Many of Koch's twins, according to their mothers, had shown a left preference in the early years but had shifted to dextrality upon reaching school age. This shift was more or less spontaneous, not a product of family pressure, though it may have been subtly influenced by the many direct and indirect dextral pressures a child is bound to experience in a right-handed society. Nevertheless, this shift was not observed in all the twins. In some 15 percent left-handedness was still present by school age (p. 226). Koch was impressed that left-handedness often persisted in one twin even though the other was definitely right-handed by school age. Such persistence runs counter to a general observation that right-handedness increases during the preschool years. Koch found thirty-two pairs of twins in which only one member followed this trend and wondered how to account for the resistant left-handed member.

Koch recalled a paper on infant laterality written by Wayne Dennis in the 1930s. Dennis (1935) had been able to observe for close to a year a pair of twins who were shielded from conventional efforts to foster dextrality. Intertwin stimulation was kept to a minimum by a screen placed between the adjacent cribs. However, shortly after birth each infant was inadvertently exposed to a laterality preference in feeding, because the nursing bottles were placed next to the infants on pillows—on the right for one child and on the left for the other. Bottle feeding had been started when the twins were about seven weeks old, and what Dennis referred to as a "habit" emerged at this time; in less than two days of feeding a preference was established for being fed from a given side. According to Dennis, the babies cried if the bottle was not placed in the same position as on the two previous days. One baby wanted the bottle on his right and other wanted it on his left, indicating laterality at least with respect to feeding. As Koch observed, it is possible that such dominance extends to other situations because of the way twins are so commonly treated. Each twin is placed in a crib regarded as belonging to him, and the mother tends to approach the crib from the same side each time. Laterality would also be reinforced by having one twin routinely nurse at one breast and the other at the opposite breast and by placing them side by side in high chairs and strollers. Thus twins, in contrast with singletons, are apt to have right/left preferences reinforced. Since parents are urged not to interfere with a child's spontaneous sinistrality, these early chance preferences may be given inadvertent encouragement.

These considerations do not rule out the influence of genetic factors in twin behavior, and their role is being given special attention in an ambitious investigation of twins now under way at the University of Minnesota. According to an interim report by Holden (1980), the investigation is concentrating on twins reared apart. An enormous mass of data is being assembled, and its analysis and evaluation will take some years; but one investigator suspects they will find that "more human behavior is genetically determined or influenced than we ever supposed" (Holden 1980, p. 59). Of course this does not negate the relevance of experiential or nongenetic factors in right/left preferences on specific tasks. Thus some right-handed individuals are left-footed when kicking a ball, and some left-handed individuals are right-eyed when sighting a rifle or using a microscope. People may also be right-eared or left-eared—even a newborn reacts to right/left auditory stimulation, which may have had some bearing on the Dennis study.

Auditory Stimulation of the Newborn

In the Dennis account the twins were described as demanding that the nursing bottle be placed in accord with a right/left postural preference, regarded as indicating contrasting lateral dominance for the two twins. However, such dominance may have been influenced by the sound of approaching footsteps as the bottle was brought to the side of the crib. Michael Wertheimer reported an interesting observation of a newborn's responsiveness to auditory stimulation. The baby was delivered by natural childbirth and no anesthetics were used, so the infant's nervous system was unaffected. Wertheimer was present at the delivery and had arranged to test the baby's hearing by clicking a toy "cricket" next to each ear in a series of trials made in a predetermined order. The trials were started "three minutes after birth" with the baby lying on her back. Two observers independently recorded the baby's ocular responses to each click. The infant's eyes moved in a well-coordinated manner right from the start, and in response to each click they either moved in the direction of the sound or did not move at all. The two observers substantially agreed about these movements. Fifty-two successive clicks were given, about eight per minute. As Wertheimer described it (1961, p. 1692): "As soon as the first click was made, the neonate, who had been crying with eyes closed, stopped crying, opened her eyes, and turned them in the direction of the click; it was clear to both observers that the movements occurred in response to the click. . . . When the experiment was over the subject was only ten minutes old."

It thus seems clear that at birth the eyes respond in quasi-reflex fashion to right/left auditory stimulation. This is at variance with a traditional teaching that oculomotor orientation requires a long period of postnatal experience. Wertheimer's demonstration suggests an inborn foundation for the development of space perception. Bower (1977) interprets this demonstration as involving more than rudimentary nativistic reactions to bilateral sounds; in discussing the newborn's perceptual world (pp. 18–26) he says such reactions mean that the baby expects to *see* something upon *hearing* the click, implying rudimentary sensory awareness as well as an innate linkage between auditory and visual processes. If this is so, then the position preference established so rapidly by the Dennis twins may have been promoted by instinctive orientation to approaching footsteps, which led one twin to expect food from the right and the other to expect it from the left.

The part such auditory factors play in the right/left orientation of twins depends on consistency in the placement of the cribs. It may apply where one twin is right-handed and the other left-handed, but of course often both twins are right-handed. Koch's sample included such pairs as well as pairs in which both twins were left-handed. She reports that there were "a few" such pairs, "very slightly more among identical than fraternal twins" (p. 175). The effect of auditory factors on handedness thus is restricted and is not related to genetic or prenatal causes of handedness either in singletons or in twins. Such causes, as suggested by Teng et al. (1976), seem to be "associated" with increased left-handedness among twins (p. 1148). This important study will be considered further in the next section.

Wertheimer's observation of the neonate's reaction to auditory stimulation has been interpreted as suggesting that the baby *expected* to see something when she turned her eyes toward the click. Does such expectation imply an inherent tendency to perceive auditory space as related to visual space? McGurk and Lewis raised this question when they asked whether there is "perception within a common auditory-visual space" in early infancy (1974, p. 649). They defined early infancy as the period from one month to seven months, and they tested infants at three ages during this period. Their sample consisted of thirty-five babies: eleven were tested at one month, twelve at four months, and twelve at seven months. The infants were individually tested while propped in a semiupright position that permitted them to turn in different directions. Each mother sat directly in front of her baby and was instructed to talk to the child in a normal voice for two minutes. As she talked her voice was shifted from a center speaker to a speaker on the right and then to one on the left. The baby's facial, ocular, and bodily reactions were noted by different observers and recorded with a television camera.

This experimental setting calls for a word of explanation. Ordinarily we take it for granted that a person's voice comes from his open mouth; hence for the voice to sound far off to one side would strike us as extraordinary, a startling departure from a fixed association between face and voice. How early in the course of development is this association established? Or is it an inborn association? The McGurk and Lewis study was prompted by an earlier investigation in which the experimenters had concluded that this association is present at birth or at least by one month of age. Their study repeated the earlier work using what they deemed an improved method.

Contrary to the earlier findings, McGurk and Lewis failed to find this audiovisual association even by the seventh month, so they had to leave the question of its eventual emergence unsettled. As they put it (1974, p. 650):

> The nature and development of audiovisual coordination during early infancy remains an open question. The assumption that such coordination initially occurs within a unified audiovisual space is unsupported by our findings. Similarly, there is no evidence from our study that modifications of the normal spatial relationship between face and voice are experienced by the young infant as violations of a preexisting expectancy for face and voice to occupy the same spatial location.

The latter conclusion is altogether in accord with current studies of the young infant's grasp of spatial relations. In his account of the subject Bower (1977, pp. 115–20) summarizes some of the evidence showing the infant's failure to understand how one *object,* such as a toy held in his mother's hand, is related to the same toy placed *on* the table or *in* a cup. Even at nine months he continues to have trouble dealing with the spatial changes when objects are placed *upon, behind, below,* or *in front* of other objects. How much more difficult it must be to fix the locus of intangible, invisible voices.[4]

The neonate's ocular response to a click in the Wertheimer study was different from babies' reactions to the human voice. In the latter instance the infants' eyes were already focused on the mother's face at the time of auditory stimulation; in the Wertheimer study there was no such prior ocular fixation. This constitutes an important difference. Had Wertheimer

---

4. This refers to voices spatially separated from the mother's face and projected from empty space. The task would be different were the mother's voice projected from a stranger's mouth. One experiment cited by Bower (1977, p. 34) confronted two-week-old infants with their mother's faces and a stranger's face through the openings of a partition above their cribs. A special device made it possible to transpose the mother's voice to the stranger's face and vice versa. During these transpositions both adults talked and both were silent so that the infants' reactions could be observed as the mother spoke in her own voice or the stranger's voice. The babies fixated on their mothers more frequently than on the stranger, which was taken as proof that a baby recognizes his mother at as early as two weeks. When the mother's voice was transposed to the stranger the babies averted their gaze by turning their heads, which was interpreted as an attempt to avoid having to focus on the face with the wrong voice. In the absence of more supporting evidence this interpretation seems questionable.

substituted the sound of his own voice for the metallic click, it seems likely that the infant's ocular reactions would have been the same. Such reactions, regarded as native or instinctive ear-eye coordinations, are in accord with the biological teaching that vigilance is a native endowment.[5] Animals do not have to be taught to be startled and look around in response to sudden sounds.

Handedness in a Chinese Population

The study by Teng et al. (1976), mentioned earlier, used Chinese subjects to investigate handedness because the use of the left hand for eating and writing is not tolerated in China as it so commonly is in Western culture. In Taiwan, where the investigation took place, both parents and teachers insist that children use the right hand for these tasks. Consequently, even those regarded as "naturally" left-handed are taught to manipulate chopsticks and writing instruments with the right hand. Other manual skills are not subject to such social pressure and are thus left free as inherent expressions of hand dominance. Teng et al. found that such expressions had not been affected by the forced training of the right hand for eating and writing.

The investigation included schoolchildren and university students. More than two thousand boys and girls from fourth and fifth grades and an equal number of university men and women participated for a total of 4,143 subjects. Of these, 18 percent said they had experienced repeated correction for using the "wrong" hand. At the time of the investigation only 1.5 percent continued to eat with the left hand, and only 0.7 percent wrote with the left hand. These subjects were regarded as "naturally" left-handed. The degree to which social pressure had been effective in making subjects right-handed writers is indicated by comparing the 0.7 percent with percentages from a Berkeley, California, study of left-handed writing in schoolchildren—6.5 percent for Chinese youngsters and 9.9 percent for non-Chinese (p. 1149).

The social pressure was aimed at eating and writing, but there was some question about the specificity of this influence. Was it restricted to these two activities, or did it generalize to other manual activities? Answers were supplied by an elaborate questionnaire the subjects filled out. They reported on which hand they used for such tasks as striking a match, using a toothbrush, unscrewing jar lids, hammering nails, and opening doors. Statistical analysis of the data enabled Teng et al. to calculate what they

5. An older but still valuable account of the significance of vigilance is Liddell's 1950 article on vigilance as a factor in animal neurosis. In terms of neurology, vigilance is directly related to the arousal reaction of the reticular activating system. For details see Guyton (1976, p. 731).

termed a *laterality quotient* for each subject to estimate his natural or spontaneous handedness by determining the hand used in activities other than eating and writing. They found that training to promote use of the right hand for eating and writing had no significant influence on the use of the left hand for other activities. There was little or no transfer of training to these other maneuvers.

In the absence of substantial transfer effects, handedness was regarded as not basically a product of training or habit formation. Instead, the very limited amount of transfer was held to demonstrate "a certain degree of tenacity of the biological predilection involved in handedness." In the biologically left-handed, the investigators noted, this tenacity is directly related to lateral dominance. Their natural left-handedness results from control by the right hemisphere. However, as a result of training from early years such subjects are competent in manipulating chopsticks and pencils with their right hands while retaining their preference for the left hand in other actions like throwing balls, cutting with scissors, or brushing teeth. Does this mean that control of eating and writing has been shifted to the left hemisphere while other manual acts remain right-hemisphere functions? Or has an "ipsilateral pathway" been "established only for the socially censured activities"?

There may be no need to postulate such ipsilateral pathways. Even the definitely right-handed employ their left hands in manipulating knife and fork, typing, swimming, playing golf, and kindred skills that require the joint control of both hands. Lateral dominance does not preclude such synergic activities. The left hand of the right-handed pianist moves in harmony with the right hand, and violinists execute precise fingering with the left hand while bowing with the right. Such integrated functioning of both hands in musical performance has recently been subjected to experimental study.

Lateral Dominance and Musical Performance

The idea that musical performance might be related to lateral dominance was an outgrowth of clinical observations, not a product of abstract theorizing leading to experimental study. Clinical study of cases of brain injury came before experimental studies. The nature of such clinical cases is explained in the reports of the Russian psychologist A. R. Luria (1902–77), who examined victims of different kinds of brain injury resulting in psychological disturbances. By way of introduction he noted that circumscribed cortical injury disrupts some mental processes while leaving others undisturbed. He pointed out that "a local focus" of injury in the parietal area of the left hemisphere gives rise to disturbances of spatial orientation so that the victim has trouble telling time or reading a map. Such patients also have difficulty grasping the meaning of phrases like "father's brother" as contrasted with "brother's father." Yet they have no trouble with "the understanding and playing of musical instruments" (Luria 1973, p. 40). A striking example is the case of an outstanding composer, reported by Luria and his associates in 1965. After a vascular accident in the left temporal region, this composer was unable to understand spoken words; nevertheless he was able to continue with his creative work in music. This indicates, Luria noted, that hearing language and hearing music "depend on the working of quite different areas of the brain" (p. 41). Though he lost his verbal competence, the composer's musical competence remained intact.

These clinical observations of the preservation of musical ability despite the loss of linguistic competence have been confirmed by the neurologist Joseph Bogen in a summary review of the history of these observations (1973, pp. 104–6). The cortical independence of language and music is not a recent observation. Bogen cites a case reported in 1745 of an aphasic patient, a victim of right hemiplegia, who could sing hymns. Another aphasic patient, despite his impaired speech, was able to conduct an orchestra. The British neurologist Henry Head is quoted as writing that aphasic patients can reproduce melodies and recognize tunes, though they have trouble reading musical scores or producing the words of a song. In all these cases the left, not the right, hemisphere was injured. Conversely, patients with lesions in the right hemisphere may suffer impairment of musical skills but no loss of linguistic skills.

Bogen cites some experimental support for this attribution of musical skills to the right hemisphere—research by a Canadian investigator who administered the Seashore tests[6] of musical aptitude to patients whose temporal lobes had been excised. In some the operation involved the right temporal lobe and in others the left. Those lacking the left lobe had little trouble with the musical tests, but the other group of patients had definite problems. A close relation between music and the right hemisphere seemed clearly established. It appears that musical sensitivity per se requires an intact right temporal lobe.

This does not mean, however, that the left hemisphere is totally uninvolved in musical skill. Quite the contrary. Bever and Chiarello (1974) raised an interesting question about music and laterality—whether laterality

6. These tests are named after the "measures of musical talent" devised by Carl Seashore (1866–1949), one of the first experimental psychologists to be trained in this country, who received his doctorate at Yale in the 1890s. The tests required the subject to listen to a series of phonographic recordings of various combinations of tonal stimuli designed to measure ability to detect tonal differences in consonance, pitch, timbre, rhythm, and related components of musical sensitivity.

is affected by musical sophistication. This query was based upon the realization that musically experienced listeners "hear" things in music to which the inexperienced are "deaf" or unresponsive. The question was also an outgrowth of the observation that, despite serious disruption of speech following damage to Broca's area, some aphasics can still sing the words of a song.[7]

To answer the question, Bever and Chiarello presented various musical stimuli to right-handed subjects selected for their level of musical sophistication. Those deemed sophisticated listeners were active as instrumentalists or singers and had taken music lessons for at least four years. The other group, deemed unsophisticated or naive, had had fewer than three years of music lessons at least five years earlier; these subjects had markedly less musical experience and were not engaged in musical activities at the time of the investigation — they were relatively, rather than absolutely, inexperienced.

Each subject was tested individually, wearing earphones so that music could be directed to either the right or the left ear, right-ear stimulation thus involving the left temporal lobe and left-ear stimulation involving the right temporal lobe.[8] There was, of course, systematic involvement of both hemispheres as each ear was subjected to monaural stimulation. The stimulation consisted of simple melodies and two-note excerpts from the melodies. The researchers hypothesized that recognizing such excerpts depended upon the subject's ability to analyze a melody's internal structure and thus called for musical sophistication. This hypothesis was confirmed, since the experienced musicians were able to recognize the excerpts while the inexperienced subjects failed to do so.

Both groups of subjects recognized the simple melodies, but with an important difference concerning lateral dominance. The outcome for each group depended on the ear being used: the naive subjects did better with stimulation of the left ear, and the sophisticated subjects did better with stimulation of the right ear. Thus the right hemisphere was dominant in the naive and the left hemisphere in the sophisticated. The two groups of listeners were thus reacting differently to melodies. The naive listeners were hearing each melody as an organized whole, oblivious of its internal

---

7. In the words of Norman Geschwind, a leading student of aphasia, "a person with aphasia of the Broca type who can utter at most only one or two slurred words may be able to sing a melody rapidly, correctly and even with elegance" (1972, p. 76).

8. There may also have been some involvement of ipsilateral lobes, since some fibers of the auditory nerve terminate in these lobes while the remaining fibers cross over to the contralateral lobes. This partial crossing is also true of the optic nerve but not of motor nerves or of sensory nerves accounting for cutaneous and joint sensitivity, in which the crossing, or decussation, is complete. In the auditory nerve the contralateral fibers are regarded as dominant over the ipsilateral ones; the experimental implications of this are made clear in Doreen Kimura's article on the asymmetry of the human brain (1973, p. 72).

composition, which had to be perceived through analysis of its tonal constituents, the two-note excerpts. To perceive the excerpts as intrinsic to the melody as a whole calls for more musical knowledge than that needed for simple recognition of the melody itself.[9] It is like understanding the grammatical structure of a sentence as well as its meaning.

Bever and Chiarello's findings suggest that with increasing musical sophistication there is more left than right hemisphere involvement, but Gordon has questioned this interpretation, noting that their "data did not give an independent measure of hemispheric participation" (1975, p. 69) and advising that studies of this kind be conducted on subjects known to be "right-brained" or "left-brained" either through experience or through natural endowment. This implies studying a musically sophisticated population divided into two groups, one predominantly right-handed and the other predominantly left-handed, and comparing the results with those from similar groups of musically naive subjects. The nature and degree of lateral dominance in regard to music have not yet been determined.

Music and the Brain: Unsettled Issues

A basic unsettled issue is the nature of pitch. As Wightman and Green indicated, just how our perception of pitch is related to the frequency of sound waves "remains a mystery" (1974, p. 208). They noted that in listening to musicians tuning their instruments we recognize the sounds of piano, violin, and oboe as different even though their "pitch" is the same. Recognition of identity of pitch despite uniqueness of sounds is ordinarily explained in terms of uniform waveforms underlying timbre; but the crucial problem for any theory of pitch perception is nonuniform waveforms that seem to have the same pitch. There are no objective measures of pitch. Pianos are not tuned by machines. As Wightman and Green stress, "pitch is a purely subjective attribute of sound," which brings it within the realm of psychological research. It takes place inside the heads of listeners as they tell us whether two notes seem the same or whether one is higher or lower.

It now appears that pitch perception may be related to handedness. While searching for subjects to participate in an experiment on pitch perception, Diana Deutsch was struck by the disproportionate number of left-handed persons among those scoring well on her preliminary test, which

9. Recognition of music as a psychological process is both complex and distinctive. As Diana Deutsch brought out, it involves the abstraction of "the relational properties existing in tonal combinations," and such abstraction is independent of ability to perceive pitch differences. She refers to two individuals unable to master simple melodies despite possessing excellent pitch discrimination (1969, p. 300).

dealt with memory for pitch. After this serendipitous discovery, she organized her research to determine whether right-handed and left-handed subjects differ in this kind of auditory memory.

The subjects were required to judge whether test tones were the same or different. These test tones, introduced in a series of sequences, were either identical in pitch or varied by a semitone, and they were separated by unrelated tones so as to test auditory memory for pitch. Deutsch did not just compare the scores of her right-handed subjects with those of the left-handed ones. She calculated separate scores for those who were strongly right-handed or moderately right-handed and did the same for her left-handed subjects, thus providing four groups of subjects. The best scores for pitch memory were obtained by the moderately left-handed group; their scores were superior to those of the moderately right-handed to a statistically significant degree, a striking finding that would not have been brought to light had the study disregarded degrees of handedness. As Deutsch explained (1978, p. 560): "The finding that the moderately left-handed differ significantly in performance from the moderately right-handed . . . demonstrates that the "ambidextrous" should not be considered a single population, as is often assumed. Had the two groups been combined in this study, no significant differences would have been seen."

It appears that such differences had never before been reported. To account for this novel finding, Deutsch introduces a working hypothesis with implications for the concept of lateral dominance in general. Deutsch cites data from five references pertaining to cerebral speech representation of the left-handed. For the vast majority of right-handed individuals, speech is a left cerebral process, but a similar generalization does not apply to the left-handed, for about one-third of whom speech is a right-brain process. This indicates that "a considerable proportion of the left-handed have some speech representation in both hemispheres" (1978, p. 559), unlike the right-handed. Accordingly, Deutsch considered the likelihood of a dual cerebral representation of pitch for the left-handed, reflected in pitch memory as tested during the experiment. Whether the results obtained applied to other aspects of musical memory was not determined, nor was it determined whether the remaining subjects—those lacking dual representation—process pitch memory in the dominant or nondominant hemisphere.

A Brief Digression

Let me digress to call attention to the broader significance of this notion of dual cerebral representation. For many left-handed individuals language control comes to involve both hemispheres, as if they possessed two Broca's areas. What applies to language might also apply to other psychological processes regarded as altogether segregated right- or left-hemisphere functions; more critical study might reveal actual or potential dual representation. For example, Geschwind reported that children suffering from aphasia recover more readily and adequately than adult aphasics, which suggests right-hemisphere speech control at least during childhood. Additional evidence in support of this, Geschwind notes, is that some adult aphasics who recover turn out to have suffered brain damage in childhood (1972, p. 83).

Another clinical observation Geschwind made refers to left-handed aphasics deemed to lack dual speech representation, since for them the representation reflects left dominance. Even in this group aphasic symptoms averaged less severe than in right-handed aphasics. Furthermore, right-handed aphasics are not homogeneous in prognosis. Those from families with a history of left-handedness have better recovery rates than other right-handed aphasics.

Such clinical observations suggest the existence of a latent anlage for speech processes in the right hemisphere of the left-handed. This unexplained but challenging phenomenon keeps brain researchers on the alert for comparable anlagen involving space perception, rational or analytic thinking, holistic thinking, music appreciation, and many other activities now associated with either right or left lateral dominance, and it underlines the broader significance of dual cerebral representation.

Music and the Brain: Additional Issues

Issues related to music and the brain are so numerous that they call for an entire volume.[10] In recent decades, there has been a decided increase in journal articles dealing with such issues, reflected in a survey by Gates and Bradshaw (1977) concerned with the cerebral hemispheres and music. In the course of their article they mention about forty-five journal articles from widely scattered sources. They cite British, French, American, and Canadian journals in such varied fields as neurology, verbal learning, acoustics, otolaryngology, psychophysiology, and experimental psychology. Since they omitted German, Russian, and Scandinavian journals their coverage is not complete, but it is representative of the nature and scope of contemporary problems under investigation and provides a helpful point of departure. I shall sketch some of these problems by way of general orien-

---

10. Such a volume has been published by two British neurologists, Macdonald Critchley and R. A. Henson, entitled *Music and the Brain: Studies in the Neurology of Music* (Springfield, Ill.: Charles C. Thomas, 1977).

tation; the original journal references are listed at the close of the Gates-Bradshaw article.

Central questions in this examination of pertinent literature are the degree to which the components of musical sensitivity are related to lateral dominance and whether *all* musical experience reflects such dominance. Are some components of musical experience right- and others left-hemisphere processes? Or are they all right-hemisphere processes? Components to be considered are rhythm, harmony, pitch, intensity, and timbre, along with such frequent concomitants as emotional and ideational reactions. Experienced musicians differ from the inexperienced in their awareness of these components, and a listener may react differently to the same melody on different occasions according to his mood, expectations, and mental set. Such variations in reaction have to be taken into account when dealing with the broad question of music and lateral dominance. Many students of the question, as might be expected, attribute analytic attention to the components of a tonal sequence to left-hemisphere involvement as contrasted with right-hemisphere involvement in nonanalytic, holistic enjoyment. Whether these contrasting modes are mutually exclusive is a separate question. It is altogether likely that both contribute to the music lover's enjoyment.

Interest in and knowledge about lateral dominance largely arise from cases of aphasia that have come to the attention of physicians, particularly neurologists. By the turn of the century medical textbooks referred to motor aphasia and sensory aphasia, but they were not likely to use *motor amusia* and *sensory amusia* to describe musical disorders corresponding to the two forms of language impairment.[11] A reason for this neglect is that victims of musical disorders seldom consult physicians unless their disabilities are incidental to strokes or language disorders. The vast majority of doctors never come across amusia as an independent clinical entity.

Deficits in musical ability do exist without concomitant language deficits, but they are uncommon. In a recent (1973) examination of forty-nine cases of amusia, language deficits were found in 65 percent. Just as there are cases of *alexia,* or loss of ability to read printed words, so there are cases of musical alexia, or loss of ability to read music. Sometimes both kinds of alexia occur, but some patients can still read music though not words.

The issue of lateral dominance is of special concern where victims of motor aphasia are able to sing, but not say, the words of a song—an unusual occurrence. According to one theory, the emotions aroused in song may account for the difference. Under strong emotion aphasic patients

11. The same statement holds true for current medical texts. Guyton's widely used *Textbook of Medical Physiology* devotes space to language and to various aphasic disorders (1976, pp. 747–49, 755–56), but says not a word about amusia.

have been known to give vent to a "go to hell" or "damn you." Several theorists attribute emotionalized language to right-hemisphere influences.[12] And one patient was able to sing the words of common songs with few errors of pronunciation after his left hemisphere had been totally removed, suggesting some latent or residual potential for right-hemisphere control of speech.

That any aphasics can sing words they cannot say indicates such a potential. Thus one ought to guard against overly rigid hemispheric segregation of abilities, attributing all language functions to the left hemisphere and all music functions to the right. Linguistic and musical abilities are not mutually exclusive in all respects. They have in common such properties as perception of duration of sounds, rhythm, and temporal order. Shifting the positions of a few notes may change a familiar melody into an unfamiliar one just as shifting the order of words in a sentence may cause drastic changes in meaning. "The boy hit the ball" has the same words but a different meaning from "The ball hit the boy." Duration is obviously common to both music and language; music has long and short notes, and language has long and short vowels. In one study, aphasics' scores on the Seashore battery of music tests were all lower than the scores of normal subjects except on the time test, where scores varied with the severity of the language disturbance. When trying to estimate the passage of time in seconds or minutes we count in some way—a cognitive process involving language.[13] Counting and estimating also require implicit awareness of the spatial aspects of time. We talk about a long time or a short time, and we measure time by pointers moving around the face of a clock. Duration as a concept thus reflects the time-space continuum in which we are all engulfed—the music student following the beat of a metronome and the motorist checking his speedometer. Common to the world of music and the world of technology, this continuum involves both brain hemispheres.

Tonal changes also involve both hemispheres, and they are common to both music and language. Though their role is not as obvious in language

12. The common impression is that the singing of birds expresses emotion, and Geschwind reports that a Rockefeller investigator "has found unilateral neural control of bird-song" (1972, p. 76).

13. Yet counting does not always involve language. Woodworth, for example, reports counting without using words (1939, pp. 9–10): "I found by experiment that I could count by rhythmical groupings and could group the groups and so work up to over 100, converting the rhythmical result afterward into ordinary numbers. I have returned to this subject a number of times, as in considering the curious discrepancy between colors as seen and colors as named, and again as incidental to the work on imageless thought; and recent attempts to revive and modernize the old theory that training consists in speaking have always found me skeptical, mostly because my own experience convinces me that there are modes of thought besides the verbal, and that these other modes are more direct and incisive."

as in music, everyday speech is replete with such changes. They are evident in the rising inflection of "How much did it cost?", the preemptory tone of "*Watch out!*", and the solemn tones of "Be brave" or "I'm so sorry." These tonal changes are part of the prosody of speech. According to one recent investigation, tone control in speech may be more of a left-hemisphere process than tone control in singing. The investigators temporarily inactivated one hemisphere by injecting sodium amytal or a similar drug into one of the carotid arteries. Depressing right hemisphere functions disturbed the melodic aspects of singing but not tone control in speech. This has been interpreted as evidence that tone control of speech is more a left- than a right-hemisphere process, but in view of the rhythmic and tonal implications of this kind of control, it may also mean that musical functions are not exclusively right-hemisphere properties. The prosody of speech, as reflected in the accenting of certain syllables, in the sounds of words, and in the *Satzmelodie,* or melodic quality, of whole sentences is paralleled by the patterning of music as reflected in the pitch of given notes, in the sounds of chords, and in the melodic quality of the whole composition. Additional evidence that rhythm involves both hemispheres is that when the Seashore rhythm subtest was administered to patients after surgical removal of one temporal lobe the results were the same with both right and left lobectomies.

The cerebral localization of musical data is too complex a question to answer by making music a function of just one hemisphere. The large number of articles dealing with this issue date back to the 1880s and reflect three general trends: music as a right-hemisphere function, music as a left-hemisphere function, and music as a bilateral function. More clinical reports support right-hemisphere involvement than either left-hemisphere or bilateral involvement, but this does not settle the question. Possible failure to publish reports of many clinical observations bearing on this issue is suggested by two kinds of existing reports: those showing no musical disturbance despite lesions in the right hemisphere and those describing musical deficits resulting from left-hemisphere lesions. Reports of the second kind show that musical experience requires left-hemisphere participation. Thus we can definitely conclude that not all components of music are controlled by the right hemisphere.

A Digest of Current Findings

We can now see that the research material Gates and Bradshaw dealt with concerned, either directly or indirectly, these two questions: To what extent and in what ways is the perception of musical stimuli governed by lateral dominance? And What is the effect of musical training on such dominance?

Gates and Bradshaw asked this second question in connection with a series of experiments they had recently conducted. They employed both rhythmic and melodic stimuli and measured perception of these stimuli in terms of both speed and accuracy of recognition of simple changes. They found that accuracy of recognition indicated left-hemisphere superiority while speed of recognition pointed to right-hemisphere superiority. These laterality differences did not appear to reflect differences in musical sophistication. When experienced musicians were pitted against nonmusical subjects recognizing excerpts from familiar and unfamiliar melodies, musical training had no influence on the outcome. For both groups the left ear was more responsive to familiar tunes and the right ear to unfamiliar ones. Factors unrelated to musical training per se thus seem to bear on the laterality of music perception.

Another set of factors pertaining to the laterality of music as experienced was not mentioned in the Gates-Bradshaw survey but ought to be included here — emotional or affective reactions to music. Not all of these are products of musical training, nor are they entirely products of the temporal regions of the brain cortex. Some of them involve the thalamus in a rather unusual fashion. The thalamus is bilaterally symmetrical, with each half anatomically and functionally related to the opposite side of the body. Physiologically the thalamus has long been recognized as intimately related to affective consciousness. Thalamic activity is under some cortical control in that its intensity is reduced by impulses stemming from the brain cortex. Disease or injury in the region of the thalamus blocks these inhibiting cortical impulses so that thalamic activity may be intensified to a distressing degree.

Such distress from blockage or loss of cortical control has been clinically observed for many years. It is not limited to musical stimuli, but is associated with the affective tone of cutaneous and other stimulation. Among the first to call attention to the existence and nature of these disturbances of affect and feeling tone was the British neurologist Sir Henry Head (1861–1940). For example, one of his patients said he could not attend church because hymns agitated one side of his body. Another patient said his right hand needed consolation. The following excerpt from Head's clinical notes deals with thalamic injury in a man of sixty-five (1920, pp. 623–24):

> Music, of which he used to be unusually fond, is now intensely disagreeable; even favorite tunes "now work me up till I can't bear them" and excite involuntary movements to great amplitude and violence. On the day he traveled to London the noise of the railway train was so intolerable to him that he attempted to throw himself out of the train. No musical sounds are now capable of giving him pleasure.

All appreciation of temperature is abolished on the left half of the body. Ice produces an uncomfortable sensation of the affected parts, which he describes "as if something pricked me and made me jump," and the reaction is greater than from the normal side. No temperature between 10 C. and 50 C. produces any reaction.

These instances demonstrate thalamic involvement in music as an emotional experience and show that this kind of experience is subject to laterality in that the emotional reaction is localized in one side of the body. However, such affective localization is limited to cases of thalamic pathology. In individuals with an intact thalamus, emotional reactions to music are diffuse and holistic. Musical enjoyment and musical annoyance, like other emotional experiences, are never confined to one side or one region of the body in the undamaged organism. When angry or sad, we are angry or sad "all over," not in the localized way associated with lateral dominance.

In other phases of musical experience, as brought out in the Gates-Bradshaw survey, there appears to be "a pattern of laterality differences" varying with musical components. A 1955 study based upon factor analysis mentioned two such independent components: a rhythmic factor and a melodic factor. The melodic factor has often been linked to right-hemisphere dominance. However, according to a 1974 study, as rhythm and time begin to play a more important role in differentiating among tonal patterns, recognition of melodies becomes less subject to right-hemisphere dominance.

Even with reference to these factors of rhythm and melody the question of lateral dominance has no facile answer. Differences in the ways people listen to music must be considered. A listener who responds to the total pattern or "contour" of the sequence of pitches recognizes a melody differently from a listener who responds to each separate change of pitch. Similarly, sensitivity to the tonal rhythm pattern is different from recognition that depends on attention to individual beats or the duration of individual notes. The latter, it might be said, would involve left-hemisphere dominance and the former right-hemisphere dominance or mediation. Whether such hemispheric specialization holds true for ordinary listening is to be questioned, as is evident from the way Gates and Bradshaw end their review (1977, p. 423):

> In a normal music situation, perception depends on the synthesis of pitches and rhythms, and, thus, both processes are involved, not in terms of the specialization of one hemisphere "dominant" for music, but as an interaction of both hemispheres, each operating according to its own specialization, in the complex process of music perception.

This conclusion is not limited to the perception of music; it also applies to the execution of music by pianists, violinists, harpists, and others whose performance entails concurrent use of both hands. This activation of both hands in the "normal music situation" necessitates "an interaction of both hemispheres." Moreover, in playing a stringed instrument like the violin or cello more *dexterity* is involved in the left hand's fingering than in the right hand's bowing, which suggests teamwork or integrated action rather than lateral dominance. Since lateral dominance also suggests hemispheric specialization, we might ask whether and to what degree such specialization yields to nondominant integrated action. This question has important implications for views about the organization of consciousness or the nature of mind and will be dealt with in a separate chapter.

Concluding Comments

I began this chapter by calling attention to the brain's underlying asymmetries and the reversed laterality of its outward bilateral symmetry. Ordinarily we are not aware of these through introspective observation. We recognize handedness independently of these neurological facts, and its relation to the brain's asymmetries was discovered only in recent decades. Most of us are conscious of being right-handed but are not conscious of it as a product of left brain dominance. Similarly, we are cognizant of being able to talk without any awareness of language as a function of one hemisphere. Consciousness thus appears to be independent of lateral dominance, and hence the title of this chapter might seem misleading, at least to those unacquainted with the neuropsychologist's professional concerns.

From the viewpoint of the neuropsychologist it is important to study how conscious events, both sensory and motor, may be related to hemispheric specialization — the broad problem of consciousness as a function of lateral dominance. For example, music appears to be a predominantly right-hemisphere activity and language predominantly left-hemispheric. In terms of a division of labor, the left hemisphere is seen as the arena for one kind of conscious process and the right hemisphere for another kind. This bifurcation has not been restricted to language, handedness, and music. In their recent study of sex differences Seward and Seward (1980) devote a whole chapter to cerebral asymmetry, citing some forty studies concerned with its relation to gender. They focus on cognitive style, or the degree to which males are analytic in their approach to problems while females are more global. Although the evidence is inconclusive, they believe it suggests "that a difference in cerebral asymmetry may prove to be partly responsible for a sex difference in cognitive style" (p. 71). This hints at right-brain dominance as feminine and left-brain dominance as masculine.

Cognitive style governs a good deal of our polarized thinking as we react to events as good or bad, logical or illogical, clean or dirty, radical or conservative, or — in general — *x* rather than *y*. The radical/conservative antithesis brings to mind the left/right or bicameral organization of our legislatures. This raises an interesting question: Does attributing one set of conscious processes to the left hemisphere and a different set to the right hemisphere mean that consciousness is bicameral? This seems to cast doubt on the doctrine of mind or consciousness as integrated and to endow us with two minds — a left-hemisphere analytic mind and a right-hemisphere global mind. Whether this striking possibility is more mythical[14] than factual is far from settled. The issues involved are very complex, and much of the evidence cited is persuasive rather than coercive, often clouded by contradictions. Evaluating this evidence will prove challenging.

References

Bever, T. G., and Chiarello, H. J. 1974. Cerebral dominance in musicians and nonmusicians. *Science* 185:137–39.

Bogen, J. E. 1973. The other side of the brain: An appositional mind. In *The nature of human consciousness,* ed. R. E. Ornstein, 101–25. San Francisco: W. H. Freeman.

Bower, T. G. R. 1977. *A primer of infant development.* San Francisco: W. H. Freeman.

Corballis, M. C. 1980. Laterality and myth. *American Psychologist* 35:284–95.

Dennis, W. 1935. Laterality of function in early infancy under controlled developmental conditions. *Child Development* 6:242–52.

Deutsch, D. 1969. Music recognition. *Psychological Review* 76:300–307.

———. 1978. Pitch memory: An advantage for the left-handed. *Science* 199:559–60.

Galaburda, A. M.; Le May, M.; Kemper, T. L.; and Geschwind, N. 1978. Right-left asymmetries in the brain: Structural differences between the hemispheres may underlie cerebral dominance. *Science* 199:852–56.

Gates, A., and Bradshaw, J. L. 1977. The role of the cerebral hemispheres in music. *Brain and Language* 4:403–31.

Geschwind, N. 1972. Language and the brain. *Scientific American* (April), 76–83.

Gordon, H. W. 1975. Hemispheric asymmetry and musical performance. *Science* 189:68–69.

Guyton, A. C. 1976. *Textbook of medical physiology.* 5th ed. Philadelphia: W. B. Saunders.

14. The word *myth* is used advisedly in this context. In a recent article entitled "Laterality and Myth" Corballis (1980) has presented an informative and insightful survey of ancient and contemporary beliefs concerning the brain's duality. In his wide-ranging survey he cites from the Bible, folklore, anthropology, neurology, animal studies, psychology, and neurosurgery. In general he urges a "biological approach to laterality" as a safeguard against uncritical acceptance of alluring beliefs or myths.

Head, H. 1920. *Studies in neurology.* Vol. 2. New York: Oxford University Press.

Hicks, R. E., and Kinsbourne, M. 1976. Human handedness: A partial cross-fostering study. *Science* 192:908–10.

Holden, C. 1980. Twins reunited. *Science* 80:54–59.

Kimura, D. 1973. The asymmetry of the human brain. *Scientific American* (March), 70–78.

Koch, H. 1966. *Twins and twin relations.* Chicago: University of Chicago Press.

Liddell, H. 1950. The role of vigilance in the development of animal neurosis. In *Anxiety,* ed. P. H. Hoch and J. Zubin, 183–96. New York: Grune and Stratton.

Luria, A. R. 1973. *The working brain: An introduction to neuropsychology.* New York: Basic Books.

McGurk, H., and Lewis, M. 1974. Space perception in early infancy: Perception within a common auditory-visual space? *Science* 186:649–50.

Seward, J. P., and Seward, G. H. 1980. *Sex differences: Mental and temperamental.* Lexington: D. C. Heath.

Teng, E. L.; Lee, P.-H.; Yang, K.; and Chang, P. C. 1976. Handedness in a Chinese population: Biological, social, and pathological factors. *Science* 193:1148–50.

Wertheimer, M. 1961. Psychomotor coordination of auditory and visual space at birth. *Science* 134:1692.

Wightman, F. L., and Green, D. M. 1974. The perception of pitch. *American Scientist* 62:208–15.

Woodworth, R. S. 1939. Autobiography. In *Psychological issues,* 3–25. New York: Columbia University Press.

8 / Is Consciousness Bicameral?

*T*his chapter will elaborate on the central theme of the previous one, presuming that consciousness is related to lateral dominance. Despite outward bilateral symmetry, histological measurement has revealed hemispheric asymmetries, which, along with other evidence, suggest differences in function. This other evidence suggests that handedness, language, and logical analysis are functions of the dominant hemisphere while emotionality and aesthetics, manifested in music and art, are functions of the nondominant one. Each hemisphere thus seems to be a clearinghouse for different conscious processes. If so, then such hemispheric specialization implies a splitting of consciousness and duality of mind—two kinds of consciousness or two kinds of mental life, one for each hemisphere. However, such bifurcation of brain and mind is at variance with traditional neurological and psychological teachings that stress integration as a basic principle.

Integration in Neurological Perspective

We may be quite confident that when the layman first examines a fragment of brain tissue under a microscope he will see a chaotic tangle of interlacing fibers. He might even wonder whether such a tangle can be related to the nervous system, since *system* refers to an ordered arrangement of elements forming an organized whole. Our perplexed observer might turn to a textbook of neurology. There he would learn that the massed brain fibers are not the basic constituent elements of the system. Instead the fibers are outgrowths of nerve cells and glial cells, and the nerve cells, or neurons, constitute the fundamental units of the nervous system. As he reads on he learns that the brain contains ten billion neurons enmeshed within fifty billion or more glial cells, nonnervous supporting elements that act as a kind of sticky lattice. (*Glial* is derived from the Greek word for glue.) In addition these glial or neuroglial cells may serve the metabolic functions of providing nutrients and destroying waste products by phagocytosis. There is some question about the precise nature of these functions, but there is no question about their clinical importance, since brain tumors are glial tumors.

Our unsophisticated observer might despair as he tries to conceive of sixty billion cellular units forming a system in his skull. This is far more than the number of people in the world, which he can at least classify by country, race, social class, occupation, religion, and so on. As he continues his neurological study he will begin to cope with the myriad brain units by localizing them in different lobes of the brain, in certain horizontal levels of the cortex, and in a vast array of fiber tracts. He will begin to perceive these tracts as connecting parts of the brain with other parts as well as with different segments of all subcortical structures from the brainstem down to the spinal cord.

Before long he will think of tracts as transmitting agents for neural impulses, linking different levels of the nervous system from the brain down to the spinal cord and from the spinal cord up to the brain. These vertical or *projection* tracts will come to be differentiated from the horizontal or *association* fibers that connect each part of one hemisphere with every other part of it. Then he will learn about the *commissural* fibers that connect the two hemispheres, in particular the *corpus callosum,* along with two subordinate commissural structures. These structures permit reciprocal interhemispheric communication, and their severance has a direct bearing on bicameral consciousness. An intact corpus callosum and an undamaged cerebrum therefore ought to assure a unicameral mind, since an intact or healthy brain promotes unity of mind and consciousness. Accordingly, integration appears to be a regulative function of the brain.

The myriad projective, associative, and commissural fibers connect every cortical and subcortical area with every other one either directly or indirectly, suggesting a neural foundation for integrated behavior. Recall the close reciprocal interaction between brain and thalamus, with efferent tracts from cortex to thalamus and afferent tracts from thalamus to cortex. This anatomical arrangement has a direct bearing on sensory awareness, because every sensory nerve except the olfactory passes through the thalamus before reaching its cortical terminus. Thus the cortex and thalamus are of coordinate influence in the neurophysiology of consciousness and are sometimes described as the *thalamocortical system.* This description exemplifies the integrative connotation of the word *system,* especially in allusions to the nervous *system* per se.

The integrative function of neural action was brought to the attention of neuropsychologists early in the century by Sir Charles Sherrington (1857–1952), particularly in his classic volume *The Integrative Action of the*

Nervous System, published in 1906 and based on a series of lectures delivered at Yale University the year before. Psychologists of the time assimilated Sherrington's key ideas and passed them on to subsequent generations of psychologists. Now many of these ideas are enshrined in psychology textbooks, though their origin in Sherrington's work has been forgotten. Sherrington coined the terms *extroceptive, interoceptive,* and *proprioceptive* to describe basic characteristics of our sense organs. He first appreciated the dynamic implications of the concepts of the synapse and reciprocal innervation, and he posited that every posterior spinal nerve root refers to a definite segment of skin. Still another of his outstanding findings, based upon his intensive investigation of reflex action, replaced the notion of a reflex as an isolated segmental mechanism with the concept of interrelated or coordinated reflex units serving the integrative function of the nervous system. Living creatures as *organisms* are not just collections of autonomous cells or organs, as Sherrington trenchantly pointed out (1947, p. 2):

In the multicellular animal, especially for those higher reactions which constitute its behavior as a social unit in the natural economy, it is nervous reaction which *par excellence* integrates it, welds it together from its components, and constitutes it from a mere collection of organs an animal individual.

This integrating function of "nervous reaction" was later elaborated upon by Wilder Penfield on the basis of his experience as a brain surgeon. In one of his books he refers to this reaction as *centrencephalic integration.*[1] This term, he explained, is intended to indicate that the coordination of neural processes is not an exclusive cortical function but also involves a subcortical area concerned with convergence of nerve impulses and with "neural circuits in which activity of both hemispheres is somehow summarized and fused—circuits the activation of which makes conscious planning possible" and which "serve the purposes of inter-hemispheral and intra-hemispheral integration" (Penfield and Roberts 1959, pp. 20–21). Penfield associated such integration with the diencephalon and thus with the thalamocortical system. Since all sensory nerves except the olfactory pass through the thalamus, this brain area might readily accommodate Penfield's enlarged concept of neural convergence or sensory integration.

There were a few more distinctively psychological approaches to this problem during the 1950s, when men like Halstead, Hebb, and Lashley

[1]. This term was introduced in chapter 2 of Penfield and Roberts (1959, pp. 20–22; the chapter was written by Penfield). It is also explained and defended in Penfield (1975, pp. 44–45). Somewhat later Eccles wrote about the term in Popper and Eccles (1977) and concluded that the centrencephalic integrative process "may be a necessary, but is not a sufficient condition for consciousness" (p. 330).

were writing on such topics as brain and intelligence, the frontal lobes and learning, and thinking as affected by minimal brain damage. A critical review of these approaches was published by Alan Ross in an ambitious article covering more than one hundred references. As a psychologist, Ross agreed with Penfield, the neurosurgeon, that integration is "the basic cerebral function" and that "brain damage to any area" is apt "to disrupt optimal integration" (1955, p. 197). This implies that integration may be conceived of as a psychoneural process.

Integration in Psychological Perspective

Just as neurologists regard integration as a basic function of the brain, psychiatrists appear to regard it as a basic function of mind. They equate optimal mental health with optimal personality integration and poor mental health with disintegration as evidenced by disorientation, delirium, delusions, obsessive ideation, manic behavior, and so on. They perceive their patients as disorganized in thought and feeling—victims of confused thinking, conflicting desires, and clouding of consciousness. Such confusion, conflict, and clouding amount to perplexity about appropriate courses of action; hence the maladaptive and irrational behavior so common among psychiatric patients. Such patients are sometimes said to be out of their minds; but they are never said to be out of their consciousness. Everybody recognizes that loss of mind is very different from loss of consciousness in dreamless sleep.

In dreamless sleep we are unconscious in not knowing what is taking place around us or inside our bodies. James referred to this kind of knowing when he denied the existence of consciousness as an entity. He pointed out that thoughts "do exist" and that *consciousness* "does stand for a function," namely, "a function in experience" performed by thoughts; then he concluded, "That function is *knowing*."

James's stand is supported by the derivation of the word *conscious*—from *com*, "with," and *scire*, "to know" or "to be informed." This root meaning implies that to be conscious means to be informed of something—whether a noise, an odor, or anything else, factual or emotional. As Guilford once pointed out, even "feelings and emotions may be regarded as varieties of information" (1962, p. 9). As a process, consciousness constitutes a transitive relation. One is conscious *of* objects and bodily conditions. As Guilford also noted, "psychologically, an individual is an information-processing agent" (1974, p. 88).[2] The processing requires integration

2. Guilford has carefully worked out a system of informational psychology based upon a long series of factor-analytic investigations. The resulting *structure of intellect model,*

of items of information being experienced. Thus a child's emerging consciousness of the concept of *orange* implies the perceptual organization of sensory information about color, shape, texture, taste, and fragrance. Similarly, reasoning or daydreaming as a conscious process entails mobilizing and integrating relevant information. Informed minds are more conscious than uninformed minds.

From this informational perspective consciousness in the abstract ceases to be a meaningless or mysterious state of bare sensitivity. Instead, as James noted, in place of a nonexistent abstract consciousness there are images, thoughts, feelings, percepts, and other products of receptor stimulation traditionally classified as conscious contents but now regarded as items of information. Thus our feelings of fatigue, excitement, grief, confidence, helplessness, boredom, calmness, and apprehension are informing us of our organic condition and our readiness for action. Learning to control gastric contractions or blood pressure by biofeedback techniques can be seen as becoming informed of hitherto unnoticed autonomic events — becoming conscious of what had been unconscious. Information has replaced ignorance.

Equating consciousness with information dissipates the mystery associated with consciousness seen as an entity. This mystery is frequently associated with so-called altered states of consciousness caused by hypnosis, meditation, Zen rituals, or LSD and other psychedelic drugs. But if we regard these states as providing different kinds of information, they are less likely to seem like esoteric transformations of some mystical stuff called consciousness.[3] By such an interpretation, the concept of consciousness remains embedded in a cognitive psychology.

James alluded to such embeddedness when he recognized *knowing* as the function of consciousness, for how we come to know things is the chief concern of cognitive psychology. This concern with cognition dates back to psychology's heritage in philosophy, particularly the theory of knowledge, or epistemology. As a separate branch of philosophy epistemology might be said to spring from the opening sentence of Aristotle's *Metaphysics:* "All men by nature desire to know." This makes the quest for knowledge an inherent characteristic of human nature, reflected in man's attempt to understand whatever chances to arouse his curiosity. Since this involves finding out how things are related or put together, it is an *inte-*

---

summarized in Guilford (1974), brings together and integrates many of the traditional systems of psychology, recognizing the tremendous number of ways information is utilized in cognitive operations. As Guilford brought out in another article, there is even provision for the execution of intentions and "initiation and management of motor responses" (1972, p. 279). In short, Guilford's man of intellect is a doer as well as a thinker.

3. The altered states of consciousness described by Pelletier and Garfield (1976) seem less esoteric when they are regarded as different kinds of information.

grating quest — a quest for organization and relationships — hence a quest for meaning.

This brings up a basic principle mentioned by David Rapaport in his *Organization and Pathology of Thought*. Rapaport cites an article by the Prague psychiatrist Arnold Pick (1851–1924), who calls the principle *Bowden's[4] principle* and defines it as follows (1951, p. 665): "*The mind tends to order all the material presented to it, however disorganized, so as to make it meaningful*" (italics added).

This makes the search for meaning an integrating principle. Being basic, it is reflected directly or indirectly in influential psychological systems, particularly those that stress the unity of mind and consciousness. Chapter 2 introduced some of these systems — Brentano's intentionalism, James's radical empiricism, and Stern's unity of the person. The principle is also reflected in Gestalt psychology's law of *Prägnanz*, or *precision*, which holds that experience tends to be organized into perceptual patterns that are as simple, symmetrical, and meaningful as circumstances permit. This is supplemented by the Gestalt law of *closure*, according to which a word printed in broken type is perceived as complete and interrupted undertakings tend to be brought to a conclusion. These integrating laws highlight the importance of meaningful perception for thinking in general and problem solving in particular. This recognition is not unique to Gestalt psychology. It is implicit in what psychoanalytic psychology attributes to the synthetic function of the ego and in what functional psychology taught about consciousness as a means of control in coping with difficult or novel situations. Control comes with understanding, perceptual clarity, and practice so that there is a transition from conscious confrontation with a problem to less conscious habitual reactions and then to nonconscious automatism.

This functionalist thesis is as much neurological as psychological. The neurologist Henry Head wrote, "Behind every conscious act lie many integrations most of which take place on a purely physiological level" (1926, p. 533), echoing Sherrington's classic lectures on the nervous system and integrative action. Thus the psychological perspective of this section is congruent with the earlier neurological perspective; what Bowden said about the mind can also be said about the brain. There would be no distortion of his thought were his principle paraphrased to read that the brain tends to order all information presented to it, however disorganized, so as to make it meaningful and subject to control.

Precisely how the brain orders information has troubled both neurolo-

---

4. Despite searching various reference works, I have been able to learn nothing about Bowden. Rapaport seems to have assumed his readers would be familiar with Bowden, for he mentions only the surname.

gists and psychologists. The previous chapter asked about lateral dominance and control of language, music, and other conscious events, and this chapter asks whether right and left hemispheres process different kinds of information and thus give rise to a bicameral consciousness. To answer, we must consider lateral differences and, more important, the cerebral localization of the myriad items of information experienced as distinct modes of consciousness.

Cerebral Localization Reconsidered

There is no question but that consciousness is a function of brain activity, yet the precise nature of this relation continues to be questioned, particularly specialization within brain areas, or cerebral localization. The problem dates back to the early 1800s[5] when phrenologists assigned specific mental faculties to given brain segments subjacent to variations in skull contour. Personality diagnosis according to skull convexities and concavities was taken seriously. Phrenologists believed that each of the thirty or more faculties into which they divided the mind had a fixed locus in brain tissue. In the words of F. J. Gall (1758–1828), a leading phrenologist, "the brain is composed of as many particular and independent organs as there are fundamental powers of the mind" (1965, p. 219). The power or faculty of counting, for example, was placed in the frontal region, while the faculty of amativeness was linked to the occipital region. In principle Gall held that each faculty as a unit of conscious experience was linked to a specific unit of cortical tissue, thus advocating extreme localization. Psychologists soon rejected this view of mental faculties, just as neurologists questioned the functions attributed to these brain areas, and the scientific community came to stigmatize phrenology as a pseudoscience.

A more scientific approach to localization was introduced by Pierre Flourens (1794–1867). Unlike the phrenologists, he proceeded experimentally, noting the effects on animal behavior of surgical removal of anatomically distinct cerebral organs such as the cerebellum or the corpora quadrigemina. He worked on the brains of various animals including pigeons, rabbits, and chickens. Perhaps as a reaction against phrenology, he stressed the unity of brain action, positing that each segment of brain tissue, irrespective of its unique function, also exercises a function common

---

5. Actually it dates back centuries further. Boring says that both Pythagoras and Plato regarded "the brain as the seat of the mind and the intellect" in opposition to Aristotle, who centered mental life in the heart. To some extent this view was also reflected in the teaching of Galen (ca. A.D. 129–99) "that the animal spirits flow from the brain ventricles to the heart, and are thence distributed to the body by the arteries" (Boring 1950, p. 50).

to the brain as a whole. Thus he recognized that the unique or proper function of the cerebellum is to control muscular coordination and that its common function is to activate the entire nervous system. He appears to have anticipated current surgical "split-brain" studies. This excerpt from one of his reports has a modern flavor (1974, p. 237):

> I split a hen's right cerebral lobe lengthwise; sight was immediately lost in the left eye.
>
> However, the animal saw very well with the right eye; it heard, oriented itself, and found its food in the usual way. . . .
>
> I then removed the left cerebral lobe; the animal continued to hear, to orient itself, and to feed itself, to all appearances, just as before; with the sole difference that it could no longer see except with the eye which it had first lost.

This also illustrates the way Flourens noted both the local or unique results of brain surgery and the effects on the rest of the brain. Karl Lashley echoed this twofold emphasis close to a hundred years later, independently of Flourens, in his famous theories of equipotentiality and mass action. The latter theory held that the effect of surgical destruction of brain tissue on animal behavior such as maze performance depends more on the amount of tissue destroyed than on the precise locality. Lashley was not denying functional localization, as was sometimes thought. Instead, he showed that maze learning was not localized in a sharply circumscribed segment of cortical tissue. Similarly, his principle of equipotentiality held that functions attributed to a given brain area were not minutely localized and that one group of cells within the area could function in place of other cells, making the groups equipotential so that localization was fluid rather than fixed. Just as Flourens had argued for unity of brain action, Lashley argued for neural integration. In summarizing the results of his many studies of brain injury he wrote, "The mechanisms of integration are to be sought in the dynamic relations among the parts of the nervous system rather than in details of structural differentiation" (1929, p. 176). Thus in view of the constant flux of neural currents precision of localization is not to be expected, though one might expect some localization of an imprecise or shifting nature.[6]

Broca's own account of the brain region now identified as Broca's area

6. In commenting on a paper by Libet at a conference, Penfield called attention to an example of such shifting in connection with his discussion of the "stream of consciousness electrically reactivated" (1975, pp. 21–30). What he describes as memory "flashbacks" shifted from case to case. In one case, for example, thirty repetitions of electrical stimulation of the same cortical point elicited the same memory flashback. "In other cases, different 'flashbacks' might be produced from successive stimulations of the same point" (p. 22). Verbatim accounts of such electrically provoked experiences are to be found in Penfield and Roberts (1959, pp. 50–54).

also describes imprecise boundaries. When his famous case of motor aphasia came to autopsy, far more than loss of speech had occurred. The patient lost his speech at age thirty and died at fifty-one. Speech never returned, and there were additional neurological changes during the intervening twenty-one years. By age forty, the arm and leg on the right side were paralyzed, but those on the left could be moved despite some weakness. Later there was diminished cutaneous sensitivity on the right along with some visual difficulty. Because of such changes Broca was unable to determine the exact nature of the original brain lesion. As shown in Broca's report, pathology was not restricted to the brain area now called by his name (Broca 1965, p. 228): "Anatomical inspection shows us that the lesion was still progressing when the patient died. The lesion was therefore progressive, but it progressed very slowly, taking twenty-one years to destroy a quite limited part of the brain."

Whether speech is limited to this part of the brain, as Broca taught, has been questioned. In the words of Rosenblueth, "the initial assumption of localization which was implied when Broca's area was designated as the speech center should be relinquished" (1970, p. 37). Rosenblueth noted that other brain areas are involved, as becomes evident in the way areas governing vision and voluntary movement are engaged in reading aloud. He also mentioned the need for more critical attention to the concept of localization with reference to voluntary movement. Ordinarily we assume that voluntary movement is a consequence of activation of the motor area in the precentral gyrus; but, as he sees it, this is not a tenable assumption because what is experienced when the area is electrically stimulated differs from comparable voluntary experiences. In the former experience the movements resemble voluntary ones, but the subject is aware that they are extraneously imposed, not voluntarily executed. There is an absence of the "mental concomitant of volition" associated with intentional behavior. Consequently the motor area per se does not account for voluntary movement. Other centers must be activated.

This is not to say that volition is localized in these other centers. Neither volition nor any other psychological process is to be conceived of as having its own fixed abode in some brain center. Broca's area is not literally the residence or seat of one's knowledge of spoken French, English, or other language. Ladd and Woodworth warned against such mistaken literal interpretations of localization, saying that all such expressions as "resides in," "seat," "localization," and kindred terms *must be understood only as involving a convenient figure of speech*" (1911, p. 215; italics added).

This brings up an important but neglected point about the localization of sensory impressions. Sights, fragrances, sounds, and such are experienced as external to, not within, the brain, as are cutaneous experiences. The pain of a wounded finger is localized in the finger, just as the cold of an icy shower is diffused over the skin surface. The sensation of roughness is localized not in a brain center but in the tip of the exploring finger or perhaps the tip of a cane scraping gravel. It thus appears that afferent neural impulses do not rest in some terminal cortical habitat but are projected to the periphery in the case of contact receptors and to external surroundings in the case of distance receptors. In this sense consciousness is localized not in the brain but in these projected places or spaces.

If consciousness is not localized in the brain, what is occurring there? What is meant by cerebral localization? There is no simple answer. Let us take a seemingly simple instance of sensory localization such as a negative afterimage as a paradigm of the problem. An observer who stares at a bright red patch for a minute or so and then focuses upon a white surface will report seeing a green patch, the negative afterimage, localized on the white surface. It is a private experience not shared by others who glance at the same surface, hence its imaginal status. But does calling it an image mean that the visual experience per se is localized in the brain? Not as a private experience, for it is sensed out on the white surface. However, its status as a conscious phenomenon depends on an intact retina, optic nerve fibers, and terminal occipital tissue. Without them there can be no afterimage, but the image as *image* is not present in them as a visually sensed impression. At best one might say that neural changes *processed* there give rise to the impression, an imprecise formulation intended to provide a serviceable description of cerebral localization. Thus in terms of the afterimage paradigm the visual impression as *sensed* is extracerebral while the neural *processes* are intracerebral.

This distinction between extracerebral sensing and intracerebral processing is another way of expressing cognizance of our thoughts and surroundings as contrasted with our lack of awareness of concomitant brain events, the same distinction made in chapter 7 regarding lateral dominance. We never have introspective confirmation of lateral dominance and are never conscious of such dominance as we are conscious of noise, lights, pains, and other sensory events. The dominance is intracerebral, while the sensory events are extracerebral.

Extracerebral as applied to sensory events does not mean independent of cerebral involvement. Obviously these events entail activation of optic, olfactory, auditory, and other sensory nerves. Each of these nerves terminates in its own brain area, but the resultant sensory impression is never experienced as taking place within the brain. Instead, the impressions as neural events are projected to the source of stimulation as psychological events. This projection has nothing to do with neural tracts known as projection tracts, which connect the different vertical levels of the central nervous system. It concerns associating what is being sensed with the "cause" of the sensation. Such associating as a brain process is not conscious. What is taking place has been well summarized by Ruch et al. in a passage on "somatic sensation" in their *Neurophysiology* (1965, p. 315):

> The ultimate event in the sensory process occurs in the brain, but in no case are we aware of this. On the contrary, our sensations are projected either to the external world or to some peripheral organ in the body, i.e., to the place where experience has taught us that the acting stimulus arises. Sound seems to come from the bell, light from the lamp, etc. Pain, muscle sense, labyrinthine sensations, hunger, thirst, sexual sense, etc. are projected to the interior of the body. The temperature senses may be projected either to the air or to the skin, according to circumstances.

This extracerebral projection or localization also applies to every other conscious process. Our plans, recollections, intentions, anxieties, and hopes are not experienced as brain events when they occur; they are experienced as external to the brain, not as taking place within the brain tissue. In this sense mind qua mind is extracerebral, which explains why Aristotle failed to regard the brain as the organ of mind. Presumably he never experienced his giant intellect as localized within his skull. Apart from interludes of neurological speculation, modern man also is unaware of the brain's involvement in what he chances to be conscious of. When he thinks of himself as right-handed, he is not aware of being left-brained. Until introduced to brain anatomy, he remains ignorant of the existence of left and right brains, and even then he will not experience mental events as emanating from one side of his head or the other, even if he knows about "split-brain" patients.

The Split-Brain Story

The two brain hemispheres are bridged by the corpus callosum. For a long time the function of this thick bundle of commissural fibers remained undetermined. According to Sperry, as recently as 1951 Karl Lashley hazarded a tongue-in-cheek guess that its chief purpose was to prevent "the hemispheres from sagging" (Sperry 1968, p. 60). There was a sound reason for regarding the corpus callosum as an inert structure, since surgical severance of the linkage between the hemispheres in animals failed to cause any significant change in behavior. After monkeys recovered from split-brain surgery they appeared to be normal; hence uncertainty regarding the function of the corpus callosum.[7]

7. This uncertainty, as Geschwind brought out (1975), was not as prevalent among German brain specialists shortly after the turn of the century, who were familiar with "a series of remarkable papers" by the neurologist Hugo Liepmann, the first to describe disabilities

Even after special testing appeared to have established such a function, a question was raised about the need for a corpus callosum by the chance discovery of healthy individuals whose brains lacked this structure. Sperry was able to examine such a case, a nine-year-old boy who, despite lacking a corpus callosum, displayed "almost none of the impairments" that special testing had shown to characterize split-brain patients. It seemed that the congenital absence of a corpus callosum resulted in compensatory development within each hemisphere of functions ordinarily attributed to the opposite hemisphere. Thus language centers were no longer restricted to the left nor music centers to the right hemisphere, and there was a high degree of ambidexterity. In cases of this kind, with all functions equally under control of each half of the brain, one might say that each hemisphere is a whole brain, not just half a brain. But such cases are extremely rare, and most of those mentioned in the older medical writings were not subjected to the kind of tests later introduced in split-brain studies, so there is no way of knowing how they would have reacted to these refined procedures. We cannot regard the corpus callosum as a vestigial organ like the vermiform appendix.

There no longer is any question that behavioral changes result from split-brain surgery—they can be detected by special tests. This kind of surgery was first employed in animal experimentation; only later was it introduced as a therapeutic procedure for carefully selected human patients whose severe epileptic convulsions could not be controlled by conventional treatment. Surgery produced dramatic improvement; attacks were ended or significantly reduced in frequency. When patients recovered from the operation their everyday behavior appeared altogether normal to the casual observer, with no evidence of severed brain hemispheres. The patients themselves mentioned no changes in feeling or ideation that indicated such severance. Nevertheless, special testing procedures showed that split-brain behavior is not normal behavior. When the two hemispheres were examined unilaterally, significant differences were brought to light.

Unilateral Hemispheric Testing

Decussation of sensory and motor nerves renders it possible to test hemispheric involvement separately. For example, looking at items in the left

---

resulting from damage to the corpus callosum. He gave special recognition to the loss of control of ordinary acquired muscular skills—skills like kicking a ball, hammering a nail, or using a toothbrush. Liepmann introduced the word *apraxia* to designate this loss of ability to control or manipulate common objects. His conclusions were based not upon split-brain studies, which were introduced years later in this country, but upon clinical observations of motor disabilities and subsequent findings of corpus callosum pathology.

visual field involves the right occipital area and vice versa. The muscles of the left hand are controlled by the right precentral gyrus, and the corresponding left gyrus governs those of the right hand. Ordinarily, with all commissural links intact there is ready interchange of hemispheric data, but severing the corpus callosum and the lesser commissural fibers eliminates such interhemispheric communication.

When right and left visual fields are concurrently stimulated after such elimination, there is no interchange of information. If a word like *armband* is exposed so that *arm* is projected to the right occipital area and *band* to the left area, the patient will not perceive the word as a whole. Since speech is under left hemispheric control, he will report seeing the word *band*. When asked what kind of band, he will not mention the word *arm*. As a right-hemisphere experience, there is no spontaneous manifestation of its existence. But, though cut off from vocal expression, the word can be written. When such a patient's left hand was concealed from his view by a screen, he succeeded in writing the word *arm*.

The written word could not be seen, so the vocal left hemisphere was kept ignorant of what the right hemisphere could write but not pronounce because the surgical severance of the commissural structures prevented the word written by the nondominant right hemisphere from being communicated to the left hemisphere. Whether this means elimination of *all* interhemispheric communication is questionable, for there is some transfer of emotional experience from the nondominant to the dominant hemisphere. As reported by Eccles,[8] this was demonstrated by presenting to a patient's right visual area, through the left visual field, a picture of a nude woman. This precipitated blushing and other signs of embarrassment for which the patient was unable to supply a reason, but which Eccles thought might be due to "cross-communication . . . effected through subcortical structures such as the superior colliculus, thalamus, hypothalamus and basal ganglia whose commissural connections remain intact" (Popper and Eccles 1977, p. 321). Eccles was thus attributing the cross-communication to intact brainstem connections.

Transfer of emotion from one hemisphere to the other also came to light in the course of olfactory testing. Unlike all the other sensory nerves, the olfactory nerve is entirely ipsilateral. Since there is no contralateral decus-

---

8. Eccles was reporting not one of his own studies, but a study done at California Institute of Technology by Sperry and Gazzaniga. His description of the subcortical structures as intact commissural connections is based upon Sperry's recognition of their role. In one of his accounts of this emotional arousal Sperry mentioned that the left or language hemisphere experienced the right hemisphere's emotion but had no idea what had precipitated the emotion. As Sperry explained it: "Apparently, only the emotional effect gets across, as if the cognitive component of the process cannot be articulated through the brainstem" (1968, p. 732).

sation, it is possible to transmit odors to one hemisphere by an olfactometer without involving the opposite hemisphere. Odors presented to the right nostril activate the right hemisphere's olfactory area, but they are neither named nor described. Nevertheless, as shown in one test, their emotional impact may give rise to the left hemisphere's ohs, ahs, grunts, or other vocal expressions. In response to a putrid odor the patient might make a sound like "pfui!" but be unable to specify whether he is smelling rancid butter, limburger cheese, a rotten egg, manure, or decomposed garbage. The unpleasantness experienced by the right hemisphere is transmitted to the left hemisphere, but the cause is not transmitted. That the cause is known by the right hemisphere can be demonstrated by having the concealed left hand select appropriate objects. Thus a cube of butter might be chosen from a group of other objects. Since in this case the right hemisphere possesses information not at the disposal of the opposite hemisphere, active utilization of information as a cognitive process is not to be regarded as belonging exclusively to the left hemisphere.[9]

Furthermore, emotional sensitivity is not exclusively a right-hemisphere process, even though some investigators have so regarded it. Sackeim, Gur, and Saucy (1978) found emotions to be expressed more intensely on the left side of the face and interpreted this as indicating hemispheric asymmetry. This suggests right-hemisphere dominance in emotional expression but not an emotionless left hemisphere, since the right side of the face was not expressionless.

Although both hemispheres are involved in emotion, they differ in ways other than intensity. According to one study, deactivating the left brain with sodium amytal results in "depressive" emotions, while "euphoric" emotions follow right-hemisphere deactivation. In another study horror films were presented to each hemisphere separately. There were no "euphoric" reports; all reports were of unpleasantness, with those seen by the right brain judged more unpleasant.

Both hemispheres participate in emotional processes, and both also participate in language processes, though the left hemisphere is frequently designated as the verbal brain while by implication the speechless right hemisphere is deemed nonverbal. Such a conclusion is now known to be unwarranted. This was demonstrated by having a split-brain subject put his left hand into an enclosure containing a hidden assortment of objects

9. Whether each hemisphere processes distinctive classes of cognitive material is a separate question. On a priori grounds some writers hold that thinking that directly depends on language must be left-hemisphere cognition while nonverbal thinking means right-hemisphere cognition. In this computer age it has even been suggested that verbal thinking indicates digital versus nonverbal or analogic codification. Bogen has surveyed a variety of other cognitive dichotomies and refers to them as "two different ways of thinking" (p. 101), suggestive of mind's duality and cerebral lateralization.

and try to find a specific thing. When he was asked to "find a piece of silverware," his left hand would soon locate a spoon. The meaning of the request was thus definitely understood by the right hemisphere; but the left hemisphere, having heard the same request, could not name what had been found. When asked, the subject would hazard a guess like "fork" or "knife." In the absence of an intact commissure the right brain's knowledge of the word *spoon* could not be communicated to the left brain. Although speechless, the right brain was not wordless. Nor was it thoughtless, since the left hand selected a concrete object—a spoon—upon hearing the abstract noun *silverware*.

Right-brain competence was demonstrated in another test involving left-hand control. Split-brain patients were asked to copy simple designs like a cube or the outline of a house. In one case described by Gazzaniga a right-handed patient was able to make recognizable copies of the figures with his left hand but not with his right hand. In one instance when using his right hand he wrote the phrase "with my right hand" (1967, p. 98) in cursive script. The individual letters were clearly written, showing no left-brain impairment of right-hand control of the writing itself, but when he tried to copy the figures they were unrecognizable. Since he could write clearly, the difficulty was not due to muscular damage to the right hand; it was central rather than peripheral. Unlike the right hemisphere, the left hemisphere apparently could not grasp the spatial distinctiveness of each figure. Although it could deal with a sequence of letters and words in writing a phrase, it could not deal with copying the three-dimensional picture of a cube.

It thus appeared that the left hemisphere was specializing in sequential processing and the right hemisphere in areal or spatial processing, as in the difference between describing a scene verbally by *successively* enumerating its features and presenting these features *simultaneously* in a picture. The verbal description is spread out in time whereas the pictorial one is compressed within a definite space. In terms of learning theory the two descriptions reflect the conflict between the serial or sequential implications of classical associationism and the holistic implications of Gestalt psychology. According to current doctrine, the sequential nature of associationism suggests left-brain activation while the holistic or simultaneous nature of Gestaltism indicates right-brain activation. These split-brain studies thus might shed light on the clash between rival systems of psychology and also on computer rivalries. As Carl Sagan pointed out, it appears that the right hemisphere "works" in parallel and the left in series, so that the latter "is something like a digital computer" and "the right like an analog computer" (1977, p. 169).

Bogen (1973) made a striking interpretation of these split-brain findings. Since each hemisphere performs given mental processes in distinctive ways it seemed to him that each half of the brain had a mind of its own—the brain's duality suggested the mind's duality, and the split brain implied a split mind. He wrote, "Pending further evidence, I believe . . . that each of us has two minds in one person" (p. 117). Taken literally, this makes us all schizophrenic and challenges the neurologist's view of the nervous system as integrated as well as the psychiatrist's belief in personality integration as the sine qua non of mental health. It also appears to endorse a bicameral consciousness by attributing one array of mental processes to one hemisphere and a different array to the opposite hemisphere.

These different interpretations of the results of unilateral hemispheric testing generally suggest bicameral differentiation. Directly or indirectly, they appear to regard both mind and brain as dichotomous, as if cleavage of the brain reveals a cleavage of consciousness. In other words, this challenging dichotomy comes close to endowing each hemisphere with its own psychology.

Brain and Mind as Dichotomous

The widespread publicity given to split-brain studies has made it not at all unusual for people to include references to hemispheric specialization in their casual conversation. They may confidently assert that an artistic friend is "right-brained" as contrasted with a "left-brained" mathematical friend, thus assigning different kinds of knowledge or different modes of thinking to each hemisphere in a relative, if not an absolute, dichotomy. Everyday descriptions of people as right-handed or left-handed illustrate a relative dichotomy. A right-handed pitcher always throws the ball with his right arm, but he can throw with his left arm, though the pitch will be awkward and poorly executed. Similarly, though language is predominantly a left-hemisphere function, the right hemisphere is not altogether nonverbal. The predominance is relative, not absolute. It is in this sense that mind and brain are dichotomous.

This dichotomous approach to mind and brain may have begun in the 1860s with Broca's discovery that loss of speech is a sign of left-brain pathology. Even then it was realized that such loss meant impaired thinking as well as impaired communication, a generalization evident to the ancient Greeks. Plato wrote, "thinking and speech are one and the same." This close relation is recognized in the frequent contemporary references to left-brain involvement in reasoning as a product of language. This makes reasoning a sequential affair as words are linked to form sentences and sentences are linked successively to express unfolding ideas. In reading the eyes move along the lines of print to grasp the sequence of thoughts symbolized by the succession of words and sentences. Reading is thus a linear process, but, as in reading difficult expository material, it is also a logical, analytic, judgmental process. Thus the left brain arrives at a belief or conclusion or truth not all at once, but by a series of inferences, a step-by-step affair of thinking matters through, as in presenting an argument, evaluating evidence, proving a theorem, or outlining the plot of a detective story. Such familiar cognitive affairs, viewed as verbalized and sequential left-brain processes, strike some as more temporal than spatial—at least in contrast to nonverbal right-brain cognition.

That the right brain has better control over spatial relations than the left was shown when split-brain patients were asked to copy figures. The left hand succeeded but the right hand failed, indicating right-brain success and left-brain failure. Right-brain control of acts of spatial discrimination is also demonstrated as the fingers of a trained violinist flit from point to point along the strings with measured precision. This left-hand superiority may not be altogether a consequence of practice; it may have an inherent basis. According to some investigators, as noted by Doreen Kimura, "the tactual perception of Braille dot patterns by blind people is more rapid with the left hand than with the right." She also cites an investigation in which it was "found that when one arm is used to locate a point out of sight under a table on which the location of the point is indicated, the left arm performs more accurately than the right" (1973, p. 76). Thus in this respect the right hemisphere might be said to outstrip the left.[10] It follows that neither hemisphere is dominant in every regard.

Common allusions to the left hemisphere as dominant refer to right-hand control as well as verbal control. The idea of right connotes straight, dextrous, and auspicious, while left connotes gauche, sinister, and menacing. Concomitantly, mastery of language connotes cognitive development, the life of reason, and skill in communication. The sequence of words in verbal communication, whether speech or writing, is usually thought to indicate ideational sequence. Consequently, sequential ideation has come to be regarded as a predominantly left-brain process. Since critical thinking and logical analysis are inherently sequential, they too are taken to be left-brain processes. As cognitive operations they may be presumed to characterize the thinking of scientists and mathematicians, making scientific and mathematical thought more of a left- than a right-hemisphere operation and successive and linear rather than simultaneous and spatial.

By contrast, the right hemisphere is deemed to specialize in antithetic cognitive operations, to be more proficient in dealing with situations requiring nonlinear or concurrent apprehension—the kind variously

10. Another function in which the right brain outstrips the left brain is depth perception. Kimura found the right hemisphere's judgment of the third dimension more accurate than that of the left (1973, p. 73).

described as intuitive, holistic, artistic, configurational, and insightful. Our aesthetic reactions to paintings or to natural scenery exemplify the kind of thinking involved, especially when the reactions are immediate, spontaneous, and nonreflective. Sometimes our aesthetic appreciation is so instantaneous as to defy verbal description. Such ineffable experiences are thus congruent with the predominantly nonverbal nature of right-brain processes.

In historical perspective these verbal/nonverbal and other left-brain/right-brain contrasts look like elaborations of proverbial antitheses such as reason versus emotion, the refined versus the boorish, the classical versus the romantic, and even the provocative Apollonian/Dionysian dichotomy of Nietzsche. Seeing the contrasts as reflecting commonsense distinctions makes them less novel, but whether it enhances their validity from the viewpoint of neuropsychology is a separate issue.

A Critique of Brain/Mind Dichotomies

The left brain's involvement in language is the main reason it is regarded as dominant over the right brain. The close relation between thinking and verbal expression, or between reason and language, makes the left hemisphere appear more cognitive than the right hemisphere as well as more logical, more analytic, and more sequential in its operations. Since such sequential operations are indispensable to science, the left hemisphere has come to be associated with scientific thinking. For similar reasons mathematicians have come to be thought of as left-brain workers, governed by the demands of critical thinking, standards of logic, and precision of language.

By contrast, the nonverbal right brain has come to be regarded as more intuitive in its cognitive operations, involved more with spatial than logical relations. It is considered more synthetic than analytic, more simultaneous than sequential, and more holistic than divisive. Accordingly, aesthetic appreciation has often been regarded as a predominantly right-brain process. Presumably visits to concert halls and art galleries activate this unilateral process, as does the work done by musicians and artists. It follows, as Ornstein has noted, that right-brain lesions may ruin the careers of professional musicians (1973, p. 88) and that left-brain damage may ruin the careers of scientists, mathematicians, and others whose work entails rigorous logical controls. Such inferences are justified in terms of the specialized processes attributed to each hemisphere.

But is such sharply sundered segregation of left/right processes in accordance with fact? It is important to distinguish between the impression we gain from reading a published article in chemistry or mathematical theory and the impression created by reading an account of the writer's thinking as he did his research. The finished copy reveals the logical progression and steady sequential thinking ascribed to left-brain, scientific thinking. But false leads, tentative guesses, hours of indecision, checks and rechecks of data, rejected hunches, and whatever else may have gone into preliminary drafts, although excluded from the final copy, cannot be excluded from detailed accounts of the psychology of scientific thinking. Such accounts are apt to reveal retrogression as well as progression and balked as well as sequential thinking. Moreover, when the thinker arrives at an "elegant" finding or proof he, like the right-brained artist, may experience an aesthetic thrill. In their quest for elegant proofs, workers in science and mathematics are as much right-brain as left-brain thinkers. Interest in the aesthetics as well as the logic of proof is not uncommon among mathematicians. The mathematician and physicist John Von Neumann (1903–57) referred to this in the following passage (1956, p. 2063):

> I think there is a relatively good approximation to truth . . . that mathematical ideas originate in empirics, although the genealogy is sometimes long and obscure. But, once they are so conceived, the subject begins to live a peculiar life of its own and is better compared to a creative one, governed by almost entirely *aesthetical* motivations, than to anything else and, in particular, to an empirical science. (Italics added.)

In view of the creative drive thus assigned to "aesthetical motivations" of mathematicians, one might assume that right-brain damage would also ruin their careers. In such *spatial* branches of mathematics as topology or stereography, the need for intact right-brain functions would be imperative, as it would be for specialists in stereochemistry, the chemical field concerned with the spatial arrangement of submolecular atoms. Spatial thinking is also inherent in the work of surveyors, cartographers, civil engineers, and architects, which makes these applied sciences as dependent upon right-brain as upon left-brain processing. Scientific work is thus not an exclusively left-brain province.

Advances in technology as contrasted with pure science also appear to be contingent upon right-brain integrity. As Ferguson brought out, inventors and designers do their creative thinking pictorially and nonverbally (1977, p. 827):

> It has been nonverbal thinking, by and large, that has fixed the outlines and filled in the details of our material surroundings for, in their innumerable choices and decisions, technologists have determined the kind of world we live in, in a physical sense. Pyramids,

cathedrals, and rockets exist not because of geometry, theory of structures, or thermodynamics, but because they were first a picture — literally a vision — in the minds of those who built them.

The nonverbal thinking of technologists, though regarded as a right-brain process, is no less cognitive than the verbal thinking commonly regarded as a left-brain process. Its cognitive nature has long been recognized in the distinction between mechanical and abstract intelligence. At the same time these two domains of intellect have been deemed different from the hypothesized domain of social intelligence. This third domain, when subjected to factor analysis, as was done by O'Sullivan, Guilford, and de Mille (1965), is seen to be decidedly complex. It may involve as many as thirty factors having to do with social awareness, empathy, and understanding the intentions and feelings of others. In attempting to measure social intelligence experimenters asked subjects to state the significance of facial expressions in photographs, to judge the meaning of cartoons, and to interpret emotive sounds like sighs, whistles, and laughs. To the degree that such interpretations and judgments are nonverbal and intuitive, spatial and empathic, they imply right-brain dominance. On the other hand,[11] left-brain dominance is indicated by competence on the verbal tests employed, which included tests of ability to fit a list of words into a meaningful sentence, to formulate questions pertinent to a given situation, and to supply plot titles of "high quality" for short stories, with the proviso that "only clever titles are to be credited" (p. 15). In these measurements of social intelligence both hemispheres were brought into play; hence getting along with people as a cognitive enterprise is a bicameral affair calling for a whole brain, not half a brain.

Whether abstract intelligence, with its intimate involvement with verbal and mathematical symbols, is basically a left-brain, unicameral affair is to be questioned, even though its finished products in books and technical articles exhibit sequential thinking, logical controls, and verbal mastery. Though mathematics stands out as a paradigm of abstract intelligence, particularly as reflected in mathematical publications, such finished products fail to reflect the researcher's cognitive processes as he developed his original insights and discoveries. In his creative probing he may have disregarded the restrictions of logic, toyed with transient hunches, and been swayed by sudden aesthetic insights. In the published report the vagaries of his probing are lost as his tenable conclusions are brought into

---

11. "On the other hand," as a familiar trope, illustrates the polarized nature of cognitive orientation. The left/right antithesis of handedness reflects the same sort of polarization. There are many others, such as right/wrong, logical/illogical, radical/conservative, affirmative/negative, masculine/feminine, convex/concave, and white/black. Much of our thinking is influenced by such antithetic categories, but we may be misled by neglect of the grays in the white/black polarization.

conformity with standards of logical rigor and descriptive accuracy. Consequently, the final report gives a misleading picture of research in mathematics by excluding factors alien to the paradigm of abstract intelligence. The operation of contrasting factors is summarized by the mathematician Rees (1962, p. 9):

> In the history of mathematics the emphasis in research is sometimes on constructive intuition and the acquisition of results without too much concern for the strict demands of logic, sometimes on the insights gained by the identification and study of abstract systems within a carefully designed logical framework. But over the years the body of mathematics moves forward inevitably with growth in both directions. An individual mathematician chooses to work on one frontier or the other and the emphasis changes from one period to another, but mathematics as a whole and the community of mathematicians have their obligation to the total spectrum.

Later Rees notes that "mathematics is both inductive and deductive, needing, like poetry, persons who are creative and have a sense of the beautiful for its surest progress" (p. 12). It thus appears that this progress needs both hemispheres and is bicameral, not unicameral. The progress is bicameral also because of the presumed left-brain *sequential* nature of numeration as contrasted with the presumed right-brain *holistic* nature of spatiality. This contrast between the sequential and holistic has become familiar; one comes across it repeatedly in current writings on the split brain and related topics, and its validity appears to be taken for granted. Nevertheless, it may be a spurious belief.

The Sequential/Holistic Antithesis Questioned

Cognition as a sequential process suggests smooth progression from one thought to the next as ideas follow one another in the sequential pattern expressed on the printed page. But the actual course of cognitive events is regressive as well as progressive, uncertain as well as confident, irrelevant as well as relevant—not a smooth sequence of coherent ideas ready for left-brain verbal expression. This assumes a distinction between ideation and its verbalization, but according to a traditional view ideation itself is verbal in that thinking involves vocal or subvocal speech. This traditional teaching might be cited to support a thesis that the language hemisphere is the arena for sequential thought, making language indispensable for thinking in general and problem solving in particular. This assumes that without a minimal vocabulary one cannot think about breakfast, admire a painting, or even decide whether five is larger than three.

Can one think about numbers without having names for them? W. H. Thorpe, an animal ethologist, has stated that it is possible, and in an essay entitled "Ethology and Consciousness" (1966) he cited experimental evidence for this. As he put it, animals can "think unnamed numbers" and thus can be said to possess "a prelinguistic number sense" or, within given limits, to engage in wordless thought. He introduced the following account of a bird's recognition of numerical differences (p. 478):

> A raven, confronted with a series of boxes with a varying number of spots on the lids, was taught to open only that box which had the same number of spots as there were objects on a key card in front of it. This bird eventually learned to distinguish between five groups indicated by two, three, four, five, and six black spots on the lids of the boxes, the key being one of those numbers lying on the ground in front. The raven learned to raise only that one of the five lids which had the same number of spots as the key pattern had objects.[12]

The bird's wordless counting of the spots was more sequential than spatial, since the spots were not presented in a fixed pattern, but at the avian level this does not suggest left-brain dominance in the sense of verbal control. Birds are never victims of aphasia, and their vocalizations are unrelated to Broca's area. Whether lateral dominance applies to the bird brain in any respect is questionable. In the raven's counting, both sides of the brain may be said to have been brought into play, since birds' vision is predominantly ipsilateral because they receive only monocular stimulation. Birds compensate for this by their characteristic rapid right/left head movements, which provide for successive stimulation of each eye. The counting probably entailed such alternating movements, resulting in binocular equivalence and thus bilateral equivalence. Thus the raven's sequential counting was bilateral, not a unilateral left-brain process. It was sequential because, as already noted, the spots were not presented in a fixed order or pattern.

When humans count they have names for each number, and such naming makes counting a left-brain process. It can also be described as sequential. In counting by twos or threes or tens, one number follows another in predictable sequence. One can reel off the sequence from one to a hundred almost without thinking, as automatically as reciting the alphabet. But when the counting requires thought, sequential progress is apt to be balked. For example, in supplying the series of one to ten each raised to the third power—one, eight, twenty-seven, and so on—progress is not likely to be automatic or sequential in the sense of steady forward progress with no hesitation or reversals. Difficult thinking is never sequential in this sense.

12. The raven was reacting to the *number* of spots, not to any fixed pattern, since the relative position of the spots was changed from trial to trial.

Analogously, in reading a difficult text there is virtually no sequential thinking. There is repeated hesitation over phrases, occasional recourse to a dictionary, and frequent regression to earlier passages. Even the reading of easy texts is not smoothly sequential. The eyes move in successive jumps, or saccadic movements, along the line of print from one fixation pause to the next. Comprehension takes place at the pause, not during the saccadic transitions. The shifts from one fixation to the next indicate sequential progress, but regressive shifts do not.

Each fixation pause can encompass only a limited number of letters or words. Even the most competent speed reader cannot take in a whole page. The span of items that can be encompassed is rather small, as was established years ago. Wrenn and Cole (1935, p. 3) reported that: "The maximum that can be read at one fixation is 4 unrelated letters or 2 unrelated words—10 letters or 1 phrase—6 related words—30 letters. The reason for this increasing efficiency of a single fixation lies in the more meaningful nature of words as compared with unrelated letters and of a phrase as compared with unrelated words."

This brings up a commonly overlooked phenomenon; strictly speaking, reading a familiar phrase is more holistic than sequential. Consider the phrase *the United States of America.* This is read as a unit in a single fixation, without sequential attention to the successive letters or words. Actually the thirty letters that constitute the phrase can be telescoped into the three letters *USA* without loss of meaning or awareness of the telescoping. We read most words without explicit awareness of the successive letters; otherwise good readers could never read three hundred or more words per minute, as is not unusual. And when we see the symbol USA there is immediate understanding without explicit awareness of any of the fifty states. *Nor is there need for sequential mental review of the states.* We can think about *America* or *Europe* without rehearsing states or countries. The latter might be implicit in the thinking, but this is different from our being conscious of them. It is in this respect that the thinking is more holistic than sequential. Such holism is implicit in the use of abstract nouns. A word like *dryness* is understood without awareness of specific states of desiccation, and a word like *furniture* stands for myriad household articles without their conscious restatement. Particular instances are preconscious as conceptualized in psychoanalytic theory; they can easily be brought into consciousness by a momentary effort of attention. They are always potentially conscious; but to render them conscious necessitates a pause in the sequential flow of speech. In telling her youngster a fairy story a mother chances to say, "The queen had pretty furniture and . . ." but cannot complete the sentence because the child interrupts by asking, "What's furniture?" Mother has to pause to explain that the queen had tables, chairs, sofas, and kindred articles. What had been implicit and preconscious is made explicit and conscious, but at the expense of an ideational block in the otherwise smoothly sequential development of the story. Thus an undercurrent of potentially available preconscious holistic ideation is a concomitant of the sequential ideation in the stream of consciousness.

Just as there are reasons to question whether the verbal left brain's processing is entirely sequential and nonholistic, so there are reasons to question that the nonverbal right brain's processing is entirely holistic and nonsequential. The right brain has been found to be more proficient than the left brain in apprehending spatial relationships; the patient's left hand could draw a recognizable cube whereas his right hand could not. Thus space perception has come to be regarded as a right-brain specialty. Often this is interpreted as gaining an immediate impression of the totality of some scene such as a sunset, a cartoon, a diagram, a stranger's face, a painting, or a new car. Such initial immediate perception of a spatial totality has been regarded as holistic and nonsequential, but even prolonged inspection of such scenes has been so regarded, as in such common reports as "I kept staring at the sunset" or "His eyes were fixed on the dog in the window." The precise nature of such protracted ocular fixation is a separate issue directly related to the holism attributed to right-brain spatial dominance.

The issue has been raised independently of its bearing on hemispheric specialization. A study in the late 1940s dealt with subjects' ocular changes as they examined the ten cards of the Rorschach test. Twenty student volunteers were given the usual Rorschach instructions, and as they inspected each card their eyes were photographed. To apprehend any one of the blots as a whole, a single ocular fixation theoretically should have sufficed. But according to Blake, the investigator, there were no single ocular fixations (1948, p. 162): "An irreducible number of fixations are necessarily made in examining the blots. Theoretically the minimum is one; actually no subject produced a response with fewer than eight. Some subjects, on the other hand, searched extensively, expending as many as 110 fixations prior to producing a response."

If the successive ocular fixations are considered sequential inspections of the blot, they indicate why accounts of right-brain spatial processing as holistic and nonsequential are to be questioned. No one of the ten blots was surveyed as a whole in a single glance, as might have been expected from the usual interpretation of holism. Nor is this an exceptional finding unique to amorphous blots. The same has been reported about pictures of the human face and diagrams in a geometry text. Brandt (1945) found that in gazing at pictures of the human face there were as many as thirty-nine fixations for a large picture or as few as four for a smaller one (p. 69). Again, no single fixations took place. The same was true for geometry students. For good students the average number of ocular fixations was four, and for poor students it was eleven, with no student perceiving the whole diagram in just one fixation (Brandt 1945, pp. 132–33).

A third line of evidence, concerning art appreciation, bears on the aestheticism sometimes attributed to the right hemisphere, though it was gathered independent of questions of hemispheric dominance or bicameral consciousness. In 1935 G. T. Buswell published *How People Look at Pictures: A Study of the Psychology of Perception in Art*, a study of the photographic recording of eye movements during inspection of paintings. Of the 200 subjects who participated, 12 were elementary school children, 44 were high school pupils, and 144 were adults. Among the adults were 47 who had received from two to five years of training at an art institute. The subjects thus ranged widely in age and in sophistication about art. Despite the wide range, one finding was common to all; every record showed saccadic movements and fixation pauses. As Buswell described it (1935, pp. 15–16):

> In looking at a picture, just as in the process of reading, the eye moves in a series of quick jerks and pauses. The eye does not slide over the picture, as many people think it does. The duration of the fixation pauses varies a good deal, a pause of 3 thirtieths of a second being very brief, one of 8 to 10 thirtieths being quite common, and pauses of more than 20 thirtieths of a second occurring only in approximately 5 per cent of the cases.

Although the fixation pauses averaged less than a second in duration, their frequency for each picture was not comparably meager. More than 120 pauses per picture were common. There were marked differences in the duration of the pauses, but, quite unexpectedly, these were not due to differences in the pictures. Instead, in Buswell's words, they were "more directly related to characteristics of the individual looking at the picture" (p. 143). Also somewhat unexpectedly, those with advanced training in art averaged shorter fixation pauses than those lacking such training. Seemingly the training permitted speedier evaluation of the merits of the paintings. That all subjects made such evaluations was suggested by the fact that the duration of the pauses tended to increase in the course of viewing the picture, as if initial hasty impressions were being rectified by more considered examination. In the initial shorter pauses the eyes appeared to focus on the picture's main features, while in the later fixations they seemed to focus on subordinate features, indicating more detailed scrutiny.

Multiple fixations characterized the perception of pictures; in no instance did a single glance suffice. As in the previously cited studies using Rorschach cards and geometric diagrams, there was a succession of saccadic movements akin to ocular activity in reading. Although they concerned different perceptual tasks, all three studies showed perception of spatial figures to be sequential as well as holistic. This does not imply merging of right- and left-brain processes but indicates concurrent right-brain control of the sequential along with the spatial.

This kind of concurrent control is evident in the way the fingers of a violinist's left hand make contact with successive points along the strings. The notes as played are spread out temporally and spatially; each has its time and place of production. *When* produced is the same as *where*, since the fingers are moving in a time-space continuum. To endow either the temporal or the spatial aspects of the continuum with independent existence by an act of abstraction would involve Whitehead's *fallacy of misplaced concreteness*—the "error of mistaking the abstract for the concrete." To regard perception of space as a right-brain process and perception of time as a left-brain process is to be guilty of this fallacy.

The entire question of the hemispheric localization of cognitive functions has not yet been settled. According to recent findings it may be that no cognitive function is ever localized in a single hemisphere—that all such functions are bicameral, not unicameral.

Bicameral Localization

Knowledge of localization in the human brain has largely been gathered by studying the sick and injured. The speech difficulties of Broca's patient were accounted for by the postmortem discovery of damage to a definite region of the left hemisphere, Broca's area, which came to be regarded as the locus of motor speech. The aphasia and right hemiplegia of later stroke victims repeatedly confirmed Broca's findings,[13] which were supplemented by study of other kinds of brain damage associated with concussion, brain tumor, gunshot wounds, alcoholism, hydrocephalus, meningitis, and epilepsy. Severe epileptic attacks unresponsive to anticonvulsant medication were treated surgically, sometimes by excising segments of cortical tissue, which demonstrated the tissue's importance for certain skills or cognitive operations. For example, one of Penfield's epileptic patients was so disoriented following the operation that he became lost as soon as he turned the corner and was out of sight of his house. In this case there had been "complete removal" of tissue from the right temporoparietal region with consequent "loss of awareness of body scheme" and of "spatial relationships" (Penfield 1966, p. 223).

Similar losses were found in the famous "case Lanuti" reported by Hanf-

---

13. Broca's area is not involved in all cases of aphasia. Goldstein and Marmor reported a case of aphasia in which autopsy revealed "destruction of the entire superior temporal gyrus" and other portions of the left hemisphere, but "Broca's area, and the middle temporal and superior parietal convolutions were not involved" (1938, p. 331).

mann, Rickers-Ovsiankina, and Goldstein (1944), noteworthy because of the many psychological tests employed. The patient, Lanuti, had been in an automobile accident and later tumbled down a flight of stairs. He became an employee of the hospital and thus was under observation for almost a decade. He suffered marked spatial disorientation and had trouble finding his way around the hospital: "Even after having made the trip from the ward to the laboratory dozens of times, he was still unable to find his way by himself" (p. 24). Like Penfield's patient, he lacked an intact "body scheme." When asked to point to his ear, for example, he often just moved his palm in a wide sweep across "the side of his head which may or may not include part of the ear." Even questions regarding the number of toes, eyes, and other body parts gave him trouble.

Since findings from pathology were presumed to shed light on normal functioning, language functions came to be considered left-hemisphere processes and spatial functions right-hemisphere processes, implying that verbal ability is located in one half of the brain and spatial perception in the other half. This amounted to saying that the consequences of damage are manifested at the site of the damage, but this argument is questionable. An engine loses power if the spark plugs are damaged, but this does not prove that power is located in the plugs. Similarly, though loss of consciousness follows brain hemorrhage from a ruptured artery, it does not follow that consciousness resides in the blood or in the artery.

Cerebral Blood Flow and Consciousness

A basic function of the cerebral arteries is to bring oxygen to the brain tissues, and drastic curtailment of oxygen may cause permanent brain damage. But oxygenation varies with the activity of given brain areas, diminished amounts of blood going to areas of low activity and increased amounts to those of heightened activity. Since such activity underlies all cortical events of psychological importance, knowing how blood flow affects them might shed light on cortical localization. This promising possibility has already been experimentally investigated, with encouraging results.

Lassen, Ingvar, and Skinhøj (1978) supply a clarifying account of this kind of investigation. The method employed in measuring the flow of blood from one brain area to another was tried out in animal studies before being considered safe for use with humans. This technique involved injecting a radioactive isotope into an artery and then using radiography to record fluctuations in cerebral blood flow. By means of a small digital computer the fluctuations were shown graphically on a color television screen. Average rates of blood flow appeared in green, those 20 percent below the average in blue, and those 20 percent above in red. Thus when a subject watched a moving figure the occipital region appeared in red and Broca's area in blue. There were corresponding shifts as subjects were asked to flex their fingers, attend to spoken words, or remain quietly relaxed.

In some respects cerebral blood circulation differs from the blood supply to other organs. For healthy functioning the brain seems to require more blood than the other organs. Although it approximates only 2 percent of the body's weight, it utilizes some 20 percent of the total blood supply. Thus activation of brain cells is directly dependent on increase in blood flow and concomitant metabolic changes.

The studies reported by Lassen and his associates are of particular value because, unlike most other studies of cortical localization, they were not all based upon brain-damaged patients. Of the close to five hundred patients subjected to these radiographic brain examinations, the vast majority showed definite pathology incident to strokes, seizures, or tumors. But for some eighty patients the neurological complaints proved unrelated to brain damage, as was established by these blood-flow measurements as well as by EEG recordings and other procedures. Consequently, with reference to these patients the investigators were able "to draw some conclusions about *the localization of function in the normal cerebral cortex*" on the basis of their "studies of the regional cerebral blood flow" (p. 65; italics added).

One conclusion, especially significant because of its bearing on the concept of consciousness, was based on a rather unexpected finding. A normal level of uniform blood flow throughout the cortex had been anticipated when the subjects were resting comfortably on their backs, awake but with eyes closed, under conditions of complete silence. Contrary to expectations, there was a much higher concentration of blood in the frontal region than in other brain regions — almost 50 percent higher. This engorgement apparently affected both the left and the right frontal or prefrontal areas.

In commenting on the greater blood flow to these areas the investigators stated that such "hyperfrontal" engorgement "may contribute to an understanding of conscious awareness" because these areas have to do with "the planning of behavior"[14] while the other cortical areas relate to sensory and motor processes. In support of this interpretation they mentioned the resting consciousness as subjectively experienced. When resting one is apt to think about future actions or to reflect on past actions, though real

---

14. A detailed exposition of the nature of such planned behavior as a function of the frontal lobes is found in chapter 7 of Luria's book on neuropsychology. By a series of examples of the effects of frontal-lobe damage, he justifies the following conclusion: "*The frontal lobes . . . therefore constitute an apparatus with the function of forming stable plans and intentions capable of controlling the subject's subsequent conscious behavior*" (1973, p. 198; his italics).

action is inhibited. Under these conditions motor and sensory cortical activity is markedly reduced, with corresponding reduction in blood supply to motor and sensory areas of the cortex. Terminating the rest period by activating these primary areas brought increased blood flow to them, as shown by shifts to red on the television screen.

Lassen and his associates investigated in detail the relation between language and the cortical areas activated. In general both hemispheres were found to be involved; both the right and the left auditory cortex were activated when the subject listened to words. When he talked additional areas were brought into play, particularly the two Broca's areas — "Broca's area in the lower rear part of the left frontal lobe and the corresponding part of the right frontal lobe" (p. 69). However, there was a difference in the amount of flow to the supplementary parts of the two motor areas, indicating greater activity on the left than on the right. In general it was concluded that the right hemisphere does contribute something — possibly nonessential — to the final integration of neural processes accounting for left-brain control of active or motor speech.

When patients were tested with different kinds of problems, easy problems resulted in localized blood flow and difficult ones in diffuse blood flow; there was close to a 10 percent increase in flow with hard problems and no such increase with easy ones. This discrepancy is congruent with an established neurophysiological distinction between nonspecific and specific brain pathways — nonspecific pathways are diffuse, while specific ones are restricted to circumscribed sensorimotor connections. Easy questions thus entail specific pathways and difficult questions nonspecific ones. To illustrate: finding the opposite of the word *poor* is easy compared with answering a question like "Why is it wrong to commit suicide?" The easy item can be disposed of with the automatism of a reflex reaction, but the difficult question might involve one's total being. As Lassen and associates interpreted it, such involvement, being unrestricted and nonspecific, is as much subcortical as cortical. Unlike simple tasks, "demanding tasks activate larger cortical areas over diffuse pathways that fan out from the reticular formation of the brain stem and the thalamus of the midbrain." This seems to be the same as Penfield's view of centrencephalic integration discussed earlier. The diffuse neural circuits thus activated make "conscious planning possible" and also "serve the purposes of inter-hemispheral and intra-hemispheral integration" (Penfield and Roberts 1959, pp. 20–21). Coping with difficult tasks entails conscious planning; hence Penfield and these investigators of cerebral blood flow converged on a common problem and independently arrived at the same conclusion. What Penfield ascribed to interhemispheral integration Lassen, Ingvar, and Skinhøj (1978) ascribed to total cerebral activation. As they put it, "it appears that for the brain to 'understand' the surrounding world, to perceive its meaning and to take action in difficult tasks the cerebral cortex must be activated not only locally but also totally" (p. 71).

Total activation means that processes in both hemispheres work together as parts of an *integrated* nervous system. Such unity means *one* mind, not a verbal mind on the left and a separate spatial mind on the right. It is doubtful that such rigid segregation of function is to be found in the undamaged healthy brain,[15] and undue preoccupation with the notion is apt to obscure the essential unity of mind and brain.

The Unity of Mind and Brain

To regard one brain hemisphere as dominant over the other in a master/slave relationship governed by a law of lateralization is an unjustified interpretation with a deceptive connotation. Dominance in the sense of mastery over a rival suggests hostility and coerced subservience, with reluctant obedience and the potential for revolt. Such dominance portends disunity rather than unity and is altogether at variance with the facts of cerebral dominance. Cooperative interdependence, not antagonistic rivalry, is the hallmark of interhemispheric relations. The hemispheres work together in unison, and even lateralization often involves a sharing of responsibility. Some right-handed people are left-footed, and others may be left-eyed; about one-third of left-handed and three-quarters of right-handed individuals are right-eyed in using a microscope or sighting a rifle. Complete left cerebral dominance is found in only one-quarter of the population, marked or pronounced left dominance in barely more than a third, and relatively weak left dominance in the remainder. Moreover, "in one-tenth of all cases the dominance of the left hemisphere is totally absent" (Luria 1973, pp. 78–79).

Even when the dominance of one hemisphere is marked there is no conflict in the execution of bilateral movements. Irrespective of the degree of lateralization, the arms and legs of good swimmers move through the

15. This entire issue of the relation between a normal brain with undamaged hemispheres and mind as single was touched upon by Ornstein (1978). After reviewing work with split-brain subjects, he introduced an account of work with normal subjects. He and his co-workers had subjected ten healthy subjects to a variety of tasks and checked concomitant brain changes by EEG recordings. Among the tasks was a reading assignment that required subjects to deal both with technical and factual reading matter and with literary and imaginative stories. That the EEG tracings induced a less rigid interpretation of the familiar verbal/spatial dichotomy is evident in the following conclusion (p. 82): "Stories can involve the right hemisphere, and spatial tests the left—if people choose to use their brains that way. It seems apparent from our research and from the work of others that the human being has a single mind and that the brain's hemispheres are not specialized for different types of *material* (verbal and spatial), but for different types of *thought*."

water smoothly and efficiently. The arms of rowers exhibit the same co-
operative efficiency. Markedly right-footed individuals have no trouble
walking, running, or dancing. Those who are markedly left-handed may
nevertheless strike piano keys or typewriter keys competently. Deaf people
use both hands in signing, and most of us, when engaged in animated discussion, supplement our talk with bilateral gestures. Harpists must use
both hands, and so do cellists and violinists. The eyes exhibit similar synergistic activity as they converge on objects, adjust for distance vision, and
move conjointly in following movement, with no indication that one eye
is dominant.

Such interhemispheric unity accords with the views of Paul MacLean,
a noted student of brain development from the evolutionary standpoint.
In an interview published in *Science* he declared, "The hemispheres are
equipotential" (Holden 1979). The interview was prompted by MacLean's
original research on brain organization manifested in the biology of neural
growth. He stressed neural development from primitive to more advanced
animal phyla through eons of time and recognized three successive levels
of change, giving rise to what he termed the *triune* brain. These three levels
are characterized by progress from a low reptilian stage to a middle limbic,
or paleomammalian, stage and on up to a neomammalian, or neocortical,
stage. Broadly considered, the earliest stage has to do with instinctive and
ritualistic behavior, the limbic stage with emotional factors associated with
the thalamus, the pituitary, and related structures, and the neocortical stage
with thinking, planning, and the cognitive regulation of behavior. According to this view the human being's triune brain is really three brains in
one, each contributing to the unified action of the whole. MacLean warned
against the tendency to overemphasize the neocortical or hemispheric contribution (Holden 1979, pp. 1067–68):

> And although he has hailed the neocortex as "the mother of inven-
> tion and the father of abstract thought," he finds that much business,
> human and animal can be done without it. "People don't like to hear
> this business about the neocortex," he observes. "We have been
> brought up being told the neocortex does everything," an assump-
> tion that has filtered up from the days of John Locke, who saw the
> mind as a *tabula rasa,* and later the behaviorists, whose contention
> that all behavior is learned is a way of dismissing the evidence that
> subcortical structures already have their own ways of dealing with
> the world. MacLean believes that the people who are enamored of
> theorizing about the differences between the left (rational, verbal)
> and right (nonverbal, intuitive) cerebral hemispheres are missing the
> boat somewhat. "I think they've got a lot of stuff maybe too high
> upstairs"—that is many of the creative, emotional, and spiritual
> impulses ascribed to the right hemisphere are more properly attrib-

utable to the limbic system. *"The hemispheres are equipotential,"*[16] he asserts. (Italics added.)

Such hemispheric equipotentiality is another way of describing the co-operative and synergistic interdependence of the two hemispheres. This equipotential and synergistic teamwork is exemplified by any skilled typist as the fingers of right and left hands strike the spatially separated keys in whatever sequence the spelling chances to require. There is no question of spatial discrimination and sequential ideation being right- and left-brain prerogatives. All ten fingers are dealing with both space and sequence. And to the degree that spelling is a phase of language the typist's right brain is just as verbal as the left brain, as if a single mind is doing the spelling.

MacLean is not unmindful of this unity of mind and brain. His triune brain is a recognition of a triune mind, with each of the three stages of evolutionary neural development indicating concomitant mental development. It is also biological recognition of the age-old view of mind as tripartite, as in Plato's dividing the human soul into three: a rational soul in the head region, a noble irrational soul in the heart region, and a base irrational soul below the diaphragm. Later classical psychology envisioned man as a creature capable of thinking, desiring, and willing. These cognitive, orectic, and conative aspects are reflected in sentences like I know, I wish, and I must. In the idiom of grammarians these constitute indicative, optative, and imperative sentences, and in the idiom of psychoanalysis they constitute man's ego, id, and superego.

These tripartite levels are often equated with higher and lower levels of man's nature. Probing into such hypothesized lower levels has been called depth psychology, but no school of height psychology has yet come into existence. However, it is not uncommon for reason to be given a higher rating than emotion. Everyday speech reflects this by referring to the gut reactions as contrasted to brainwork, and in general visceral reactions are considered inferior to the superior brain reactions.[17]

Such ratings of some reactions as higher in location and value than others are embedded in MacLean's concept of the triune brain. From his evolutionary perspective vertical differences in structure from brainstem to neocortex stand out as of greater significance than possible horizontal differ-

16. MacLean's use of this term is not to be confused with Lashley's theories of equipotentiality and mass action alluded to earlier in this chapter.

17. The relations between brain and viscera are complex and have given rise to investigations of biofeedback interaction as well as of the influence of consciousness on visceral changes. As Grings explained, the goal of these and related investigations "is to relate thinking and emotion, to find better means for bridging the gap between the higher mental processes as we see them in the human subject, and the subtleties of internal organismic behavior such as that mediated by the autonomic nervous system" (1973, p. 256).

ences in the brain's bilateral symmetry. The great changes in behavioral endowment are expressed not in left/right modifications of neural structure but in successive vertical emergent developments, from primitive notochords to increasingly complex neural elaborations in later phyla. It was in terms of this perspective that he saw the hemispheres as equipotential.

The Hemispheres as Equipotential

In such activities as walking, running, and swimming right and left brains work together in synergistic harmony. This is as true of man as it is of dogs and horses, and with respect to these activities the hemispheres are obviously equipotential. This does not appear to have been questioned in animals, which are not described as right-pawed or left-hoofed. Their brains are not influenced by lateralization, and no distinctive functions are attributed to their hemispheres. Barking and neighing are not ascribed to a left-brain homologue of Broca's area. For animals hemispheric specialization and right/left dominance are irrelevant, and their hemispheres are altogether equipotential. In many respects the undamaged hemispheres of man are also equipotential, as is to be expected in view of the continuity of evolutionary development.

The concept of hemispheric equipotentiality is not at odds with the fundamentals of cortical localization. For both man and beast the cranial nerves have their characteristic places in each hemisphere. In both, optic nerves terminate in occipital regions, auditory in temporal areas, and olfactory in hippocampal tissue, while the array of motor nerves have their points of departure in the precentral gyrus.

It is customary to list twelve cranial nerves, but in reality there are twenty-four, since each hemisphere has its own set. But in normal circumstances these two sets operate as one. Consequently they may be regarded as equipotential in their influence on hemispheric activation. This is particularly evident in arousal of optic, olfactory, and other sensory nerves. Their bilateral stimulation does not give rise to a doubling of sensations. When confronted with a flower we are not conscious of two fragrances, one from each nostril, or of two flowers, one from each retina.

With intact commissures each hemisphere "knows" what the other is sensing, so that with undamaged sense organs and normal brains there is no double vision, double hearing, or double olfaction. Despite a bicameral brain, the result is a unified consciousness. Such undivided consciousness is largely a product of the equipotential participation of both hemispheres, even when hemispheric dominance is marked. A right-handed person can sign his name with his left hand; though it may look strained and somewhat childish, the signature will be recognizable. One might say the right brain knows what to do but has trouble doing it or that the left brain's knowledge has been shared with the right brain. This interhemispheric sharing, called cross-education or bilateral transfer, has been known as a psychological phenomenon at least since the 1850s, when such transfer was found to characterize cutaneous stimulation. An experimental subject was taught to discriminate between two stimulating points applied to his left arm. As the points were brought closer together, he could still perceive them as two, not as one. Training reduced the two-point threshold, and this reduction transferred or crossed over to the homologous region of the right arm.[18]

More than one hundred years after this investigation of the cutaneous threshold, we find it has unanticipated implications. At the time nobody had thought of spatial discrimination as a right-brain process, so the left/right transfer of cutaneous sensitivity was not regarded as related to lateral dominance. But in view of current teachings regarding right-brain specialization in spatial perception, the contralateral transfer of the lowered two-point threshold suggests that the right brain shares its spatial information with the left brain, as if the left brain *knows* about spatial distance. Had the experiment involved transfer from the right arm to the left we would probably be considering left-brain spatial information shared with the right brain. Thus in processing this kind of information the two hemispheres are equipotential.

Hemispheric equipotentiality, interpreted as a sharing of "knowledge," is thus a product of cross-education, and with equality of information neither hemisphere appears to be dominant over the other. This raises a question about the origin of such dominance.

Concerning Hemispheric Dominance

Hemispheric dominance pertains to the human brain but not to the animal brain. Animals like dogs and horses run, jump, swim, and engage in other acts involving synergistic neuromuscular control. Their forelimbs and hind limbs function as an integrated organic unit with no front/rear or left/right rivalry or dominance. As yet there have been no assured reports of handedness among the higher anthropoids. Chimpanzees, for example, are reported to be ambidextrous, though they can doubtless be trained to prefer one hand just as dogs can be trained to use one paw when "shaking

18. An account of this early work and somewhat later work, along with bibliographical references, is found in Ladd and Woodworth's discussion of transference of learning (1911, pp. 565–68).

hands."[19] Lateral dominance is of no interest to veterinarians. Nor is it of interest to pediatricians treating babies in the prelingual months. Except for the degree to which handedness is congenital, the hemispheres of prelingual infants, like those of animals, appear to be nondominant and reflect a unicameral consciousness in their cooperative interdependence.

Interest in hemispheric dominance was largely an outgrowth of findings associated with language pathology such as aphasia, amusia, alexia, and agraphia. Later studies of left/right specialization attributable to lateralization, particularly split-brain studies, are derivatives of these earlier investigations of loss of verbal control. Aphasic patients "know" what they want to say even though no words can be produced, as one can know how to perform an act without having the strength or skill to accomplish it. In this sense there are nonsprinting track coaches who know how to sprint just as there are nonsinging voice teachers who know how to sing. And even in instances of pronounced right-handedness the left hand "knows" how to imitate the right hand's motions in pantomime. Thus a right-handed tennis player can go through the motions of serving with his left hand, though he cannot deliver an effective serve. His right brain "knows" what to do without being able to do it; it cannot duplicate the left brain's dominance.

Most people are unlikely to think about dominance as a neurological phenomenon unless some family member suffers a stroke and becomes aphasic or hemiplegic. Even the medical profession was not aware of cerebral dominance until nineteenth-century investigations of brain pathology by men like Flourens and Broca. Interest in cerebral dominance in undamaged brains is largely a twentieth-century development, a result of what had previously been learned about damaged brains.

Dominance in normal brains presupposes some language development, so neither animal nor infant psychologists have much interest in it. The hemispheres of prelingual infants are fully equipotential, nondominant, and not yet lateralized. Thus study of how infants react to particular modes of stimulation should shed light on the basic question of untutored brain organization and thus on consciousness as unicameral or bicameral.

Experimental Study of the Newborn

This section is concerned with the psychological rather than the pediatric study of the neonate's reactions—not the hybrid field of pediatric

19. In a brief article on the subject Keller wrote that, according to one investigator, "both lower and higher apes are ambidextrous" even though "individual animals can develop a certain degree of handedness for special, frequently performed acts" (1942, p. 1147).

psychiatry.[20] I shall focus on this question: Does the neonate experience meaningful perceptions or only meaningless sensations? In a long tradition dating back to Aristotle the mind of the newborn has been compared to a tabula rasa upon which the effects of experience are inscribed. This tradition was endorsed by Locke and by all later empiricists. In their view, crediting the infant with unlearned meaningful perception would be endorsing the existence of innate ideas. In terms of the tabula rasa, or blank slate, metaphor, the neonate is born with a blank mind, and initial exposure to sights, sounds, and other sensory impressions results in chaotic confusion. Perceptual clarity is out of the question.

The empiricists' endorsement of the blank slate metaphor was a priori, not based upon empirical tests designed to determine its validity. On theoretical grounds they were contending that the newborn must *learn* to sort the early mass of confusing sensory impressions into recognizable objects. He would be unable to perceive his mother's hands as hands or her face as a face. All such distinctive perceptions would require many weeks of experience to emerge from the initial jumble of sensory impressions.

However, direct testing of infant behavior has shown that this empiricist teaching is contrary to fact. Fantz (1963) found that infants less than five days old focused on black-and-white patterns more consistently than on unpatterned surfaces. One of the patterns was a schematic face, and in seven of eight exposures an infant less than twenty-four hours old chose to look at the face. Fantz interpreted this and related findings from the eighteen babies tested as indicating an "innate ability to perceive form" and as calling "for a revision of traditional views that the visual world of the infant is initially formless or chaotic and that we must learn to see configurations" (p. 297). Since both eyes focused on the surface, it may be presumed that both hemispheres participated in the configurational perception in what may be considered the dawn of a unicameral consciousness.

Additional support for this conclusion is found in a study by Meltzoff and Moore (1977), intended to find out whether newborn infants would imitate adults' facial expressions and hand movements. Hand movements consisted of alternately extending and flexing the fingers. Three facial expressions were introduced: protruding the tongue, opening the mouth wide, and pursing the lips. Each infant's reactions to hand and facial changes were videotaped so that the results could be scored by outside judges rather than by the investigators. The subjects were eighteen infants ranging in age from twelve to twenty-one days, evenly divided by sex.

20. This field, the product of the joint efforts of child psychiatrists and pediatricians, came into existence once the two groups realized that their professional responsibilities overlapped. As Shirley noted, "the fostering of mental health in children is the province of both pediatrics and child psychiatry" (1963, p. 22).

The authors refer to their "recent observations of facial imitation in six newborns—one only 60 minutes old," but in evaluating the data only the twelve- to twenty-one-day range was used.

On the basis of the outside judges' evaluation of the videotaped data, it was concluded that the infants had been imitating both the manual and the facial gestures. A similar picture of tongue protrusion by a six-day-old infant is found in Bower (1977, p. 28). Bower also mentions imitation of mouth opening and eyelash fluttering as reported in a University of Edinburgh doctoral dissertation and comparable findings as reported in a University of Geneva doctoral dissertation. Thus three independent studies from different countries all confirm the existence of innate imitative behavior. Whether such confirmation settles the issue or is merely evidence in its favor is another question,[21] but in view of such presumptive evidence the innate imitation thesis may be judged a plausible working hypothesis having provocative psychological implications.

What Innate Imitation Implies

According to the empiricist tradition, the newborn perceives initial sensory impressions as meaningless confusion. The hypothesized tabula rasa was deemed to be not an existing mind but a kind of neutral surface upon which the effects of postnatal experience were impressed—a noncognitive surface. Consequently the newborn was presumed to be mindless. Nor is this presumption altogether outmoded. In his paper on "the brain-consciousness problem" Gomes (1966) maintained, "when a human baby is born, his mind, and with it, his capacity to control his behavior, are practically nonexistent" (p. 464). Like his empiricist predecessors he cited no specific evidence to support this a priori contention. However, the neonate's reported imitation of gestures makes his assertion dubious. The newborn certainly manifests "capacity to control his behavior" when he imitates tongue protrusion.

How does innate imitation bear on the question of bicameral consciousness? To imitate tongue protrusion the infant must perceive the adult's protruding tongue and at the same time experience what appears to be spontaneous awareness of its likeness to his own tongue, since he has never seen his own in a mirror. The newborn seemed to visually recognize the

21. Current interest in this question was precipitated by the Meltzoff and Moore article, which appeared in *Science* on 7 October 1977. The issue of 13 July 1979 contained three articles critical of the Meltzoff-Moore findings, in a section entitled "Interpreting 'Imitative' Responses in Early Infancy" (pp. 214–19). In a closing article Meltzoff and Moore dealt systematically with each of the points raised by their critics. To me it appears to be a persuasive rebuttal; but each person will have to decide this for himself after examining all the articles.

adult's protruding tongue as akin to his own proprioceptively experienced tongue—and to know that his could also protrude. How is this to be explained? One might postulate a neural linkage between the infant's optic nerve and the nerves mediating the tongue's kinesthetic impulses, similar to the neural mechanism involved in the innate pecking behavior of precocial birds. Immediately upon hatching a chick begins to peck at kernels of corn. The eye-beak coordination suggests a linkage between the optic nerve and the nerves responsible for pecking, perhaps even a connection between what the bird sees and what it does. This might be construed as attributing the rudiments of conscious content to the bird brain. To the layman with no mentalistic inhibitions, this would seem an obvious and unobjectionable interpretation.

Conscious content can also be attributed to the brain of the infant who imitates tongue protrusion, thus implying that the protrusion is not an unconscious reflex or a primitive tropistic, forced movement. Since both eyes are focused on the adult's face, visual processes are being activated, resulting in consciousness of the protruding tongue. The resulting binocular vision involves both hemispheres, but there is no double vision, merely a single consciousness of the tongue implying unicameral consciousness. Though the muscles of the tongue are bilaterally symmetrical and thus under control of both hemispheres, the tongue is not subject to lateral dominance. Voluntary tongue protrusion indicates integrative neural control, interhemispheric congruence, and a single or unicameral consciousness. This conclusion is equally applicable as the newborn imitates yawning, lip pursing, or eyelid fluttering—there is no interference between the muscles on the right side of the face and those on the left. As in spontaneous crying, smiling, grimacing, and frowning, the facial muscles reflect equipotential hemispheric innervation. One side of the face is more expressive than the other only in cases of nerve injury.

These studies of imitation by the newborn suggest there is perceptual clarity and hence a dawning of consciousness at the start of postnatal existence. Neither the mind nor the brain is a tabula rasa.[22] Despite the existence of two hemispheres, there is no evidence of two minds or two kinds of consciousness; there is no double vision or double hearing. The equipotential hemispheres imply an integrated brain, which implies an integrated mind, active at birth through the complex process of neural maturation initiated from the moment of conception.[23] Nor does such matura-

22. Nor did Locke consider the tabula rasa a nonconscious blank surface. He endowed the infant with the capacity for reflection, implying an incipient mind and consciousness ab initio.

23. For an informative account of neural maturation see Sperry's chapter "Mechanisms of Neural Maturation" (1951), in the *Handbook of Experimental Psychology,* edited by S. S. Stevens. Although written more than thirty years ago, it still is an informative introduction to the subject. It should be supplemented by the more recent account in Cowan (1979).

tion cease at birth; not all postnatal brain changes are due to learning. It is altogether likely that later changes interpreted as evidence of lateralization are fundamentally maturational changes, and hemispheric specialization is not mutually exclusive. There does not appear to be a sharp division of labor so that the left brain has a monopoly on sequential thinking and the right brain on intuitive and holistic ideation. The same is true of hemispheric motor control. According to clinical reports, the youthful aphasic patient is more likely to recover than the older patient, implying right-brain potential for motor speech control—thus the right-brain homologue to Broca's area is not inert.

Of course in the healthy brain with intact commissures, unlike the split brain, nondominant interhemispheric communication is the rule. As Kinsbourne noted in a recent article (1982, p. 142):

> There are no discontinuities in the brain, no independent channels traverse it, nor is its territory divisible into areas that house autonomous processes. The suggestive contours of the forebrain, when viewed as an anatomical specimen, and the separate hemispheres are a deceptive guide to how it works. Functional systems overlap sulci, traverse gyri, and even straddle hemispheres via the great forebrain commissure.

Despite the vast amount of research on lateralization, *rigid* segregation of cognitive skills in music or language or art or mathematics has not come to light, and without such segregation there can be no bicameral consciousness. The evidence is cumulative and definitive in support of a unicameral consciousness.

Concluding Comments

Studies of imitation in newborns suggest that the neonate starts life with an integrated brain and a unicameral consciousness. Nor does subsequent lateralization of linguistic and other skills mean two kinds of brains and two kinds of consciousness.[24] Regardless of the specialization attributed to each hemisphere, neuropsychological integration is not endangered in the healthy brain with intact commissures. An undamaged bicameral brain accommodates a unicameral consciousness.

I chose the verb *accommodates* because of its vagueness, to call attention to an important unresolved issue from psychology's philosophic

24. Interesting studies of such development of lateralized linguistic and other skills have been reported. For example, Cioffi and Kandel (1979) consider a possible sex difference in the processing of verbal and other material. Their work supplies helpful references to related studies.

past[25] — the brain/consciousness relation. To call this relation accommodative is not the same as calling it causal or interactive or labeling it a double-aspect or a parallel relation. It is prudent to avoid endorsing any of these proposed explanations, since the precise nature of the relation has not yet been established. This relation lies at the heart of the mystery of consciousness and, since conscious events are never experienced independent of brain tissue, appears indissoluble. The quest for understanding of behavior disorders has given rise to the specialties of psychiatry and neurology, whose very existence reflects the mystery of consciousness.

Both psychiatrists and neurologists must consider the transition from electrochemical brain events to conscious events, which is as much a mystery of the brain as of consciousness. As I said at the beginning of this book, a volume exploring this subject would require the collaboration of numerous experts, including neurochemists, electroencephalographers, brain surgeons, neuropathologists, hematologists, endocrinologists, anthropologists, philosophers of science, social psychologists, clinical psychologists, and possibly metaphysicians. We might envisage the mystery as an intricate jigsaw puzzle, with each expert possessing some of the pieces.

Recognizing the complexity of the mystery itself constitutes progress. This complexity is a far cry from what John Locke glimpsed as he reflected on the neonate's tabula rasa, or from what Paul Broca saw as he gazed upon the exposed brain of his famous patient. Although the mystery is still with us, great advances have taken place, accounting for the fascination of the research endeavors that persist from generation to generation. Progress may be slow and uneven but it is still progress.

References

Blake, R. R. 1948. Ocular activity during administration of the Rorschach test. *Journal of Clinical Psychology* 4:159–69.

Bogen, J. E. 1973. The other side of the brain: An appositional mind. In *The nature of human consciousness,* ed. R. E. Ornstein. San Francisco: W. H. Freeman.

Boring, E. G. 1950. *A history of experimental psychology.* New York: Appleton-Century-Crofts.

Bower, T. G. R. 1977. *A primer of infant development.* San Francisco: W. H. Freeman.

Brandt, H. F. 1945. *The psychology of seeing.* New York: Philosophical Library.

25. Shortly after writing this sentence I came across Garcia's 1981 article in which he too appears to recognize Locke's understanding of the tabula rasa as reflective: "First, let us dispense with the canard that he was a radical environmentalist wedded to the 'tabula rasa.' " This blunt introductory statement is followed by quotations from Locke's *Essay* (1981, p. 156).

Broca, P. 1965. On the speech center. In *A source book in the history of psychology,* ed. R. J. Herrnstein and E. G. Boring, 223–29. Cambridge: Harvard University Press.

Buswell, G. T. 1935. *How people look at pictures: A study of the psychology of perception in art.* Chicago: University of Chicago Press.

Cioffi, J., and Kandel, G. L. 1979. Laterality of stereognostic accuracy of children for words, shapes, and bigrams: A sex difference for bigrams. *Science* 204:1432–34.

Cowan, W. M. 1979. The development of the brain. *Scientific American* (September), 113–33.

Fantz, R. L. 1963. Pattern vision in newborn infants. *Science* 140:296–97.

Ferguson, E. S. 1977. The mind's eye: Nonverbal thought in technology. *Science* 197:827–36.

Flourens, P. 1974. Experimental studies on the properties and functions of the nervous system in vertebrates. In *The roots of psychology: A source book in the history of ideas,* ed. S. Solomon, 236–38. New York: Basic Books.

Fodor, J. A. 1981. The mind-body problem. *American Scientist* (January), 114–23.

Gall, F. J. 1965. On phrenology, the localization of the functions of the brain. In *A source book in the history of psychology,* ed. R. J. Herrnstein and E. G. Boring, 211–19. Cambridge: Harvard University Press.

Garcia, J. 1981. Tilting at the paper mills of academe. *American Psychologist* 36: 149–58.

Gazzaniga, M. S. 1967. The split brain in man. In *The nature of human consciousness: A book of readings,* ed. R. L. Ornstein, 87–100. San Francisco: W. H. Freeman.

Geschwind, N. 1975. The apraxias: Neural mechanisms of disorders of learned movements. *American Scientist* 63:188–95.

Goldstein, K., and Marmor, J. 1938. A case of aphasia, with special reference to the problems of repetition and word-finding. *Journal of Neurology and Psychiatry* 1:329–41.

Gomes, A. O. 1966. The brain-consciousness problem in contemporary scientific research. In *Brain and Conscious Experience,* ed. J. C. Eccles, 446–69. New York: Springer-Verlag.

Grings, W. W. 1973. The role of consciousness and cognition in autonomic behavior change. In *The psychophysiology of thinking,* ed. F. J. McGuigan and R. A. Schoonover, 233–62. New York: Academic Press.

Guilford, J. P. 1962. An informational view of mind. *Journal of Psychological Researches* 1:1–10.

———. 1974. A psychology with act, content, and form. *Journal of General Psychology* 90:87–100.

Hanfmann, E.; Rickers-Ovsiankina, M.; and Goldstein, K. 1944. Case Lanuti: Extreme concretization of behavior due to damage of the brain cortex. *Psychological Monographs* 57:1–72.

Head, H. 1926. *Aphasia and kindred disorders of speech.* Vol. 1. New York: Macmillan.

Holden, C. 1979. Paul MacLean and the triune brain. *Science* 204:1066–68.

Keller, R. 1942. Handedness among apes. *Ciba Symposia* 3:1146–47.

Kimura, D. 1973. The asymmetry of the human brain. *Scientific American* (March), 70–78.

Kinsbourne, M. 1982. Hemispheric specialization and the growth of human understanding. *American Psychologist* 37:411–20.

Ladd, G. T., and Woodworth, R. S. 1911. *Elements of physiological psychology.* New York: Charles Scribner's Sons.

Lashley, K. S. 1929. *Brain mechanisms and intelligence: A quantitative study of injuries to the brain.* Chicago: University of Chicago Press.

Lassen, N. A.; Ingvar, D. H.; and Skinhøj, E. 1978. Brain function and blood flow. *Scientific American* (October), 62–71.

Libet, B. 1966. Brain stimulation and the threshold of conscious experience. In *Brain and conscious experience,* ed. J. C. Eccles, 165–81. New York: Springer-Verlag.

Luria, A. R. 1973. *The working brain: An introduction to neuropsychology.* Trans. Basil Haigh. New York: Basic Books.

Meltzoff, A. N., and Moore, M. K. 1977. Imitation of facial and manual gestures by human neonates. *Science* 198:75–78.

Ornstein, R. E. 1973. Right and left thinking. *Psychology Today* 6:86–92.

———. 1978. The split and the whole brain. *Human Nature* 1:76–83.

O'Sullivan, M.; Guilford, J. P.; and de Mille, R. 1965. The measurement of social intelligence. *Reports from the Psychological Laboratory: University of Southern California* 34 (June):3–39.

Pelletier, K. R., and Garfield, C. 1976. *Consciousness: East and West.* New York: Harper and Row.

Penfield, W. 1966. Speech perception and the uncommitted cortex. In *Brain and conscious experience,* ed. J. C. Eccles, 217–37. New York: Springer-Verlag.

———. 1975. *The mystery of mind: A critical study of consciousness and the human brain.* Princeton: Princeton University Press.

Penfield, W., and Roberts, L. 1959. *Speech and brain mechanisms.* Princeton: Princeton University Press.

Popper, K. R., and Eccles, J. C. 1977. *The self and its brain.* New York: Springer International.

Rapaport, D. 1951. *Organization and pathology of thought.* New York: Columbia University Press.

Rees, M. 1962. The nature of mathematics. *Science* 138:9–12.

Rosenblueth, A. 1970. *Mind and brain: A philosophy of science.* Cambridge: MIT Press.

Ross, A. O. 1955. Integration as a basic cerebral function. *Psychological Reports* 1:179–202.

Ruch, T. C.; Patton, H. D.; Woodbury, J. W.; and Tow, A. L. 1965. *Neurophysiology.* Philadelphia: W. B. Saunders.

Sackeim, H. A.; Gur, R. C.; and Saucy, M. C. 1978. Emotions are expressed more intensely on the left side of the face. *Science* 202:434–35.

Sagan, C. 1977. *The dragons of Eden: Speculations on the evolution of human intelligence.* New York: Random House.

Sherrington, C. 1947. *The integrative action of the nervous system.* New Haven: Yale University Press. First published 1906.

Shirley, H. F. 1963. *Pediatric psychiatry*. Cambridge: Harvard University Press.

Sperry, R. W. 1951. Mechanisms of neural maturation. In *Handbook of experimental psychology*, ed. S. S. Stevens, 236–80. New York: John Wiley.

———. 1964. The great cerebral commissure. In *Frontiers of psychological research: Readings from the Scientific American*, ed. S. Coopersmith, 60–70. San Francisco: W. H. Freeman. Originally published January 1964.

Thorpe, W. H. 1966. Ethology and consciousness. In *Brain and conscious experience*, ed. J. C. Eccles, 470–505. New York: Springer-Verlag.

Von Neumann, J. 1956. The mathematician. In *The world of mathematics*, ed. J. R. Newman, 4:2053–63. New York: Simon and Schuster.

Wrenn, C. G., and Cole, L. 1935. *How to read rapidly and well: A manual of silent reading*. Stanford: Stanford University Press.

9 / Consciousness: A Progress Report

*T*oward the end of the previous chapter, I compared the mystery of consciousness to a jigsaw puzzle being worked on by experts from diverse disciplines, making slow but steady progress. It is in this spirit that the title of the present chapter is to be understood. This is not a formal listing of impressive successes but an account of constructive changes in outlook — both enlightening and subject to verification.

This progress report will center on consciousness as cognitive, an outlook that goes back to the rational soul of Aristotle's *De anima*. For the founding fathers of modern psychology cognition was only one of the many attributes of consciousness, some of which had misleading connotations; hence they were reluctant to define psychology as the science of consciousness and sought a definition congruent with their scientific aspirations.

On Defining Consciousness

John Dewey was just twenty-seven in 1886 when his *Psychology* was published. In it he defined psychology as "the Science of the facts or Phenomena of Self." He did not deny the existence of consciousness, for he made psychical phenomena "facts of consciousness," evidently expecting his readers to understand, though, as he put it, "consciousness can neither be defined nor described." Nevertheless, in his view psychology was to study "the various *forms* of consciousness showing the *conditions* under which they arise," as biologists study various forms of life even without a prior formal definition of life. Even today biologists disagree on whether viruses are a form of life or a complex lifeless protein.

But long before Dewey *consciousness* had been defined. In 1690, with the publication of Locke's classic *Essay concerning Human Understanding,* the word *consciousness* was first introduced as an abstract term and given this explicit definition: "Consciousness is the perception of what passes in a man's own mind." The word *mind* was taken for granted, not defined or explained. Since it seems to have been an alternative to the word *understanding,* Locke's central thesis may be reduced to the contention that mind is a product of the conjoint influence of sensation and reflection. The latter was deemed a conscious process, since when engaged in reflection man is "conscious to himself that he thinks." Locke elaborated upon reflection as follows:

> [It] is the perception of the operation of our own mind within us, as it is employed about the ideas it has got; which operations . . . are perception, thinking, doubting, believing, reasoning, knowing, willing, and all the different actings of our own minds; which we being *conscious* of, and observing in ourselves, do from these receive into our understandings as distinct ideas, as we do from bodies affecting our senses. (1901, p. 207; italics added.)

I include this quotation to call attention to Locke's seven examples of the "operations" of reflection. Of these seven acts only one is cast as a noun, while the other six are participles or gerunds. The exception is the word *perception* — not *perceiving* — because for Locke perception is the consciousness "of what passes in a man's own mind," making perception and consciousness synonymous. Reflection, perception, and consciousness all supplied the understanding with "the different actings of our minds," illustrated by such verbal nouns as doubting, reasoning, and believing. These and others such as abstracting, judging, hoping, analyzing, daydreaming, concentrating, and theorizing are all cognitive processes. All have to do with knowing, for the word *cognition* is derived from *gnoscere,* "to know," just as *consciousness* is derived from *scire,* "to know," the root of the word *science.*

Locke as Cognitivist

Although Locke is usually identified with the history of British empiricism, his psychology was not so nonrationalistic and objectivist. He did place great emphasis upon how external sense affected ideational development, but he also recognized the influence of reflection or "internal sense." His empiricism thus was both objective and subjective, as is evident in this passage from the *Essay* (1956, p. 296):

> *Our knowledge of our own existence is intuitive.* As for our own existence, we perceive it so plainly and so certainly that it neither

needs nor is capable of any proof. For nothing can be more evident to us than our own existence. I think, I reason, I feel pleasure and pain: can any of these be more evident to me than my own existence? If I doubt of all other things, that very doubt makes me perceive my own existence, and will not suffer me to doubt of that. For if I know I feel pain, it is evident I have as certain perception of my own existence as of the existence of the pain I feel; or if I know I doubt, I have as certain perception of the existence of the thing doubting, as of that thought which I call doubt. Experience, then, convinces us that we have an intuitive knowledge of our own existence, and an internal infallible knowledge that we are. In every act of sensation, reasoning, or thinking, we are conscious to ourselves of our own being, and in this matter come not short of the highest degree of certainty.

I said before that Locke regarded mind as a product of the conjoint influence of sensation and reflection. It now appears that he also recognized intuition. His stress on doubting is reminiscent of the *res cogitans* of Descartes and helps reveal him as a philosophic forerunner of cognitive psychology. His cognitive orientation is also reflected in his refusal "to meddle with the physical consideration of the mind." He thus belongs to what Sampson refers to as "the cognitivist tradition," though according to Sampson there is a contrast between that tradition and British empiricism (1981, p. 730):

> The cognitivist tradition is usually contrasted with the objectivist tradition of British empiricism, which has also influenced the contemporary forms of psychology but which emphasizes the properties of the object more than those of the subject. Cognitive psychology recognizes a disparity between what is "out there" and its internal representation and argues that behavior is a function of the subjective world as transformed and represented internally.

For Locke, what is "out there" as mediated by sensation was contrasted with consciousness defined as "the perception of what passes in a man's own mind," and was also contrasted with the "different actings of our own minds" in reflection and with the certainty of intuitive knowledge. Locke's distinction between primary and secondary qualities of sensation was also in accord with the disparity Sampson notes. He deemed primary qualities like shape, number, and extensity to be intrinsic to the physical object and contrasted them with secondary qualities such as color, taste, and smell. In short, Locke's empiricism does not contrast sharply with what Sampson ascribes to the cognitivist tradition. The *Essay*'s treatment of human understanding makes his empiricism altogether congruent with that tradition, as does its treatment of ideation, concept formation, and other cognitive or noetic processes.

The Noetic Consciousness

To speak of consciousness as noetic might seem tautological, like referring to consciousness as conscious. As a derivative of *noesis,* the Greek word for cognition or intellect, *noetic* connotes consciousness as cognitive or intellectual in the sense of knowing that one knows.

Although Aristotle used *nous* to mean mind, he had no word for consciousness. His psychology did provide for a hierarchy of souls or "psychic powers," "the nutritive, the appetitive, the sensory, the locomotive, and the power of thinking." This power of thinking as a function of the rational soul he considered a unique human endowment, while the sensory soul was limited to animals. Had he known the concept of consciousness, he might have contrasted the noetic consciousness of man with the sensory consciousness of beasts as the difference between thoughtful apprehension and thoughtless awareness or between meaningful understanding and meaningless sentience. Kant once wrote: "The understanding cannot see. The senses cannot think. Only by their union can knowledge be produced," a formulation reminiscent of Locke's distinction between sensation and reflection.

Consciousness as noetic thus has long been recognized, though expressed differently from age to age. In *De anima* Aristotle wrote, "by mind I mean that whereby the soul thinks and judges," and he opened his *Metaphysics* with the words "All men by nature desire to know." Augustine attributed man's observation of his inner thoughts and feelings to "man's internal sense" (*sensus interioris hominis*), and Descartes wrote of "the thing that thinks," or the *res cogitans.* Somewhat later it became "the intellect itself" (*intellectus ipse*) of Leibniz, and still later Brentano sharpened the concept in the *intentionalism* of his act psychology, by which every conscious act points to or intends something so that we are always conscious *of* something. Invariably something is the object of the noetic consciousness as we think thoughts, make judgments, entertain likes and dislikes, or perform other cognitive acts. Each such act is thus a noetic process to the degree that something is apprehended or becomes known.

In denying the existence of consciousness, James was warning against its reification by those who might conceive of it as an independent entity, made of some kind of psychic stuff. For him this sort of consciousness had no existence. He viewed consciousness as a cognitive process having a "function in experience" and added "that function is knowing." This

knowing function has been receiving increasing recognition by cogniti-
vists in the sense that to be conscious is to know and to know is to be
informed. They recognize the informational implications of the noetic consciousness and thus the underlying equivalence between consciousness and
information.

Consciousness and Information as Equivalent

The words *information* and *consciousness,* though they have much in
common, differ in connotation, the former being more factual and concrete. Nobody has questioned the existence of information as James questioned the existence of consciousness. And I would guess that Dewey would
have had no trouble defining *information*. Though equivalent, the two
terms are not identical in meaning. Though we talk about bits of information, it would be nonsense to talk about bits of consciousness. A boxer
who is knocked out is said to have lost consciousness, but not information. He is called unconscious because stimulating his sense organs elicits
no reaction—he appears blind, deaf, analgesic, anosmic, and anaptic. Consciousness is said to be restored when stimulation once more elicits characteristic reactions. Years ago, in the idiom of structural psychology, light,
pain, sound, smell, and touch were regarded as attributes of sensation
and considered in terms of quality, intensity, extensity, and protensity.
Now we think of them as familiar *known* items of experience.

Today's cognitive psychologists think of such known items of experience as information and see all sensory processes as informational processes. Some biologists have seen the sensory consciousness in this same
way. The biologist Sir Julian Huxley wrote (1959, pp. 16–17):

> The brain alone is not responsible for mind, even though it is a
> necessary organ for its manifestation. Indeed an isolated brain is a
> piece of biological nonsense, as meaningless as an isolated human
> individual. I would prefer to say that mind is generated by or in
> complex organizations of living matter, capable of receiving *informa-
> tion* of many qualities or modalities about events both in the other
> world and in itself, of synthesizing and processing that *information*
> in various organized forms, and of utilizing it to direct present and
> future action—in other words by higher animals with their sense-
> organs, nerves, brains, and muscles. (Italics added.)

And the ornithologist Joel Carl Welty had this to say about the nervous
system of birds (1975, p. 68):

> The chief functions of the central nervous system are to integrate
> *information* received through sensory impulses from the body and

outside world, to store this *information* selectively in the form of memory and learning, and to integrate and coordinate outgoing motor impulses to the viscera and muscles into useful patterns of behavior. (Italics added.)

According to Welty, the informational sensory impulses are "stored" not in the bird's cerebral cortex, but in the corpus striatum. Since the bird's cortex is poorly developed and devoid of fissures, the corpus striatum becomes the dominant cerebral structure.

Guilford's Informational Consciousness

In discussing the informational consciousness, Guilford wrote that "feelings and emotions may be regarded as varieties of information" and that "psychologically, an individual is an information processing agent." Guilford's views of consciousness grew out of his investigations of the complexities of the human intellect. For thirty years he has carefully designed factor-analytic studies of human cognition, reported both independently and in collaboration with successive generations of graduate students. These many publications are scattered in different journals, but fortunately Guilford has summarized salient findings in his *Cognitive Psychology* (1979). Guilford's provocative cognitive schema, known as the structure-of-intellect or SI model, does not lend itself to succinct presentation, but in the book he outlines its essentials (1979, pp. 16–25). The model shows great promise as a heuristic contribution to cognitive psychology.

In a recent article Guilford discusses ways the model might be of help to cognitive psychology. In particular he refers to the informational view of consciousness (1982, p. 49):

> Cognitive psychology took an enormous step forward when it substituted the concept of information for that of "consciousness." Information is much more manageable than consciousness in many ways. Indeed, because of the substitution . . . a better label for this discipline would be "informational psychology." One advantage of the information-processing view is that mental phenomena, so envisaged, can be unconscious as well as conscious. In either case, observations of mental activity must be largely inferential, but this is true of atomic physics and of other natural sciences as well.

"Information processing" is a term belonging to the many disciplines involved in organizing, storing, transmitting, and communicating knowledge. It has to do with cybernetics, libraries, radio, television, calculators, computers, tape recorders, telephones, shorthand, or—in brief—any mode of communication. It is not unique to psychology. Guilford defines information as "that which organisms discriminate" and acknowledges that the definition is derived from "what information engineers call *transmitted information.*" The substitution of the concept of information for the concept of consciousness thus ought to be envisaged in the light of the vast scope of information processing. This also suggests the vast cognitive scope of the SI model.

In this 1982 article Guilford points out that the SI model can help dispose of "cognitive psychology's ambiguities." Such ambiguity, he notes, dates far back in psychology's history and pervades its basic concepts. Some are treated as unitary rather than recognized as clusters of discrete components. For example, the concept of memory involves many components. Elsewhere Guilford alludes to thirty memory functions stemming from thirty separate kinds of information (1979, pp. 77–78). On the basis of factor-analytic research, Guilford has defined intelligence as "a systematic collection of abilities or functions for the processing of information of different kinds in various ways" (1982, p. 49).[1]

In discussing such processing of information, Guilford brings up one troublesome ambiguity, the subject of *verbal* information, which he sees as pertaining to three kinds of information, not just one. The concept does include the semantic significance of words, but Guilford describes two other usages—the auditory symbolic and the visual symbolic. That these entail different cognitive abilities was shown by low intercorrelations among three kinds of verbal tests, which meant to Guilford that "the brain evidently performs in quite distinctly different ways with the three kinds of items of information."[2]

Guilford also objects to the uncritical way tests of reasoning have been used, since various tests may have close to zero correlation with one another. Are these tests to be interpreted as measuring the same cognitive process? Apparently not. According to Guilford, "there are a number of analogical-reasoning tests, each kind representing one unique reasoning ability." This is true for tests of deductive as contrasted with inductive

---

1. Some time earlier Sternberg mentioned the same idea in an article dealing with cognitive approaches to understanding mental abilities. He explained that "subjects are tested in their ability to perform tasks that contemporary psychologists believe measure basic information-processing abilities" (1981, pp. 1181–82).

2. Some support for the idea that the brain has three ways of dealing with verbal material is supplied by studies of aphasic disorders. There are failures to understand the meaning of language in semantic aphasia, failures to recognize verbal symbols in word blindness, and failures to comprehend spoken words in auditory aphasia. Broca's area in the inferior frontal convolution is associated with vocal speech, Wernicke's area in the superior temporal lobe is associated with language comprehension, and the primary visual area in the occipital region is implicated in alexia and strephosymbolia. Norman Geschwind elaborates on these aphasic disturbances in a 1970 article, "The Organization of Language and the Brain," and a 1979 article, "Specialization of the Human Brain."

reasoning and tests of convergent versus divergent production, a finding noted in the 1920s in a study of syllogistic reasoning. The study compared scores on a syllogism test with scores on an intelligence test. Although there was a marked correlation, M. C. Wilkins reported the following individual exceptions (1928, p. 30): "There seem to be individuals of good general intelligence who are able to succeed but poorly in formal syllogistic reasoning. One individual who on the intelligence test has only two individuals making a better score, on the syllogism test has 39 individuals making a better score." The intelligence test Wilkins employed had little in common with the items included in the later SI model. But the individual exceptions show a marked discrepancy between reasoning scores on the syllogism test and the reasoning tapped by the intelligence test, confirming Guilford's point.

Almost all cognitive tests are verbal in nature, and many are presumed to reflect the informational significance of consciousness. But exclusive reliance upon such tests overlooks the possibly equal significance of nonverbal cognitive processes.

Is Language Necessary for Thinking?

Thinking as used in this question refers to any ideational process, not only to reasoning. Such unrestricted usage includes "I think I'll take a walk" or "I think it was the telephone" or "I think he means well" or "I think the boy looks sad" or "I think it's my fault." The word *think* thus refers to judgments, perceptions, inferences, guesses, intentions, or any ideational process. Of course language is involved even in such processes as daydreaming or soliloquizing. But is language indispensable for thinking? If so, then the infant or preverbal child cannot think. But if the concept is enlarged to include nonverbal ideation, one must grant the infant this capacity. Babies soon recognize and reach for the bottle with evident intention. Is it doing violence to language to say the baby is thinking of the bottle? Similarly, the infant soon knows his mother's face and voice, indicating ideation.[3]

Conceding nonverbal thinking in infancy does not gainsay the tremendous role of language in cognition. Civilization in all its phases is immersed in and regulated by linguistic communication, which maintains and perpetuates the entire social order. Earlier in this century, in conjunction with the hybrid study of psycholinguistics, Benjamin Lee Whorf (1897–1941)

---

3. Recognizing faces is now known to involve a distinctive perceptual process. According to Geschwind, this process appears to center in what he calls the facial-recognition area of the brain. It has a bilateral location on the "underside of the temporal and occipital lobes" (1979, p. 191).

proposed that the nature of a culture is determined by the language of its people. In his view language governs the nature of thought, in contrast to the ordinary view that thought determines linguistic expression.

Whorf was not a psychologist but was connected with an insurance company, and the study of language was his avocation.[4] Whorf was struck by the diversity of vocabulary, word order, and other linguistic characteristics in the languages of different cultures. Such diversity, he held, determines how people perceive the world. The Eskimo has many words for snow, each indicating some feature important to him. Accordingly, for him snow is not the same as for an Englishman who has very few words for snow. Whorf studied the language of American Indians and there found much of the evidence he cited to support his cultural hypothesis. For example, he found the Navajo employing a single word for green and blue, as if they overlooked a chromatic difference obvious to us, and the vocabulary of color determined its perception. To Whorf this meant that language determines consciousness and that without words there can be no thinking. Titchener also argued this way: "there is no thought without words."

Many have questioned this dictum of no thought without words, among them the pioneer Gestalt psychologist Max Wertheimer (1880–1943), in his *Productive Thinking* (1959). Wertheimer devotes a chapter to his long talks with Albert Einstein, starting in 1916, when Einstein recounted "the story of the dramatic developments which culminated in the theory of relativity." In the course of these talks, Wertheimer probed Einstein regarding the precise kinds of ideational processes that characterized his thinking through the many years he worked on the relativity theory. Einstein was a gymnasium student of sixteen when the work began, and it grew to be the occupation of a lifetime. When asked how he had come to think about some axioms, Einstein said: "These thoughts did not come in any verbal formulation. I very rarely think in words at all. A thought comes, and I may try to express it in words afterward" (1959, p. 228).

Wertheimer did not elaborate upon Einstein's observation, and he does not mention the relation of language and thought in his account of productive thinking, though implicitly he devotes a whole chapter to it. Chapter 2 discusses Wertheimer's work with deaf-mute children at the Psychiatric and Physiological Institute of Vienna, undertaken at the request of the head of the children's clinic, who was confronted with educating these children. A psychologist and a pediatrician who had been studying the problem had not been encouraging, for they felt that "since the children lacked language, their intellectual abilities were extremely low" (1959,

---

4. A fuller account, and a critique of Whorf's thesis, is found in chapter 7 of Roger Brown's *Words and Things* (1958). His critique examines the thesis from the standpoint of psychology.

p. 79). The director engaged Wertheimer to find out whether the children were uneducable.

In dealing with the children Wertheimer stated that he used neither gestures nor language. Since the children are said to have "lacked language" we may assume they had not acquired the sign language of the deaf.[5] Wertheimer used building blocks of various sizes, shapes, and colors. He would sit at a table with one of the children and build a simple structure with three of the blocks, then knock it down. Most of the children would stack the blocks up again. Or Wertheimer would take the structure down and let the child find the right blocks to duplicate his model. He varied the blocks used so he could note how the child dealt with the changes. In watching a child reach for and manipulate the blocks Wertheimer looked for evidence of understanding, planning, or insight—in a word, thinking. Even when their efforts failed, Wertheimer noted, the experiences were not futile. It was evident that the children had learned something positive about why a structure collapsed (p. 82). Wertheimer repeatedly interprets these experiments with wordless children as indicating thinking.

These experiments with deaf-mute children are congruent with Einstein's unverbalized thinking, with what the Würzburg psychologists said about their imageless thoughts, and, I am tempted to add, with what W. H. Thorpe said about the counting of his raven (1966, p. 549). Whorf's ideas notwithstanding, nonverbal ideation does occur.

What Makes Thinking Informative?

The common distinction between superficial and profound thoughts shows we recognize thoughts as more or less meaningful or informative. As I pointed out in chapter 3 in connection with insight, knowing how to turn on lights, drive a car, or boil an egg does not mean we have insight into electrical circuitry, automotive engineering, or colloids. Nor was Sultan, Köhler's ape, to be credited with insight just because he fitted jointed sticks together to retrieve a banana. Insight requires understanding the mechanism of the jointed sticks.

The same principle holds for the informational interpretation of consciousness: the more information, the more consciousness. Let us assume

5. There is no question about the importance of exposing deaf children to language during the early years. As Moskowitz reported, lack of exposure means a later "handicap of little or no language" (1978, p. 108). This handicap, she points out, can be avoided. It is not found among deaf children of deaf parents who have been exposed to American Sign Language. By age three their fluency in sign language approximates the verbal fluency of the hearing child of three. Furthermore, the deaf child with a command of sign language learns English as a second language more easily than a deaf child first learns English taught by oral speech or lip reading.

that a junior high school science teacher has his students briefly define the words *eclipse* and *litmus*. He picks up two of the papers. On one he reads, "I think you explained about eclipse when we had the moon lessons. About litmus I'm not sure. I think we had it on our chemistry homework." The second paper reads as follows: "By eclipse is meant the way one planet or body in the sky seems to cover or cast a shadow on another. When the planet earth in its orbit comes between the sun and the moon, there would be an eclipse of the moon. Litmus is a special paper treated in such a way that it can be used to find out if a chemical solution is an acid or a base. I think if it turns blue the liquid is base and if it turns red it is an acid." The second paper reveals a consciousness and mind far better informed than those revealed in the first paper.

Or assume that an arithmetic teacher promises a prize to any student who can write a sequence of numbers after hearing them read slowly just three times, with a slight pause between each pair: 25 36 49 64 81. This series of ten numbers is beyond the average memory span for digits, and many more than three readings would be required to retain them by rote memory. But recognizing the series as the squares of each digit from five to nine would make it easier. Two readings might suffice. This is an example of productive thinking—insightful thinking—in contrast to the thinking of pupils who depended on uncomprehending rote memory. The former thinking is more conscious and more informative—rather than relatively meaningless.

Informative thinking enhances understanding and reveals a grasp of underlying principle. It is informative in being productive. Data in the telephone directory are informative but not productive; learning telephone numbers does not enhance human understanding. Promotion of productive or informational thinking is an important but somewhat neglected pedagogic challenge,[6] and the centrality of this kind of thinking in the work of cognitive psychologists should not be overlooked.

The equivalence of productive thinking and consciousness as informative appears to have been unrecognized until the past few decades. Its recognition shows growth in our understanding of consciousness and is part of an accelerated progress in recent years.

Accelerated Progress in Recent Decades

The American Psychological Association was founded in 1892. Since that date, as Fishman and Neigher noted, "organized psychology in America

---

6. Despite the lapse of years, Wertheimer's *Productive Thinking* is still a stimulating repository of enlightening suggestions for coping with this challenge.

has grown at a continuous and explosive rate, reflected in APA's membership increase over the past 60 years—from 393 in 1920 to 52,440 today" (1982, p. 545). These APA members have diverse interests, as is shown by their affiliation with one or more particular APA divisions, which have recently proliferated. Every few years a new one seems to appear. In 1982, by actual count,[7] there were forty divisions. Moreover, some twenty have been formed since the 1960s, so 50 percent of the divisions have come into existence within the past two decades, reflecting the enlargement of psychology's specialized interests. I think this growth implies enhanced understanding of mind and consciousness and thus constitutes accelerated progress.

Each of these divisions is investigating some segment of the total field of psychology. Every bit of successful research, no matter how small, sheds light on the mystery of consciousness. One division is concerned with psychotherapy, another with adult development and aging; still another deals with religious issues; and still others take up such diverse interests as psychopharmacology, psychology of women, clinical psychology, personality and social psychology, experimental psychology, psychology and law, psychological hypnosis, and some twenty other specialties. Yet there is no Division of Consciousness because, directly or indirectly, each of the forty divisions is concerned with phenomena of consciousness. This is what they have in common, and it accounts for their unified interest in psychology.

This interest is expressed in experimental research, field studies, counseling, clinical investigations, psychotherapy, educational psychology, rehabilitation, industrial management, neuropsychology, school psychology, philosophical psychology, and still other areas of research and practice. Psychologists are now officially connected with elementary schools and medical schools, with state hospitals and veterans hospitals, with aid to the blind and aid to the deaf, with courts and prisons, with highway safety and flight safety, with the business world and the armed forces—wherever psychological services might be rendered.[8]

From the informational standpoint the vast scope of this expanded psychological activity is itself evidence of progress. Each activity supplies opportunities for understanding some distinctive pattern of consciousness. School psychologists may gain insight into the dyslexic child's bewildered frustration, and military psychologists may come to appreciate the disruptive effects of barracks life on neurotic or sensitive recruits.

---

7. Although the latest division is Division 42, there is no Division 4 or Division 11; hence, just forty divisions.

8. As Kaswan (1981) brought out, this expansion of psychological services is being subjected to examination and critical evaluation.

Rehabilitation psychologists become cognizant of the catastrophic impact blindness or aphasia or paraplegia may have on consciousness. Prison psychologists learn how confinement affects the consciousness of convicts. Psychologists who deal with juvenile offenders or battered children garner similar insights, as do those who work with victims of sexual assault.[9] Let us survey some of these areas where insight is expanding.

Cognition in Children

An elaborate report on psychological studies of children edited by Sandra Scarr and published in 1979 includes a section entitled "Improving Our Knowledge of Children's Thought." In her introduction to the articles in this section Frances Horowitz reports, "our knowledge of children's thought has increased dramatically over the past 25 years" (Scarr 1979, p. 892). This generalization is supported by Leslie B. Cohen's paper, "Our Developing Knowledge of Infant Perception and Cognition"; according to Cohen, "More has been learned about infant perception in the past 15 or 20 years than in all previous years" (p. 894). In the 1950s there were just a few students of infant development; now several hundred are engaged in this kind of research.

Data on infants' visual perception are obtained by measuring the duration of ocular fixations while the baby focuses on some target. By looking through a peephole the investigator can observe the target's reflection on the infant's cornea. Considerable information has been obtained by this technique, and it has been established that infants perceive forms, colors, patterns, and faces and also that they prefer novel to familiar visual stimuli, curved lines to straight lines, solid objects to two-dimensional objects, color to colorless stimuli, and complex patterns to simple patterns. When four-month-old infants were shown a silent film simultaneously with one accompanied by sound from a speaker, the latter film elicited longer visual fixations, "thus demonstrating the ability to coordinate auditory and visual information." These impressive findings constitute a marked change from the time when the infant's visual world was thought to be an amorphous confusion.

The same visual-fixation technique has been adapted to study both memory and concept formation. In one study of long-term memory it was found that infants as young as five months retained for two weeks some memory of a face observed for two minutes. Other studies used photographs of faces to investigate concept formation and found that "30-week-

---

9. An account of psychological efforts on behalf of victims of sexual assault is found in Atkeson et al. (1982).

old infants showed not only that they could acquire a concept but that they could acquire different levels of concepts" according to changes in the photographs.

This experimental psychology of infancy is providing glimpses into the newborn's hitherto unknown perceptual impressions and cognitive stirrings. Such glimpses, as Cohen (1979) points out, may eventually contribute to the diagnosis and treatment "of specific perceptual and cognitive deficits in high-risk or retarded infants."

Striking progress is brought to light in Rochel Gelman's essay "Preschool Thought." She hints at this progress in the following summary:

> Until very recently, almost all researchers of cognitive development have made a habit of contrasting the preschooler with the older child. Preschoolers have been characterized as lacking the classification abilities, communication skills, number concepts, memorial skills, and a framework for reasoning about causal relationships between events that older children are granted. Indeed, had one written an essay on preschool thought five years ago, the conclusion might have been that preschoolers are remarkably ignorant. In this essay, I review some of the evidence that has begun to pile up against the view that preschoolers are cognitively inept. I then consider why we failed to see what it is that preschoolers can do and possible misinterpretations of the recent findings. (1979, p. 900)

The alleged shortcomings of the preschooler's cognitive development listed by Gelman typify Piaget's view of the preschool child's egocentric cognitive orientation, by which the child expects everybody to see the world as he does, as if *his* experiences are the measure of all things. When requested to choose the picture showing how a fluttering flag would look to a child across the street, he selects one that duplicates the view from his side. According to Piaget, he cannot enter the ideational world of others to appreciate how their thoughts differ from his. This Piagetian view of the preschooler's cognitive limitations is what Gelman challenged.

Gelman and a colleague found that four-year-olds, contrary to Piaget's view, did comprehend the ideational outlook of others. In talking to two-year-olds about a toy, the children used short words and simple constructions, but they used longer words and more complex constructions when talking to adults. They recognized that babies know less than adults, so they treated them differently. They merely told babies about the toy, but they engaged adults in conversation, sharing thoughts about the toy and asking questions. There was no evidence of an egocentric ignorance of or indifference to the thoughts and abilities of others.

This sharing of perspectives was also demonstrated for visual perception. Gelman describes how children from one to three, when asked to show toys to adults, presented the front of the toys. When they showed pictures, the picture was almost always turned toward the adult, while the blank back faced the child. Here too there was an appreciation of perspectives with no egocentric fixity.

In this survey of preschool thinking, Gelman reports on a wide range of cognitive abilities that investigators have brought to light—among others, the abilities to use numbers, to coin words, to think in classes or categories, to appreciate the sequence of time, and finally the preschool child's amazing ability to learn his native language. One researcher has estimated that by age six children know about fourteen thousand words, thus learning an average of nine new words each day from the time speaking begins until their sixth birthdays.

Gelman warns against misinterpreting these recent proofs of preschoolers' cognitive competence. In spite of their successes, many tasks that older children find easy baffle preschool children. Children are not miniature adults. The journey from early childhood to maturity is marked by developmental stages of preadolescence, adolescence, and postadolescence, then people must pass through young adulthood to middle age and on to old age. The progression is often hampered by retrogression, and with the advent of old age the mature adult has new problems to face.

The Aging Consciousness: Some Key Issues

Problems of aging are numerous and complex and require the collaboration of many specialists. The most informative psychological treatment of these problems is a bulky volume containing forty-three chapters written by some ninety authors, edited by L. W. Poon and entitled *Aging in the 1980s: Psychological Issues*. Its coverage exemplifies the acceleration of psychological progress in recent decades; as the volume's prologue states, "The psychology of aging has matured in the last 50 years" (1980, p. xiii). Let me mention some of the less technical topics discussed.

One chapter is devoted to the part grandparents play in family dynamics. Another deals with the hearing difficulties so common among the elderly, though there is technical discussion of the measurement of auditory sensation. Another chapter concerns the emotional disturbances associated with senility, including cerebral atrophy and its assessment. Impaired memory is a frequent gerontological complaint, so there is an account of the effects certain drugs have on memory. An especially interesting chapter concerns the problems confronting victims of reduced sensory acuity and reduced mobility and the ways these handicaps might be overcome, with suggestions about the legibility of street signs, adequacy of illumination, accessibility of bus routes, and nearness of shops, plus practical suggestions about household arrangements, including a special kitchen (p. 419) for a person confined to a wheelchair.

A chapter by Frances Cohen discusses how attitude and expectation influence the outcome of surgery.

> Physicians frequently note that despite similarities in physical condition, surgical patients (as well as patients with a variety of illnesses) often differ greatly in the course of physical recovery. It has been thought that this variability may be due in part to differences in the way patients cope with the stresses involved. Because of the greater incidence of health problems among those in their middle and later years, it is particularly important to determine what factors influence recovery and whether psychological intervention can improve the recovery process. Moreover, as the developmental literature suggests, there may be critical differences in the types of coping strategies used by different people at different stages of the life cycle. These differences may influence intervention tactics. For example, if active modes of coping are less common among older patients and yet prove to be the most adaptive strategy, health professionals might plan special intervention programs with this population to influence the ways in which they cope (p. 375).

Although the problems raised here were formulated only during the 1970s, some thirty research studies have already dealt with various aspects of them, and some promising leads have come to light.

The section entitled "Advances in the Cognitive Psychology of Aging" deals with differences in information processing between age groups, including perceptual and attentional processes, and discusses new trends in the investigation of learning and memory as influenced by age. For the past two decades most of the research in this area has been based on information processing, which regards learning as an active cognitive process in which the learner participates rather than passively being bombarded by items of information. Such active participation is very evident in memory-span studies. Tasks falling within the limits of the memory span are described as primary and those exceeding the limits as secondary. In general, primary memory does not appear to be impaired by age; but age does disrupt secondary memory. Other chapters in this section review the literature on how age affects concept formation, problem solving, and testable intelligence. The extensive references show that these cognitive issues have been a dominant interest during the 1970s.

Another gerontological subject actively pursued during the 1970s and reviewed in the Poon volume is midlife personality changes. For many the decade from forty to fifty may be a critical period of transition. For others this midlife period extends for fifteen or twenty years. Family responsibilities change as children leave to establish homes of their own. Other concerns may include retirement from work or profession, dread of aging, anxiety about aged parents, worry about midlife endocrine changes, especially as affecting sexual life, and thoughts about one's will as one comes to grips with one's own mortality. In some respects this period of personal crisis resembles the transition from puberty to early maturity, for both are apt to entail intense preoccupation with what lies ahead, provoking uncertainty, anxiety, and self-distrust. There is a relatively high incidence of suicide or attempted suicide in both periods, and such self-destructive consciousness constitutes another area of psychological study that has come to the fore in recent decades.

The Self-Destructive Consciousness

Active psychological study of suicide, especially aimed at suicide prevention, began in the 1950s. A vast amount of information has been systematized since then, giving rise to the field of study known as suicidology. Suicidologists become adept at recognizing clues to a self-destructive consciousness. In our culture suicide is regarded as unfortunate or sinful and is prevented whenever possible. Because of this disapproval people may be reluctant to acknowledge suicide attempts. They may rationalize that "the gas in the kitchen was left on by accident" or that "the poor woman was confused when she took too many sleeping pills." This reluctance is a manifestation of the tendency to regard suicide as weakness or lack of courage and thus as dishonorable.

In other cultures, however, suicide may be hailed as evidence of strength, courage, and honor. During World War II, Japanese kamikaze pilots made suicidal bombing attacks, and their suicide was a tribute to them. An older phase of Japanese culture provided for the honorable ritual of harakiri, or suicide by disembowelment, as a demonstration of fidelity to a respected superior. Monks and nuns in Vietnam at the time of the Vietnam war set themselves aflame in public as a means of social protest and died as heroes and heroines.

These cultural differences in the evaluation of suicide were recognized by the French sociologist Emile Durkheim (1858–1917). His 1897 book on suicide brought the subject within the orbit of scientific investigation. In his view there are three kinds of suicide. One kind, which he called *altruistic,* has society's endorsement, like the Japanese and Vietnamese instances just cited. Such altruistic acts are carried out for a cause or as proof of devotion. Acts of self-sacrifice in which one dies so another may live exemplify altruistic suicide. Antithetic to this is Durkheim's *egoistic* suicide, the self-inflicted death of one who has withdrawn from society, lacks family ties, and feels impelled to end a lonely, ego-centered existence. Statistically there are more suicides among unmarried men than among married men. The third kind of suicide is Durkheim's *anomic* suicide, which is attributable to the disruption of social moorings or community ties. It occurs when an individual's value system breaks down under sudden catastrophic stress such as loss of a fortune in a stock market crash, death of a family member in a car accident, or disgrace because of a divorce scandal—the list is endless. The victim may feel abandoned by God, unworthy in the eyes of family and friends, or a failure in his own eyes so that he welcomes the peace of death.

Durkheim's views are usually classified as belonging to the sociology of suicide; in his day there was no psychology of suicide worthy of the name. Even William James, in his famous chapter "The Consciousness of Self" disposed of suicide in this brief paragraph (1890, p. 317):

> When possessed by the emotion of *fear* . . . we are in a *negative* state of mind; that is, our desire is limited to the mere banishing of something, without regard to what shall take its place. In this state of mind there can unquestionably be genuine thoughts, and genuine acts of suicide, spiritual and social, as well as bodily. Anything, *anything,* at such times, so as to escape and not be! But such conditions of suicidal frenzy are pathological in their nature and run dead against everything that is regular in the life of the Self in man.

Upon superficial inspection this seems to be an a priori explanation of suicide, not the product of direct investigation. Yet this succinct comment may not have been altogether independent of personal experience. As reported in Matthiessen's biography *The James Family,* James wrote to a friend that during the winter of 1867 he had been "on the continual verge of suicide" (1947, p. 213). James was twenty-six at the time. Years later, when he was close to sixty, he delivered a series of lectures in Edinburgh that were published as *The Varieties of Religious Experience.* As an example of a "sick soul" he presented a case he said he had translated from the French. He thanked "the sufferer" for permission to quote the case and described it as an instance of "the worst kind of melancholy" or a "form of panic fear." As he later acknowledged, the "French case" was a personal experience, apparently dating back to the winter of 1867. It is thus a sophisticated psychologist's retrospective account of his own self-destructive consciousness (1902, pp. 160–61):

> Whilst in this state of philosophic pessimism and general depression of spirits about my prospects, I went one evening into a dressing room in the twilight to procure some article that was there; when suddenly there fell upon me without any warning, just as if it came out of the darkness, a horrible fear of my own existence. Simul-

taneously, there arose in my mind the image of an epileptic patient I had seen in the asylum, a black-haired youth with greenish skin, entirely idiotic, who used to sit all day on one of the benches, or rather shelves against the wall, with his knees drawn up against his chin, and the coarse gray undershirt, which was his only garment, drawn over them inclosing his entire figure. He sat there like a sort of sculptured Egyptian cat or Peruvian mummy, moving nothing but his black eyes and looking absolutely non-human. The image and my fear entered into a species of combination with each other. *That shape am I,* I felt, potentially. Nothing that I possess can defend me against that fate, if the hour for it should strike for me as it struck for him. There was such a horror of him, and such a perception of my own merely momentary discrepancy from him, that it was as if something hitherto solid within my breast gave way entirely, and I became a mass of quivering fear. After this the universe was changed for me altogether. I awoke morning after morning with a horrible dread at the pit of my stomach, and with a sense of the insecurity of life that I never knew before, and that I have never felt since. It was like a revelation; and although the immediate feelings passed away, the experience has made me sympathetic with the morbid feelings of others ever since. It gradually faded, but for months I was unable to go out into the dark alone.

James wrote this account of dread and self-loathing at the turn of the century, but it accords with an account of the potential suicide's emotional disturbance that appeared in a recent paper by the suicidologist Neuringer (1982, p. 182):

It would seem reasonable to suppose that the clinical literature on suicide is correct in assuming that the emotional tone of self-destructive individuals is extremely negative. The general suicide folklore holds that feelings of hopelessness, helplessness, self-loathing, depression, anxiety, and so forth are key constituents of the affect life of individuals who wish to terminate their existence.

James thus put into words the characteristic inner life of the potential suicide, which very few could express so accurately and effectively. James's account is not a suicide note of the kind written before death. In recent decades some of the leading suicidologists have subjected many such notes to critical analysis. As Schneidman, Farberow, and Litman report, "suicide notes offer an unusual opportunity for the investigator to obtain some important insights into the thoughts and feelings of suicidal persons, written as they are within the context of suicidal behavior" (1970, p. 216). These suicide notes are usually very brief, to the point, and devoid of stylistic elegance like James's.

As a psychiatrist and suicidologist, Litman (1975) once immersed himself in such notes to find out why people resort to suicide. He had access to a thousand suicide notes from Los Angeles covering some twenty-four months, during which about three thousand suicides had taken place. Reading the notes proved both painful and frustrating—painful because of the human suffering disclosed and frustrating because he found no explanation for suicide, though some notes gave reasons including loss of love, apprehension about illness, distress at being a burden to others, being drained of energy, and feeling unable to put up with things any longer. Hopelessness was the prevalent mood of these notes; but, Litman adds, "there are those exceptional messages that convey a confident religious faith in a happy afterlife."

In addition to analyzing suicide notes, suicidologists conduct personal interviews with those who have attempted suicide or who are alarmed by their self-destructive thoughts and feelings. These interviews often take place at suicide prevention centers, now established in many communities. Although much about self-punishing[10] and self-destructive[11] behavior remains enigmatic, progress has been made, especially in recognition of suicide risk, the place of antidepressant medication, and the role of individual and group psychotherapy in treating suicide-prone individuals. The psychology of suicide has now caught up with the sociology of suicide as started by Durkheim.

Some Concluding Reflections

In addition to these topics that I have cited as examples of recent accelerated progress in research on various aspects of consciousness, a few others are too important to be ignored.

10. Some self-punishing behavior is altogether inexplicable at present. For example, one of the characteristic symptoms of a heritable disease known as the Lesch-Nyhan syndrome is compulsive self-mutilation. The condition involves disturbances of uric acid metabolism and enzymes, but why these prompt self-mutilation remains unknown.

11. A recent enigmatic finding cited in a report from Stockholm by Träskman, Åsberg, Bertilsson, and Sjöstrand (1981) points to an association between biochemical factors and self-destructive behavior. They compared the monoamine metabolite concentrations in the cerebrospinal fluid of patients who had attempted suicide with concentrations in healthy normal controls. The suicidal group had significantly lower levels. One of the concentrations checked was for the serotonin metabolite, and those with low levels had engaged in impulsive, "seemingly unpremeditated" suicide attempts. This suggested "that the link between serotonin functions and suicidal behavior might be a deficient control of aggressive impulses." The investigators added that it would be "premature" to measure spinal fluid concentrations routinely in evaluating suicide risks, but they added that "once psychological correlates of a disturbed serotonin turnover in man are found, this knowledge might lay the foundation for a more goal-directed psychotherapeutic intervention than hitherto has been possible" (1981, p. 635).

I was struck by a statement in an article by Hicks and Ridely, "Black Studies in Psychology," that "black students perceive the psychological literature on blacks to be negatively biased" (1979, p. 600). This brought to mind Gordon Allport's *The Nature of Prejudice,* with its treatment of anti-Negro attitudes (1954, pp. 56ff., 270ff.), and suggested the topic of black studies and the prejudiced mind or some closely related theme.

A special issue of the *Journal of Abnormal Psychology* dealt with various phases of hypnosis, including the consciousness or personality characteristics of those highly susceptible or unsusceptible to hypnosis, a subject also discussed by Hilgard and Hilgard (1975, pp. 6–13). Although the journal's articles largely concerned hypnosis as related to psychopathology, one did deal with normal subjects. In "Hypnosis and Creativity" Patricia Bowers presented persuasive evidence that student subjects who are readily hypnotized are more creative than those who are not.

A third topic was suggested by a recent increase in psychological studies of creativity. Since the late 1960s these studies even have their own publication, the *Journal of Creative Behavior.* The literature on the subject is large, but an introduction is found in the bibliographical references to Rothenberg and Hausman, *The Creativity Question* (1976).

There is danger of overstating the progress that has been made. I have not dealt with research failures, intractable problems, or contemporary controversies. And though progress calls for reducing the complexity of the concept of consciousness, such reduction has not ensued; in fact the studies I have discussed have actually increased this complexity.

But perhaps the increase in complexity might actually indicate progress, as is suggested by the history of mental tests. There is a vast difference between the understanding of the nature of intelligence as revealed by Binet tests early in the century and what we have learned from contemporary factor-analytic studies. Intellect involves many more variables than suspected by the pioneering mental testers. And more variables mean increased complexity.

In both science and technology, successful solutions are apt to produce new problems. The first psychometric test engendered an avalanche of special tests to cope with hitherto unsuspected problems—culture-free tests, achievement tests, nonverbal tests, representativeness tests, analogies tests. Psychometric progress thus brought a more complex concept of intellect, enriched but not a finished concept. There is always new business on the psychometric agenda.

Likewise, our concept of consciousness is not settled or finished. Just as research rendered intellect more complex yet enriched the concept, research has rendered the consciousness in which it is embedded far more complex but definitely richer than the founding fathers of psychology suspected. And the end is not yet in sight.

References

Allport, G. W. 1954. *The nature of prejudice.* Boston: Beacon Press.

Atkeson, B. M.; Calhoun, K. S.; Resick, P. A.; and Ellis, E. E. 1982. Victims of rape: Repeated assessment of depressive symptoms. *Journal of Consulting and Clinical Psychology* 50:96–102.

Bowers, P. 1979. Hypnosis and creativity: The search for the missing link. *Journal of Abnormal Psychology* 88:564–72.

Brown, R. 1958. *Words and things.* Glencoe, Ill.: Free Press.

Cohen, F. 1980. Coping with surgery: Information, psychological preparation, and recovery. In *Aging in the 1980s: Psychological Issues,* ed. L. W. Poon. Washington, D.C.: American Psychological Association.

Cohen, L. B. 1979. Our developing knowledge of infant perception and cognition. *American Psychologist* 34:894–99.

Fishman, D. B., and Neigher, W. D. 1982. American psychology in the eighties: Who will buy? *American Psychologist* 37:533–46.

Gelman, R. 1979. Preschool thought. *American Psychologist* 34:900–905.

Geschwind, N. 1970. The organization of language and the brain. *Science* 170:940–44.

———. 1979. Specialization of the human brain. *Scientific American* 241:180–99.

Guilford, J. P. 1979. *Cognitive psychology with a frame of reference.* San Diego: Edits.

———. 1982. Cognitive psychology's ambiguities: Some suggested remedies. *Psychological Review* 89:48–59.

Hicks, L. H., and Ridly, S. E. 1979. Black studies in psychology. *American Psychologist* 34:597–602.

Hilgard, E. R., and Hilgard, J. R. 1975. *Hypnosis in relief of pain.* Los Altos, Calif.: William Kaufmann.

Huxley, J. 1959. Introduction to Pierre Teilhard de Chardin, *The phenomenon of man.* New York: Harper and Row.

James, W. 1890. *The principles of psychology.* Vol. 1. New York: Henry Holt.

———. 1902. *The varieties of religious experience.* New York: Longmans, Green.

Kaswan, J. 1981. Manifest and latent functions of psychological services. *American Psychologist* 36:290–99.

Litman, R. E. 1975. The assessment of suicidality. In *Consultation-liaison psychiatry,* ed. R. O. Pasnau, 227–36. New York: Grune and Stratton.

Locke, J. 1901. *The philosophical works of John Locke.* Ed. J. A. St. John. Vol. 1. London: George Bell.

———. 1956. *An essay concerning human understanding.* Chicago: Henry Regnery.

Matthiessen, F. O. 1947. *The James family.* New York: Alfred A. Knopf.

Moskowitz, B. A. 1978. The acquisition of language. *Scientific American* 239:92–108.

Neuringer, C. 1982. Affect configurations and changes in women who threaten suicide following a crisis. *Journal of Consulting and Clinical Psychology* 50:182–86.

Poon, L. W., ed. 1980. *Aging in the 1980s: Psychological issues.* Washington, D.C.: American Psychological Association.

Rothenberg, A., and Hausman, C. R. 1976. *The creativity question.* Durham, N.C.: Duke University Press.

Sampson, E. E. 1981. Cognitive psychology as ideology. *American Psychologist* 36:730–43.

Scarr, S., ed. 1979. Psychology and children: Current research and practice. Essays in observance of the International Year of the Child 1979. *American Psychologist* 34:809–1039.

Schneidman, E. S.; Farberow, N. L.; and Litman, R. E. 1970. *The psychology of suicide.* New York: Science House.

Sternberg, R. J. 1981. Testing and cognitive psychology. *American Psychologist* 36:1181–89.

Thorpe, W. H. 1966. Ethology and consciousness. In *Brain and conscious experience,* ed. J. C. Eccles, 470–505. New York: Springer-Verlag.

Träskman, L.; Åsberg, M.; Bertilsson, L.; and Sjöstrand, L. 1981. Monoamine metabolites in CSF and suicidal behavior. *Archives of General Psychiatry* 38:631–36.

Welty, J. C. 1975. *The life of birds.* 2d ed. Philadelphia: W. B. Saunders.

Wertheimer, M. 1959. *Productive thinking.* New York: Harper.

Wilkins, M. C. 1928. The effect of changed material on ability to do formal syllogistic reasoning. *Archives of Psychology,* no. 102.

Index